JOE SAWARD
FASCINATING FORMULA 1 FACTS
VOLUME IV

JOE SAWARD

FASCINATING FORMULA 1 FACTS
VOLUME IV

First published in 2023 by Morienval Press

3 5 7 9 8 6 7 6 1

All rights reserved

Copyright © Joe Saward 2023

The right of Joe Saward to be identified as the author of this work has asserted his right under the Copyright, Designs and Patents Act 1988.

This book is in copyright.
Subject to statutory exception and to provisions of relevant collective licensing agreements, no reproduction of any part may take place without the written permission of the author.

www.morienval.com

This book is sold subject to the conditions that it shall not, by way of trade or otherwise, be lent, re-sold, hired out, or otherwise circulated without the publisher's prior consent in any form of binding or cover other than that in which it is published and without a similar condition including this condition being imposed on the subsequent purchaser.

ISBN 978-0-9554868-6-9

Printed and bound in the United Kingdom by
Lightning Source
6 Precedent Drive, Rooksley,
Milton Keynes, Buckinghamshire
MK13 8PR

A remarkable family

Some people are born into extraordinary lives. If you write a film script about them, it would be rejected as being unrealistic. Paul Belmondo had just such a story. His grandfather Paul, after whom he was named, was from an Italian background but was born and grew up in Algeria. He survived the trenches in World War I in spite of suffering from being gassed during the battle of Saint-Mihiel, near Verdun. In the 1920s, he sought a quieter life and soon became a well-known sculptor in France, ultimately advancing to become a professor at the École Nationale Supérieure des Beaux-Arts de Paris in the 1950s. Paul's son, Jean-Paul, was a man of a rather character. Born in 1933, he was a sportsman in his youth and began his professional career as a boxer. He began appearing in films in his early twenties and made his breakthrough to stardom in 1960, in Jean-Luc Godard's A Bout de Souffle, alongside Jean Seberg, one of the films that launched the Nouvelle Vague movement in the cinema. In the 1960s, 1970s and 1980s he was one of France's biggest film stars. Jean-Paul's son Paul was born in 1963 in the Paris surburb of Boulogne-Billancourt, the home of the Renault car company. His parent split up two years later, after 13 years of marriage. His mother, the dancer Elodie Constantin, then moved to London where Paul spent three years of his childhood. He returned to France at 11 but he was not a good student, having become fascinated by cars and by the cinema. His first job was as a camera assistant in a low-budget movie but later served as a director's assistant for his father 1982 hit film L'As des As (The Ace of Aces). In the same period he raced karts but began to appear in the gossip columns because of his friendship with Princess Stéphanie of Monaco. The pair became a couple for several years, despite pressure from the paparazzi, who shadowed their every move.

He finished sixth in his first season in Formula Renault with Ecurie Elf, including a victory on the Le Mans Bugatti circuit and graduated into French Formula 3 in 1984 and finished fourth, his team-mate Olivier Grouillard winning the title. He switched to David Price Racing in 1985 and won a race at Albi but he finished the year in sixth overall and a second season with the British team proved to be even worse. In 1987, he moved up to Formula 3000 with the GBDA team and remained in the formula for the next five seasons with different teams, without much success. In 1992, however, he was able to find the budget to join the March F1 team. He qualified five times and his best finish was ninth in Hungary, but he then ran out of funding. Two years later he returned to F1 with the Pacific F1 team but the car was not competitive and he qualified only twice. After his time in F1 was over, he concentrated on GTs and, for several years, ran his own Paul Belmondo Racing.

Unlike some of his peers, Paul was never affected by his celebrity, having lived his entire life in the limelight. In fact, he was happy not to be the centre of attention and to live as normal a life as possible. In 1990, he married an Italian model called Luana Tenca. The couple had three children and, in 2010, almost by accident, Luana met one of the directors of Canal+, which then ran a channel called Cuisine TV. This resulted in her becoming a TV chef with her own programme called Bienvenue chez Luana. Later she was recruited by France 5 to appear on its nightly talk show C à vous as the resident chef, a job she did for five years.

In recent years, Paul has found himself gravitating towards the arts, and has played a variety of rules on the stage, on TV and in film. He has worked as a TV commentator on motorsport with various channels and even tried his hand directing a documentary about the life of his father. He has also worked for nearly 10 years as the ambassador for Chapal, the luxury leather goods firm associated with the Bardinon family, which also owns one of the world's greatest collection of Ferraris, and its own private racing circuit.

A family business

Brothers Claude and Georges Gachnang were both passionate about racing, even if they lived in a country where such activities were banned. They lived in the town of Aigle in Switzerland, to the south of Montreux, nor far from where the river Rhone runs into Lake Geneva, and worked as mechanics, racing whenever they could. Georges competed at Le Mans in 1960, sharing an AC-Bristol with André Wicky, but it was not a great success. Claude and Georges then decided to set up their own business called Cegga, an acronym for Charles Et Georges Gachnang, Aigle, preparing and modifying cars to use in local hillclimb races and sports car events outside Switzerland.

These included the Cegga Ferrari 3000S, which was a modified 1958 Ferrari 250 Testa Rossa. In 1961, the brothers decided that they would build their own Cegga Formula 1 car for the new 1.5-litre F1 regulations. This was a tube-framed device, powered by a Maserati sports car engine. The car as not ready until April 1962 when it was taken to Pau to take part in the non-championship Pau Grand Prix Formula 1 race. The driver Maurice Caillet did not qualify. The car was then sent to Naples for the Gran Premio di Napoli on the Posillipo circuit but again Caillet failed to qualify. The project was stopped and the car sold. It was used in local hillclimbs after that. In 1966, however, the brothers decided to try again, this time with a V12 Ferrari engine. They built a car that looked similar to a Lotus 24 and Georges Gachnang tested the car at Monza but there was never the money to go racing and the Cegga-Ferrari was used only in hillclimbs by Georges Gachnang. It was later sold to a French driver called Philippe Panis for hillclimb races. He would only use it for a few months because his wife's family forced him to stop racing, not long after he and his wife Monique had had a son, whom they named Olivier.

The Gachnangs did not have the money to make their dreams come true and Cegga was shut down in 1970. Georges set up a garage and soon became a car dealer. Georges's son Olivier and his daughter Véronique were also passionate about the sport, as was Véronique's husband Antoine "Toni" Buemi, who came from Sicilian stock. It was probably natural that Toni and Véronique's first child Sébastien would become passionate about the sport as well, as was his cousin, Natacha, Olivier's daughter, who was born a year earlier.

When Sébastien was five, his father gave him a kart for Christmas and he was soon racing around the car park outside the family's Toyota garage. As soon as he could, he began competing and was soon winning titles, often racing karts against his cousin.

Natacha, being older, was the first to jump into car racing, competing in Formula BMW in Germany in 2003, Sébastien followed in 2004. In his debut season, he finished third in the championship, behind the dominant Sebastian Vettel, who was then in his second year. Buemi then did a second year, but was beaten to the title by a youngster called Nico Hülkenberg. But he landed support from Red Bull and this took him through Formula 3 and GP2 and ultimately put him into Scuderia Toro Rosso for the 2009 season. He scored points on his debut in Australia, and again in his third race in China. Despite some solid results, Buemi fell victim to Red Bull's ruthless approach, being dropped to make way for Daniel Ricciardo and Jean-Eric Vergne. His abilities as a test driver were recognised and appreciated and he was named as Red Bull Racing's reserve driver for 2012, a job he continues to hold.

His career was far from over, however, as he was signed to race for Toyota in the WEC in 2013 and the following year he won the WEC title. He also began competing in Formula E and would win the electric series title in 2015-2016. In 2018, he won Le Mans sharing his Toyota with Fernando Alonso and Kazuki Nakajima, and scored a second victory this year – and a second WEC title.

Natacha climbed the ladder to race sports cars but in, 2010, suffered a mechanical failure while practising with her GT car at the Yas Marina circuit in Abu Dhabi. The car smashed into the barriers at the end of the straight and was badly damaged. She suffered a serious leg injury and had to be cut from the car. She has not raced since.

What could have been

Racing drivers are not always reasonable individuals. They are, perhaps by nature, not given to caution and that can get them into trouble – and worse. Robert Kubica is a good example of this. He had struggled through the ranks to get to Formula 1, the first Polish driver to compete in the sport and, in 2008, won the Canadian Grand Prix at the wheel of his BMW Sauber after his longtime rival Lewis Hamilton crashed into the back of Kimi Räikkönen's Ferrari at the exit of the pitlane. BMW quit at the end of 2009, leaving Robert without a drive and he quickly signed to race for Renault in 2010. It was not the best option as the team was in the process of being sold after the disastrous revelations about the Singapore GP in 2008 when the team fixed the race by having Nelson Piquet Jr crash, allowing Fernando Alonso to get into a position that allowed him to win. It was rumoured from the middle of 2010 onwards that Ferrari wanted to hire Kubica but Felipe Massa was retained that summer, leaving Robert to stay at Renault in 2011. Then in February that year, while competing in the Ronde di Andora rally in a privately-entered car, he had a severe accident when he hit a barrier head-on and this came into the cockpit and caused him serious injuries. For the next eight years, Robert tried to find a way back into F1, undergoing a number of operations, before finally convincing Williams to take him on in 2019. It is a sad story as Kubica was one of the most talented of his generation. It was doubly sad because a little while before his accident he had signed a deal to race for Ferrari in 2012…

He's not only driver to have had such a story. The German driver Stefan Bellof exploded on to the international racing scene in 1982, winning his first two Formula 2 races as a rookie. This put him on the shopping list of the Formula 1 teams and landed him a factory Rothmans Porsche sports car drive in 1983 and 1984. In his first year, he won at Silverstone, Fuji and Kyalami but lost out in the championship race to team-mate Jacky Ickx, although he also set the fastest ever lap at the old Nürburgring, which stood unbeaten until a couple of years ago.

At the end of 1983, Bellof had such a good reputation that he was invited to test for the McLaren F1 team, along with Ayrton Senna and Martin Brundle. The team had contracts with Alain Prost and Niki Lauda so there was little hope of a race drive, but the performances was such that he and Brundle were signed by Tyrrell for the 1984 season. That year, he won the WEC title with six wins in 11 races and made his name in F1, with a best result being a spectacular third place at Monaco, a race he might have won had it not been stopped early because of pouring rain.

Bellof remained with Tyrrell in 1985 and Ken Tyrrell was keen to stop his drivers from racing in sports cars. But because he did not pay them enough, both Bellof and Brundle raced in WEC as well. Bellof drove a Brun Porsche. At Spa, during the Spa 1,000 km, he collided with his former Rothmans Porsche teammate Jacky Ickx, going into Eau Rouge corner. The car ran into the barriers behind which was a concrete block that served as the base for the grandstands. Bellof was killed in the crash. He had signed to join Ferrari in 1986 shortly before his death....

A man called Jap Tek Lie

Go west from Kuala Lumpur, across the Malacca Strait, and you will find the city of Medan. It might seem a pretty unlikely city to have been the birthplace of a Formula 1 team owner, but Jap Tek Lie was unusual in an awful lot of respects.

When he was born in 1907, Medan was part of what was known as the Dutch East Indies, and as the Paris of Sumatra. As the name suggests, Jap Tek Lie was from a hakka Chinese family. At the time, around two percent of the population of the East Indies came from China (around 1.2 million of them) and they were treated as Dutch subjects, although there were classified as "foreign orientals", which meant that access to Dutch education was limited. In pursuit of a good education, therefore, Chinese parents would send their children to the Netherlands. It was thus that in the 1920s, Jap Tek Lie went to school in Holland. This meant that he learned a lot of languages, including six Chinese dialects, Dutch, English, French, German, Malay and even Thai. This all helped when he began a trading company after finishing his education. Initially, he ran trading companies and travel agencies. By that point, he had adopted the name of "Teddy Yip". He was always a party animal, enjoying good martinis, exotic women and very fast cars. He had charm to spare and travelled endlessly, making money. When Europe fell into war, he departed, settling in Hong Kong, although much of the trading was done in this era through Macau which was neutral because it was a Portuguese territory. In the 1950s, Macau's position was further enhanced during the Korean War when United Nations imposed a trade embargo on China. Yip did well and, by the 1950s, was already a big player in the city. He started racing in the same era, competing in the Macau GP in a Jaguar XK120.

The Portuguese government then decided to grant the rights to all leisure activities in Macau, including casinos, hotels and even the ferries to a private company. Yip became part of the Sociedade de Turismo e Diversoes de Macau (STDM) consortium that won the bid, along with his brother-in-law Stanley Ho, Henry Fok, a well-connected Hong Kong real estate developer, and Yip Hon, who ran casinos. STDM paid taxes to the government, but were also involved in many other activities, such as dredging waterways, funding construction projects, overseas tourism offices and trade shows and organising events in Macau. This organisation gradually turned Macau into a major tourist centre, focussed on gambling, but active in other respects as well, including hosting the Macau GP, in which he raced for many years, his best result being third in a Jaguar E-type. In the early 1970s, he met the team boss Sid Taylor and agreed to sponsor the team in Formula 5000, running Vern Schuppan. This led to Yip joining forces with Team Ensign in F1 in 1974 but also further Formula 5000 activity with Schuppan and Alan Jones.

In 1976, he set up Theodore Racing, run by Taylor and fielded an Ensign for Patrick Tambay. He then commissioned Ron Tauranac to build him a Formula 1 car, which was driven by Eddie Cheever and then by Keke Rosberg, who shocked the F1 world by winning the non-championship 1977 International Trophy race at Silverstone. That was the high point but Yip continued to be active both in F1 and in the United States, where he sponsored Dan Gurney. In 1979, he sponsored Ensign again without success and then ran a British F1 team for David Kennedy and Desiree Wilson, who become the first woman to win a Formula 1 race that year.

Yip decided to create another F1 team in 1981 and hired Tony Southgate and team manager Jo Ramirez. The car was driven by Tambay and later by Marc Surer. He then merged Theodore with Ensign and ran the Nigel Bennett-designed Ensign N183 as a Theodore for Johnny Cecotto and Roberto Guerrero. The team was closed after that but Yip continued to run Theodore Racing in Macau, hiring some of the best-known names to drive his cars.

He continued to enjoy racing until his death in 2003, at the age of 96.

A military man

Before Charlie Whiting was made F1 Race Director in 1997, the role was filled – albeit very briefly – by a British Rear Admiral, who had recently retired from the Royal Navy. The experiment was not very successful as military discipline and the fast-moving ducking and weaving of the F1 crowd did not combine very successfully. Roger Lane-Nott disappeared off to a life running worthy causes, initially in the offshore oil sector and later in farming. He was secretary of the British Racing Drivers' Club as well. In recent times, he has become involved in a political pressure group for veterans, campaigning for Britain to leave the European Union and stood (and lost) as a Brexit Party candidate for the South West of England in the European Parliamentary elections.

Lane-Nott was a bit of an odd appointment. Max Mosley was the FIA President and was then leading a campaign to bring a more scientific approach to F1 safety, following the deaths of Ayrton Senna and Roland Ratzenberger at Imola in 1994. It was felt that Lane-Nott's experience in a high-technology, safety-critical environment would be helpful for the sport. He was a long-time racing fan, but his experience was rather limited as he had spent a lot of his life in submarines.

Educated at Pangbourne College, Mike Hailwood's old school, he moved on to attend the Britannia Royal Naval College in Dartmouth. He was commissioned in the submarine service, then joined the nuclear-powered HMS Revenge in Scotland in 1969 and moved on to HMS Conqueror (which would become famous for sinking the General Belgrano battleship during the Falklands War in 1982). He was then selected for what was known as a Perisher course, which was the first big step towards becoming a submarine commander. His first command came in 1975 with HMS Walrus. After two years, he moved to a land posting, as a staff officer at Fleet Headquarters in Northwood, Hertfordshire, before becoming commander of the nuclear submarine HMS Swiftsure and then HMS Splendid in 1979.

The submarine was one of the first to arrive in the South Atlantic during the Falklands War in 1982, its job being to shadow the Argentine aircraft carrier 25 de Mayo. The ship disappeared into Argentine territorial waters, defined as 12 miles off the coast, and Splendid came close to attacking the ship, as its torpedoes could have been fired from international waters. In the end, this was deemed to be unwise. Splendid was sent to the estuary of the Gallegos River, off Puerto Deseado, where it sat beneath the waves, monitoring all activity at the Río Gallegos air base, which meant that the task force in the Falklands knew what to expect. As a result, he was mentioned in despatches and then posted to the United States Naval Academy at Annapolis, where he studied management techniques before returning to Britain to take command of the Third Submarine Squadron in Faslane, Scotland.

He later moved on to become assistant director of defence concepts at the Ministry of Defence and, after a staff course at the Royal College of Defence Studies in 1989, he spent a year at sea as commander of the frigate HMS Coventry. He was then made senior naval officer in the Middle East, during the latter stages of the Gulf War before becoming Chief of Staff, Submarines. A year later, he was appointed to be the Royal Navy's first Commander Operations, exercising operational command of all Royal Navy maritime operations, reporting to the

Fleet Commander, in addition to being Flag Officer Submarines. That led to a role with NATO but by then, it became clear that he was not going to get to the very top as younger men were in more senior positions. After 33 years in the Royal Navy, he retired at the age of 52.

Mosley later credited him with setting up new systems and procedures and for having brought new thinking into the sport, but it was quickly clear that it was not a perfect fit.

Boulognes and Boulognes

The name Boulogne can be rather confusing for the average non-French motor racing fan. It was a racing circuit from the very early years of the sport, between 1909 and 1928. Then the name popped up again in the late 1940s, with another circuit in the so-called Bois de Boulogne (which translates as Boulogne Wood). The only thing was that the two circuits were 150 miles apart. And then, of course, you have Boulogne-Billancourt, where Louis Renault built his first automobile in a garden shed at his parents' weekend house. Today, Renault's world headquarters located in the town, although some may know it as being a place where the comedy actor Peter Ustinov had an apartment, simply because he wanted a suitably silly address - "11 rue de Silly".

So, how does one make sense of all of this? Well, it all began with an unmanned boat floating in the estuary of the River Liane off Boulogne-sur-Mer in around 633. The thing was that, so they say, the boat was carrying a luminous statue of the Virgin Mary. This impressed the locals (as it would). They secured the boat and took the statue to the local church and soon miracles started to happen. Notre-Dame de la Mer became a popular pilgrimage destination, which made Boulogne-sur-Mer a prosperous place. In 1308, France's King Philip IV made a pilgrimage to see the statue and decided, because it was a long way to travel, that he would build a chapel with a copy of the statue in the hamlet of Menuls-lès-Saint-Cloud, in the forest not far from Paris. This was known as Notre-Dame de Boulogne la Petite and over time the area became known as Boulogne-la-Petite and later Boulogne-sur-Seine. In 1924, in an effort to make things less complicated, this was renamed Boulogne-Billancourt. By then the forest had become known as the Bois de Boulogne (Boulogne Wood) and had been transformed into a public park, featuring wide carriageways, man-made lakes and even waterfalls. It was all designed to be a place for Parisians to relax, just outside the walls of the city.

At the same time, Boulogne-sur-Mer had become something of a seaside resort, as a place for Parisians to go bathing and a port to which the English came on steamboats from Folkestone, often going on Paris. The artist Joseph Turner painted many seascapes and sunsets in Boulogne. Competition between rival seaside towns resulted in all manner of promotional ideas and Boulogne-sur-Mer hit on the idea of having a motor race in 1909 and a 32-mile road circuit was laid out in the countryside inland from the town, using the Saint-Omer road as far as Longueville and then south Brunembert, Selles and Desvres, before returning to Boulogne on the Arras road. It was fast and dangerous and, while the Coupe de l'Auto provided great victories for Lion-Peugeot and rival Hispano-Suiza, it also caused the death of Giosuè Giuppone, one of the Lion-Peugeot stars. Later it would see one of the early victories for Delage and in 1913 hosted the Grand Prix de l'ACF, with Peugeot battling the British Sunbeams. In the 1920s, the circuit was revived for the Boulogne Speed Week, a variety of races, rallies and hillclimbs with the main event being a combined voiturette/cyclecar race called the Grand Prix of Boulogne, with the winners including Henry Segrave, the splendidly-named Bunny Marshall, George Eyston and Malcolm Campbell. By 1928, however, the event run out of steam and faded quietly away.

However, down in Paris, the Bois de Boulogne began to feature in motor racing as many of the early races started from the Porte Maillot and featured sections in the park. Later there would be sprint competitions on the fast roads and even in 1927 the suggestion that the Grand Prix de l'ACF should be held in the Bois de Boulogne. In the end, it was decided to run the race at the Montlhéry speedway. "Certainly the race in the centre of Paris would have done much to popularize the sport of motor racing," Motorsport magazine reported, "and its publicity would have been so great, that it is not improbable that some of the biggest firms in the French industry, who have long regarded racing with indifference, would have returned to the arena". It didn't happen, but immediately after the war, in the summer of 1945, the Bois would become the venue for the Grand Prix de la Libération, attended by hundreds of thousands of people, who were delighted to watch Jean-Pierre Wimille win the race for Bugatti. Perhaps, one day, the French will wake up to the fact that Formula 1 cars are now incredibly efficient and host another race in the Bois, instead of at remote circuits such as Paul Ricard and Magny-Cours. Paris is, after wall, just what F1 wants – a global destination city.

Who knows, the name Boulogne might once again be at the forefront of motorsport. And who knows, perhaps Renault might even start winning again…

A very fast fellow

The coast of the Languedoc is flat, apart from a very large rock, called Mont St-Clair, which rises from the sea, a few miles to the south-west of Montpellier. Around it is the town of Sète and a sandy isthmus which divides the Mediterranean from a salt water lagoon, which marks the end of the Canal du Midi, the waterway that links the Atlantic to the Mediterranean. Sète boasts a network of canals which has given it the nickname of the "Venice of the Languedoc". It is popular seaside resort. It was there, in 1963, that Georges Raphanel, a former BP executive in Algeria, opened an ice cream shop on the Canal Royal.

Algerian independence has resulted in around 800,000 so-called Pieds-Noirs returning home to France. Georges's parents had done the same, setting up a bar called Le Dauphin at the nearby Grau d'Agde.

Georges's son Pierre-Henri, who was born in Algiers, was only two at the time the family left Algeria but he grew up as a Frenchman, attending the local school in Grau before being sent off to boarding school during the week, firstly in Béziers and then later at Pézenas. He started karting when he was young, using an engine which his father had taken from a moped, competing on a track in the vineyards, inland from the coast. It was clear that he was talented and his family decided to sell the business and concentrate on developing his career, spending their weekends on the road at kart races all over Europe. After pondering a career as a vet and then as a policeman, Pierre-Henri realised that he was best-suited to being a racing driver. But without money it was tough. Things began to move in the right direction when he won the Marlboro-backed Cherche Son Pilote scholarship scheme, which led to a fully-sponsored season in Formula Renault before he moved into French Formula 3. He was helped on his way by the town of Agde, which raised money from the local population to sponsor him.

In his second Formula 3 season he joined the mighty ORECA and won the French title and the Monaco F3 Grand Prix. It seemed like he was finally on his way but Formula 3000 was tough and he didn't have much money. There was little success but, at the end of 1988, he finally got a break in Formula 1, being offered the chance to race in Australia by Gérard Larrousse to replace Yannick Dalmas, his long-time rival, who was suffering from Legionnaire's Disease. It was not a great move and Raphanel failed to qualify. The following year he took a risk with Coloni because he had no money and then switched to Rial, but both cars were uncompetitive and his chances of an F1 career began to slip away. Rather than trying to battle on without money, he took the wise decision to accept the offer of a factory drive with Toyota, racing mainly in Japan, where he earned good money and enjoyed some success. He also raced sports cars in Europe, finished second at Le Mans on two occasions and was on the podium a third time.

He continued racing until 2000 and then returned to his home town and set up an estate agency. In 2006, he was recruited by Bugatti as a test driver and demonstrator, teaching wealthy buyers how to handle the 1,000 hp cars. In 2010, he set a world record for production cars when lapping the Volkswagen Ehra-Lessien testing facility in a Bugatti Veyron at 267 mph.

The man who got there first

Ellis Hall was an oil man, and a very successful one as well. He had plenty of money and lived in a grand house in Boulder, Colorado, with his wife Theresa and their four children: Richard, Betty, James and Charles.

Alas, tragedy struck and he lost his wife to illness at the age of just 46. The children were 18, 16, 12 and nine. It was a traumatic time. A couple of years later, he remarried. Virginia Hockenhull was 10 years his junior and her daughter Joann joined the clan. The new family spent the next three years in New Mexico.

In the summer of 1953, Ellis took his wife, two daughters and some friends on a holiday trip to Juneau in Alaska with their twin-engined De Havilland Dove. On the return trip, the plane disappeared somewhere over southern Alaska. It was a month before any wreckage was found. For the Hall brothers, it was a second traumatic blow – and it changed their lives. The plan had always been for them to follow their father into the oil business but once Ellis was gone, they could do what they wanted to do. James (known as Jim) gave up studying geology at Cal Tech and switched to mechanical engineering. He was already mad about cars and, at 14, had turned a beaten-up 1929 Model T Ford into a hot rod.

Richard (known as Dick) ran the oil business for a while and then they all agreed to sell the shares. Between them, they inherited a vast fortune, amounting to nearly $24 million, equivalent to around $250 million today. Dick moved to Texas and helped Carroll Shelby set up a sports car dealership in Dallas. Jim came home from college in the summer of 1954 and did his first races in his brother's Austin Healey at Fort Sumner in New Mexico. That was it. He was hooked on racing.

With some of his inheritance money, he built his own speedway on a plot of land outside Midland, Texas, not far from the Texas-New Mexico border. Rattlesnake Raceway was soon attracting a group of young racers, including another younger oilman called Hap Sharp. As this was being developed, another oilman Gary Laughlin asked the Hall brothers and Shelby to build him a Chevrolet Corvette with Italian-styled bodywork, designed by Sergio Scaglietti. Jim then bought a Lotus Formula 2 car, put a 2.5-litre Climax engine into it and entered it for the United States GP at Riverside. In the next three years, he raced in 11 Grands Prix in a variety of different Lotuses for various different teams.

Hall and Sharp had the ambition to build their own racing cars and in the US at the time sports cars were the thing. They approached well-known racing car builders Dick Troutman and Tom Barnes to build them a car to be called a Chaparral. It was a conventional machine and but they wanted more and so bought the rights to the name and built their own sports car, named the Chaparral 2, a mid-engined car with a monocoque chassis and a fibreglass body. At the same time in Britain, Colin Chapman was creating the first monocoque F1 car, but the difference was that Chaparral was using aerospace materials, notably fibreglass composites to build the bodywork.

At the time, the American car manufacturers had all agreed to withdraw from racing but General Motors was not playing by the rules and began to use Chaparral as a skunk works to develop new ideas. They started out with the first rear wings, and even adjustable versions of the same thing, they then invented side-mounted radiators, built lightweight aluminium engines, designed a semi-automatic transmission, did the first data-collection, built the first composite chassis and ultimately, in 1970, created the extraordinary Chaparral 2J, the first ground effect racing car, which used an small engine to drive fans that sucked air from beneath the car and used a polycarbonate plastic material called Lexan that was light, flexible and unbreakable to create "skirts" that sealed off the air flows, moving up and down as required using cables and pulleys.

If all of this sounds vaguely familiar, it is because most of these ideas eventually went into F1, where others took credit for them. Perhaps they were better developed that Hall's machinery had been, but he had got there first.

Pushing the boundaries of technology meant that Hall had many of his ideas outlawed at international level, but Chaparral enjoyed huge success at home with Hall winning the US Road Racing Championships in 1964 and 1965 and his cars winning in every series in which they competed including CanAm, Formula 5000 and IndyCar. Although there was never a Chaparral Formula 1 car, Hall's impact on Grand Prix racing was considerable.

In the end, Hall tired of fighting regulators, began to produce more conventional cars, such as the Chaparral 2K, which applied the ground effect seen in F1 to Indycars. It was designed by a certain John Barnard. In 1980 the Chaparral 2K won the Indy 500 and the CART championship in the hands of Johnny Rutherford.

Barnard then went off to F1 to create the first composite chassis and the first semi-automatic gearboxes, while Colin Chapman had previously done much work on ground-effect, and Gordon Murray had designed a car that was sucked to the tarmac using fans...

Hall turned to using March, Lola and Reynard chassis in Indycar racing and was still winning races with Gil de Ferran in the mid-1990s. He then decided he had done enough and closed the team down. He was then 62 and wanted a quieter life.

Budgetary considerations

The 2021 Formula 1 season is the first to feature a budget cap, in an effort to stop teams from spending silly money in their quest to win F1. Racers are racers and as long as they have access to money, they spend it. It's illogical, of course, in a world where automobile companies are obsessed by cost-efficiency, but the rewards for winning are great and so the big guns each burn through more than a million dollars a day - and consider this to be money well-spent.

But it is nonetheless like a nuclear arms race, with rivals spending vast amounts on futile machines that are developed only to keep them ahead of their rivals, without having much value in the real world. F1 engines today are amazing and useful for the world, but the chassis and aerodynamics are completely useless outside the sport. The money is being spent so that teams can "keep up with the Joneses".

It is now more than 15 years since a budget cap was first suggested in Formula 1 and the irony is that the idea came from a man called Parry-Jones. Richard Parry-Jones was Welsh, as the name suggests. He hails from the city of Bangor, close to the Menai Strait, which separates the island of Anglesey from the Welsh mainland. His family had been involved in slate quarrying in the region but from childhood his passion was for cars, inspired by watching the RAC Rally passing through the forests close to his house. Parry-Jones joined the Ford Motor Company as a trainee, working in product development while also studying for a degree in mechanical engineering at Salford University. He rose through the company to become Chief Technical Officer.

In 1999, the Lebanese-Australian Jacques Nasser became the boss of Ford. "Jac the Knife" had big plans and rapidly bought Cosworth and Stewart Grand Prix and in 2000 launched Jaguar Racing. This was not a success and while there were internecine fights for control of the F1 operation, Nasser fell out with Ford chairman William Clay Ford Jr and was removed from office in 2001. A year later, Parry-Jones was asked to review Ford's F1 programme and decide what to do to make it work. He took charge.

It was in Australia in 2004 that he left his biggest mark on the sport, when he proposed a budget cap.

"The cost trends in the sport are unsustainable," he said. "Other sports have successfully created ways in which costs can be capped and there is no reason that we cannot do the same in F1."

Parry-Jones said that to get everyone in F1 to agree to cap the budgets, there would need to be a high cap to begin with and strong penalties to make sure that anyone found to be overspending would face serious trouble.

The idea was laughed out of the paddock at the time because F1 team bosses argued that it was naïve to believe that spending could not be controlled and that there would inevitably be off-the-balance-sheet operations if teams had their budgets restricted. They cited the case, in the 1960s, when the American Automobile Manufacturer Association announced that, to keep down costs, none of the companies would compete in racing. But then Chevrolet secretly used the Chaparral company as a so-called "skunk works" to develop all kind of extraordinary racing technology, while pretending not to be involved.

In 2006, the then FIA President Max Mosley took up the fight, saying that F1 should scrap income-sharing deals with manufacturer teams saying that it would "entirely reasonable to offer the manufacturers that join the Formula 1 World Championship no income" and suggesting that the least successful teams should get the most money. No-one took that very seriously either, as Mosley was clearly stirring up trouble in the negotiating process to get the automobile manufacturers to sign up to a new Concorde Agreement.

Alas, there was not much patience in Detroit and, at the end of 2004, Jaguar Racing was sold to Red Bull. The rest is history, culminating in World Championship success in 2010, 2011, 2012 and 2013.

Parry-Jones remained at Ford. In 2005, he was made a CBE in the New Year honour list, for services to the automobile industry and then retired in 2007 to live as a technology and policy advisor and academic.

Ahead of their time

The Kaiser-Wilhelm-Gesellschaft zur Förderung der Wissenschaften was an independent scientific institution, established in Germany in 1911, with its goal being to promote research into the natural sciences in Imperial Germany. One of this organisations biggest successes came in the 1920s when research scientists Dr Hans Tropsch and Dr Franz Fischer discovered a process that allowed the production of liquid hydrocarbon fuels using coal as a starting point. It was, by all accounts, a complex business, which involved a thermochemical process that turned carbonaceous materials (such as coal and lignite) into gas which was subsequently transformed in a high pressure environment, using metal catalysts, into a liquid.

The reason that this was important was because Germany had very little oil of its own - but there was an abundance of coal reserves. Today the country has closed the last of its hard coal mines, but still around 38 percent of its electrical power comes from power stations which are fired by lignite, the so-called brown coal. The fuel produced with the Fischer-Tropsch process was first commercialised in the late 1930s by a company that was formed for the purpose called Braunkohlen Benzin AG, shortened to Brabag. This was created by the Nazi government which ordered the giant chemical company IG Farben to join forces with a consortium of lignite mine owners to create petroleum products.

When the war came a few years later, the Fischer-Tropsch process took on an even more important role and was used to produce around nine percent of Germany's fuel during World War II.

The easy access to oil around the world in the post-war years was such that the technology found few users but South Africa had an unusual set of circumstances. It had little in the way of oil reserves and it had a political system that would end being unacceptable around the world, leading to embargoes. As early as 1950, the South African government realized that it needed to do something to cut down on the cost of oil imports and acquired the rights to use the Fischer-Tropsch process in South Africa and set up a company called SouthAfrican Coal, Oil and Gas Corporation (Sasol), with funding from South Africa's Industrial Development Corporation.

The first production facility was opened in 1955 and, by the mid-1980s, Sasol was supplying around a quarter of South Africa's fuel needs. Its big breakthrough came in 1973 when OPEC hiked oil prices around the world, causing an oil crisis and, as a result, Sasol expanded to two extra manufacturing facilities. The government decided to float the business in 1979 and, by the 1980s, Sasol was considering foreign expansion. After the laws of apartheid were abolished in 1991, Sasol set out to increase the company's international exposure by sponsoring a team in Formula 1. The problem was that all the top teams already had big oil deals: McLaren with Shell, Ferrari with Agip, Williams with Elf and Benetton with Mobil. The best-placed team without a deal was Jordan Grand Prix, which had finished fifth in the World Championship in its debut season earlier that year. It had done a great job, but was in desperate need of money.

World Champion Ayrton Senna got involved in the process, as he was looking for ways to get his friend Mauricio Gugelmin a drive for 1992, and so he rang Eddie Jordan just before Christmas and introduced him to the South Africans. Jordan jumped (one might say leapt) at the opportunity and Sasol was happy to become the Jordan team's title sponsor for 1992. The problem was that EJ had also decided (on financial grounds) to do a deal with Yamaha to use the OX99 V12 engine. These were terrible and, that season, the team managed to score only one point in 1992. The sponsorship would last two further seasons, with the Yamaha V12 being replaced by a Hart V10 for the second and third years, which led to Jordan climbing back to fifth in the Constructors' again. During that time, Sasol developed its own fuels for F1 (although one needs to be careful because in that era there was a lot of mistruths peddled about who was supplying what fuels to whom).

For 1995 Jordan was offered a Peugeot engine deal (with a lot of money) and the French firm wanted to work with Total. So the Sasol deal was bounced on to the struggling Arrows, along with the Hart engines. The 18 percent slide in the value of the rand against other international currencies that year meant that the firm could not really compete outside South Africa.

As F1 looks more to synthetic fuels in the future, perhaps Sasol can play a role... We shall see.

Being practical

Being practical is a skill that is sometimes forgotten in modern Formula 1, with its complicated computer programmes and slightly odd boffins. One of the key elements to success is to make sure that your drivers feel confident and happy and thus in a position to perform at their very best.

Today, honesty and transparency are important, but in the old days that was not always in the best interest of a team...

Alberto Ascari was a hugely talented driver. He won the World Championship for Ferrari in 1952 and 1953. His other great victory outside F1 was winning the Mille Miglia in 1954, when he was driving for Ferrari.

The only real problem was that Ascari was extremely superstitious, something which probably related to the fact that, when he was seven years old, his father Antonio, a celebrated Grand Prix driver of his era, was killed racing in the Grand Prix de l'ACF at Montlhéry. Alberto wouldn't permit anyone to even touch the case in which he carried his racing equipment: his blue helmet, his goggles, his gloves and his favourite shirt.

For 1954, Ascari decided he would leave Ferrari in order to join a new team being put together by Gianni Lancia, with the celebrated Vittorio Jano building a car that would become known as the Lancia D50. It was late in arriving and so Ascari had to sit out most of the season. He did some sports car racing with Ferrari but it was a relatively quiet year for him. In November, the Lancia factory sent three of its D24 sports cars to Mexico, to take part in the Carrera Panamericana, the final round of the World Sports Car Championship. This was a 1,900-mile race on public roads from Tuxtla in the southern state of Chiapas to Ciudad Juarez, in the state of Chihuahua, in the very north of the country. The cars were driven by Juan Manuel Fangio, Piero Taruffi and Felice Bonetto. The drivers did reconnaissance work before the event and would often paint warning signals on the road to remind themselves of particular hazards ahead. At the town of Silao, in the central province of Guanajuato, Bonetto missed one of the warning signs and arrived in a 60 mph corner travelling at about 125 mph. He tried to negotiate the corner but the car slid into the side of a house and the impact was such that Bonetto hit his head on the side of the building. He died instantly. The car was stopped by a lamp post. When it was taken back to the factory it was found that the damage was not very serious.

Jano and his team decided that the D24 could be rebuilt for the 1954 season. The problem was that they were well aware of Ascari's superstitions and were worried that he would be spooked if he was racing a car which had previously killed its driver and so they carefully changed the chassis number from 0002 to 0006, so that Alberto would think it was a different car. The team entered the Mille Miglia in May 1954 with four new cars for Ascari, Taruffi, Castellotti and Gino Valenzaro. Ascari was on fine form and completed the 992-mile race from Brescia to Rome and back again in 11 hours and 26 minutes, a full 33 minutes ahead of the second placed.

The following year Lancia's D50 was ready for the Formula 1 World Championship, although the company was already running into financial difficulties. In Monaco Ascari had a celebrated crash into the harbour. A few days later he went to Monza and for some reason decided to test a Ferrari. He did not have his usual racing gear with him and so climbed aboard the car in a shirt and tie and with a helmet he borrowed from Castellotti. He crashed and was killed. Gianni Lancia decided to cancel his F1 programme and sold the cars to Enzo Ferrari…

Ferrari's big sponsor

The story of Scuderia Ferrari's primary sponsor begins in Germany in the 1830s. It was not a happy place, with poor working conditions, unemployment, failed harvests and increasing food prices. This led to uprisings that were suppressed violently. This unhappiness would lead to the revolutions in 1848 but before then, tens of thousands of Germans headed abroad, to countries where they thought life could be better. Many went to the United States, but a considerable number also ended up in Britain, particularly in London.

We know from records in the UK that a German who took the name Bernard Morris was born in Germany in 1793 and we can deduce from the 1841 census that he moved to Britain between 1833, when his daughter Johanna was born in Germany, and 1835 when his son Philip was born in London. The family lived in Whitechapel and was not poor, as it could afford a servant. Bernard's profession was listed as being a tobacco manufacturer. At the time, tobacco was imbibed in pipes and cigars, although chewing tobacco was also widespread.

Legend has it that Philip opened a shop on Bond Street in 1847, but he was only 12 at the time, so it was probably his father who opened the store at 22 Bond Street and began to sell cigars from Havana. Several Germans had opened cigar factories in Havana, which would explain the supply. This was followed seven years later (in 1854) by cigarettes. Legend has it that Philip Morris saw an army officer on leave from the Crimean War, smoking tobacco rolled in paper and decided that the firm should make hand-rolled, smoke-cured cigarettes, using Turkish tobacco. But the best cigarette-rollers could make only three or four a minute. Morris hired a staff of cigarette rollers from Russia, Turkey and Egypt and they manufactured an impressive 3,000 cigarettes a day, which were snapped up by customers keen on what was then called "a short smoke".

Somewhere along the way, the name of the business became Philip Morris & Co. Ltd.

In the 1860s, Don Luis Susini, a Cuban cigarette manufacturer, developed a cigarette-rolling machine that could roll up to 60 cigarettes a minute, and then as technology improved, American inventor James Bonsack built a more efficient machine able to produce 200 cigarettes a minute.

Morris's primary brands by 1870 were called Philip Morris Cambridge and Philip Morris Oxford Blues. The popularity of the cigarettes grew, with demand spreading through the British Empire. The business began to more and more money and, in 1872, Gustav Eckmeyer became the company's exclusive importer in New York.

Ironically, Morris was then struck down with lung cancer as he died in 1873, at the age of just 37, leaving his company to his widow Margaret and his brother Leopold.

That same year, Richard Benson and William Hedges opened a rival shop a few buildings further down Bond Street.

Seven years later, Leopold agreed a deal to buy Margaret's shares and continued in the business for another 14 years, taking on another partner in Joseph Grunebaum for a while. In 1381, the company initiated a public offering raising £60,000. This was oversubscribed six-fold. The money raised enabled the construction of new factories in Soho: one on Poland Street, the other on Marlborough Street. The business grew accordingly and the firm began marketing a brand called Marlborough, mild cigarettes produced in the Marlborough Street factory, which were aimed at the female customers. Later the company would also introduce a brand called Bond Street.

But Leopold Morris, by then in his mid-fifties, fell deeply in love with an opera singer and spent far too much money on her whims with the result that the business ran into trouble and ended up in receivership, with William Curtis Thomson, an accountant, getting control of the business. This all meant that when Imperial Tobacco was put together in 1901, Philip Morris was deemed to small to be a member. The firm was then appointed tobacconist to King Edward VII and became a chic and luxury product. At the same time, Eckmayer put together investors in New York to create a US manufacturing business. Ownership was split 50-50 between the British parent and American partners. The rest is history. The Americans bought out the British in 1919 and soon afterwards the firm shortened the Marlborough brand name to Marlboro and began selling cigarettes under that name.

Marlboro was one of the first tobacco sponsors in Formula 1, arriving with BRM in 1972. It began a hugely successful relationship with McLaren in 1974, which continued into the 1990s. Marlboro's links with Ferrari began in 1978 with Gilles Villeneuve and gradually the company became the primary sponsor of the celebrated Italian team. That remains the case today, despite anti-tobacco legislation that means that the Marlboro name and logo are no longer allowed.

Working in the background

Richard Cregan pops up from time to time in the Formula 1 paddock. He doesn't say much but he's clearly up to something... Cregan's story is one that is a great source of inspiration for those who want to work in the business – but don't know how to achieve their goal.

Born in County Kildare in 1960, Richard was passionate about the sport from the age of five or six because his older brother Andy competed in motorcycle trials. The family didn't have much money, their father was a blacksmith-turned-bricklayer and so the Cregan brothers had to do what they could.

At 16, Richard applied to become an apprentice with Aer Lingus, studying to become a technician at Bolton Street College (now part of the Dublin Institute of Technology) for two years before moving to the airport to complete his apprenticeship. His passion was motorsport and he did his best to compete, taking part in local rallycross, but followed the World Rally Championship passionately. At the time, Toyota was doing a lot of rallies in Africa and the enterprising Cregan managed to find the telephone number for Toyota Team Europe in Cologne, Germany, rang up and offered to work for free on the Safari Rally, telling the team that he could get to Nairobi simply enough on an Aer Lingus flight and wanted only accommodation. Not long afterwards, the TTE team manager Henry Liddon rang him.

The result was that Cregan quit Aer Lingus and went to Cologne to work as a mechanic with TTE. At the time, the team owned by Ove Andersson, had a staff of just 25. Cregan was then 24 and in the years that followed, as Toyota became a force in the World Rally Championship, winning the World Championship for the first time in 1990 with Carlos Sainz, Cregan was quietly moving up in the organisation. In 1993 Toyota bought TTE and it was renamed Toyota Motorsport GmbH (TMG). Cregan soon became operations manager for the team and overseeing the WRC successes that followed. He was then involved with the organisation of the team's Le Mans 24 Hours team, which raced at Le Mans in 1998 and 1999 before attention turned to a Formula 1 programme. By then, the team had expanded to 450 people.

Cregan was by then general manager and when Andersson retired (against his will) in 2003, Richard was made team manager of Panasonic Toyota Racing. Alas, the top management at Toyota Motorsport had little idea of how to be successful in motorsport. The team spent a huge sum of money but achieved little. A frustrated Cregan decided to leave at the end of 2008 in order to take up an interesting new role, overseeing the development of the Yas Marina racing circuit with Abu Dhabi Motorsport.

The first race took place in 2009 and Cregan moved up to become CEO of the Yas Marina circuit until the end of 2013 when he was asked by Bernie Ecclestone to work getting the Russian GP at Sochi together in time for the inaugural event in the autumn of 2014.

Having delivered the F1 race, he took time to run his own Formula 4 team, called Rasgaira Motorsports, in the UAE, with his son Robert as the driver. In 2017, with his Sochi contract coming to an end, he began working as an independent F1 consultant.

Since then, so they say, he has been working on the concept of a Formula 1 race in Las Vegas – not that he is going to say much on the subject.

Based on an idea by...

The South African Grand Prix of 1982, which was the last F1 race to take place in January, is best remembered for a drivers' strike caused by the mercurial Jean-Marie Balestre, President of the intenational federation, who inserted new clauses in the superlicence documents which meant that the drivers had to stay with the same team for three seasons, forced them to declare their salaries and made them commit to not criticising the governing body. It was all rather daft.

The race was scheduled for Saturday, January 23, and to make the most of the trip, the teams decided to test at Kyalami on the Monday and Tuesday before the race. It was during these tests that Marc Surer crashed and broke his ankles at Leeukop Corner, while testing his Arrows. The crash came two years after he had suffered similar injuries crashing an ATS at Crowthorne Corner.

A few days later Didier Pironi, the head of the Grand Prix Drivers' Association, announced that the drivers would not compete in Thursday practice and organised a coach to take them away from the circuit, to the Sunnyside Park Hotel. The race organisers tried to stop them leaving by parking a minibus across the circuit exit, but Jacques Laffite hopped off the coach, found the keys in the ignition, moved the offending machine and the drivers disappeared off to Johannesburg. Pironi remained at the circuit to negotiate. A compromise was eventually found and practice and qualifying happened as normal on Friday with René Arnoux on pole for Renault, Nelson Piquet second in a Brabham-BMW and Gilles Villeneuve third for Ferrari. Then came Riccardo Patrese

(Brabham-BMW), Alain Prost (Renault) and Didier Pironi (Ferrari), making it six turbocharged cars in the first six places, which was no surprise given that Kyalami is at 5,000 ft above sea level. The normally-aspirated cars were behind, led by the two Williams-Cosworths of Keke Rosberg and Carlos Reutemann.

There was little doubt that a turbo would win the race, if they could get to the finish. Arnoux led early on but on lap 14, Prost overtook him to take the lead. Things remained much the same until lap 41 when Prost suffered a puncture at high speed. He was lucky not to crash and drove around to the pits, taking a long time to get there. He was given new tyres but he was a lap behind when he rejoined. On his new tyres, he quickly unlapped himself and began to hunt down the cars ahead and within 20 laps was back in second place and hunting down Arnoux for the lead. René was in trouble with his tyres and could push no harder. Ten laps from the end, Prost took the lead and went on to win the race. It was a great victory, made extraordinary by the fact that Alan had fought back from being a lap behind. The key point, however, was that Prost had completed the race in a faster time than his team-mate – despite a long delay.

This got some of the designers thinking. At the time, Brabham was struggling with unreliable BMW engines, which was causing friction between team boss Bernie Ecclestone and BMW. Ecclestone wanted to race Cosworth-powered BT49s, while BMW wanted the team run BMW-engined BT50s, which were not very reliable and often not as fast as the lighter Cosworth cars. Towards the end of the season, a new fuel mix made things a lot better but at the British GP, Brabham designer Gordon Murray decided to try something a little different and started the BT50s with a light fuel load, allowing them to race away from the field using faster soft tyres. They were then called in to refuel and given new soft tyres which meant that they could run a faster race than would have been the case without having a pit stop. It was the start of F1's pit stop revolution... And was Alain Porst responsible for that?

A real all-rounder

The Chris-Craft Corporation is a manufacturer of powerboats, based in Sarasota, Florida. It dates back to the 1870s when Christopher Columbus Smith began building motorboats, but the celebrated name probably never reached the ears of Reginald Craft, a Barclays Bank manager from Romford in Essex, a devout Methodist, who went on to become a missionary in Africa. He was not into boats and so, when his second son was born, he saw no reason not to name the newcomer Christopher Craft, Christopher was, after all, a good biblical name.

Reginald had married one of his bank colleagues, Lois Logan, but their three sons: Ian, Christopher and Robert (known as Andy) were not much given to banking nor to religion. Ian became a doctor and in the 1970s, as professor of obstetrics and gynaecology at the Royal Free Hospital in London, was one of the pioneers of artificial insemination techniques in Britain. Andy was still a teenager when he became involved with a bodyshop in nearby Woodford; while Chris was briefly a buyer of ladies underwear before getting involved with the Ford Motor Company in Dagenham, where he quickly found his way into the competition department. He was keen to race but did not get the chance until he was 22, when he drove a Ford Anglia, which had come from his brother Andy's shop. There was never much money but Chris raced whenever he could and in whatever machinery was on offer. After a promising start in various touring cars he tried single-seaters with a Merlyn Formula 3 car and then a more competitive Tecno.

In 1968, he was recruited by the mighty Broadspeed team to campaign factory Ford Escorts in the British Saloon Car Championship, while he was also able to race sports cars with a Lola T70, with which he won the Martini International Trophy at Silverstone. This led him to start a long partnership with Alain de Cadenet, in his Porsche 908 and later his McLaren M8E CanAm car.

This led to the decision to acquire an ex-factory Brabham BT33 F1 car and enter it for Craft under de Cadenet's Ecurie Evergreen banner. Chris failed to qualify for the first race, in Canada, but he made it for the second race at Watkins Glen although his race ended with a suspension failure. There was no money to do more but Craft continued to compete in a wide range of machinery, including Formula 2, Formula 5000, sports and touring cars. He finished fourth on his debut at Le Mans in 1971 in a David Piper Ferrari 512M, which he shared with David Weir.

In 1973, he won the European 2-litre sportscar title in Martin Birrane's Lola and in 1976 finished third at Le Mans with De Cadenet, following up with fifth the following year. He returned to the BTCC with a Ford Capri in 1978 and 1979 when he was also working for Ford's competition department and running a second-hand car business. He continued to race into the 1980s but then turned to engineering, starting the Light Car Company, based in St. Neots in Cambridgeshire, with Formula 1 designer Gordon Murray, who he had known since his F1 days, with the goal being to build a car called the Rocket, which was shaped as a racing car and powered by a 1,000cc Yamaha motorcycle engine, but was licensed for the road.

The cars were produced until 1998 when the Light Car Company turned to classic car restoration.

A DIY Formula 1 car

Not everyone who drives a Formula 1 qualifies to be called a Grand Prix driver. There have been around 80 drivers who tried to qualify for a race since the World Championship began, but failed to do so, not least a certain Bernie Ecclestone, who tried to qualify a Connaught at Monaco in 1958. These nearly men (and women) come from wildly varied backgrounds. However, quite a few of them came from southern Africa.

Why? Well, back in the 1960s there was a fairly active South African National Drivers Championship which used all manner of machinery, ranging from cars that had been recently raced in the Formula 1 World Championship, to F1 machines that had been modified. And then there were a few home-built specials, based on the technology that the locals has seen in action. They would race one another and when Formula 1 visited South Africa each year at the end of the year (summer time in the Southern Hemisphere) there were always a few non-championship races, such as the Cape, Rand and Natal Grands Prix, which appealed to the F1 folk, who could make decent start money from race promoters and could also sell their old machinery at the end of the F1 season. As engines were hard to find, the locals relied on tuned-up versions of the 1.5-litre straight-4s which were used in the Alfa Romeo Giulietta.

Doug (Louis Douglas) Serrurier built LDS cars, based on old Coopers. They were not bad cars and consequently Ray Reed decided to build his own car, based on the LDS.

Reed had been born and grew up in what was then Southern Rhodesia, a self-governing British colony, run by a minority white government. He had recently turned 30 but had a taste for adventure. When he was 19, he had signed up for pilot training with the Southern Rhodesian Air Force at Belvedere Airport in Salisbury. For reasons that are now obscure, he did not graduate and become a jet pilot but rather ended up back at home in the town of Gwelo, halfway between Salisbury (now Harare) and Bulawayo. He focused instead on engineering, making himself enough money to consider building his own racing car. The folk of Southern Rhodesia had to be practical because they were a long way from anywhere and they were willing to give anything a try. Reed's car was called the RE-Alfa Romeo, named after his business, Ray's Engineering. The car was first raced in local events in 1963 before being taken to South Africa early in 1964. It didn't achieve a great deal but was in action in Lourenco Marques in Mozambique (now Maputo) later that year. For the end of season races in

1964, it went back to South Africa and competed in the Rand GP at Kyalami on December 12 but suffered an engine failure. It was entered for the South African GP, held on New Year's Day on the East London circuit, but Reed never showed up. Perhaps the blown engine could not be replaced, or there was no budget left. The car passed into the hands of Peter Huson, who crashed it at Kumalo in late 1966 although Reed had plans to rebuild it into a sports car for the Springbok Series, which was then becoming the major motorsport series in southern Africa. Whatever the case this was never done. Early in 1970, Reed and his three children were killed while flying in bad weather in South Africa.

A sad tale

When he was a teenager, Paul Morgan drove a 1904 De Dion Bouton around the cloisters of Gloucester Cathedral with rather undue haste. It seemed like a good idea at the time. He had rebuilt the vintage car and the cathedral was hosting an exhibition to highlight the hobbies of the boys at Gloucester School – and renovating old cars was Morgan's hobby… It was something he had picked up from his father Brian, the managing director of the Benton & Stone engineering company, who had rebuilt a string of old automobiles and was well known for having written, with Dick Wheatley, a book called The Restoration of Vintage and Thoroughbred Cars, which is still considered a classic today. Not long after the adventure in the cathedral cloisters, Morgan and his pal Robert Simpson drove the car in the London to Brighton Run. Thankfully no-one thought to ask about driving licences…

After leaving school, he won a place to study engineering at Aston University but in his spare time he enjoyed dangerous sports, including racing a 1934 Lagonda Rapier, learning to fly, going pot-holing and being one of the pioneers of hang-gliding in the UK. He graduated in 1970 and went to work for Cosworth Engineering in Northampton, where he became increasingly involved in the DFX programme, the engine soon replacing the Offenhauser as the standard engine in Indycar racing. It was at Cosworth that he began working with Swiss engineer Mario Illien, developing the engine for CART. Both men were frustrated that Cosworth was rather conservative because it had a virtually monopoly by then and did not need to push that hard. They believed that they could build much better engines and eventually decided to go it alone and do exactly that. Thy asked Roger Penske for help and he found them funding from General Motors and the four parties each took a quarter share in a new company called Ilmor Engineering – with Morgan looking after manufacturing and commercial matters and Illien running the design and development. In 1986 they entered CART with Ilmor-Chevrolet engines and in 1987 Mario Andretti gave them their first victory at Long Beach. A year later, Rick Mears gave them their first victory in the Indy 500. Between 1987 and 1991 the Ilmor-Chevrolet won 64 of 78 CART races.

In 1991, they built a V10 Formula 1 engine for the Leyton House F1 team and then added Tyrrell as a customer. This drew them to the attention of Sauber and Mercedes which were looking at doing F1. A deal was done for Ilmor to build the engines and things went well in 1993. A year later, Mercedes acquired GM's share in Ilmor and officially entered F1 with Sauber. In the US, Ilmor's new engine in 1995 was called a Mercedes. More success followed. That year Mercedes and Ilmor began a new relationship with McLaren. It took time but in 1998 and 1999 Mika Hakkinen won the World Championship using the engines.

The success allowed Morgan to indulge in his hobbies and he acquired not only a collection of vintage cars and motorcycles but also several vintage aircraft including a Harvard, a Mustang, a Corsair and a Hawker Sea Fury.

In the spring of 2001, he decided to take the Sea Fury up for a short lunchtime flight from the grass strip at Sywell Aerodrome, not far from the Ilmor factory in Brixworth. After half an hour flying he came in to land. The plane landed with a series of light bounces without the tail dropping as would normally be the case. It then ran into softer ground, which caused the plane to nose over, coming to rest upside-down, crushing the cockpit. Morgan was killed in the impact. He was just 52.

A man with a low profile

Lucio Zanon ran his family's wool business in Biella. He had inherited the business from his father Giuseppe, although the family originated in Venice.

Biella is in the foothills of the Alps and the soft water coming from the mountains was particularly effective for washing wool. The town became a centre for wool processing and textile manufacturing. With the mechanization of the industry and Biella's reputation for quality materials, the family became very rich. Lucio began to invest in other businesses, notably finance and insurance in nearby Turin.

Lucio was a man of culture and education and was keen on charitable causes. He established the Cavalry Museum in Pinerolo, and funded the reconstruction of the church tower of San Paolo in Biella, while also acquiring villas on the Italian Riviera and across the border in Saint-Jean-Cap-Ferrat. In World War II, he fought with the Italian army in France and later in Albania. He became a decorated hero and was granted the title of Count of Valguirata by King Victor Emmanuel III. He later became the Marquis di Fenera. A celebrated monarchist, he later became the Liberian consul in Turin.

His son Giuseppe, named after Lucio's father, was born in Biella in 1927 and grew up in a very comfortable world, where money was never a problem. He was known as "Gughi" and developed a passion for fast cars, which he shared with his cousin Vittorio, although the latter was more interested in historic racing cars, while Gughi enjoyed finding and helping to develop young talents.

He first became involved in Formula 1 in the 1950s and played a role in helping Italian youngsters Umberto Maglioli, Gino Munaron and Giancarlo Baghetti to get to F1. He would later become involved with Emerson Fittipaldi and Carlos Reuteman. He did a lot to help establish Frank Williams, who had spent a lot of time in Italy in his formative years, although the two later fell out later when Zanon wanted Michele Alboreto in a Williams for 1989. An agreement was basically in place (but not signed) but Williams decided that he wanted to keep Riccardo Patrese, leaving Alboreto out in the cold.

Count Zanon provided funding for Ronnie Peterson and then Lella Lombardi, paying for her drive with March in 1975, when she became the first woman to qualify for a race in F1 since the 1950s. Lombardi's sponsorship came from Lavazza, the company controlled by Zanon's wife Pucci. Lella finished sixth in her second race, the Spanish GP, which was stopped early as a result of crashes, which led to the awarding of half points. Nonetheless, her half-point marked the first (and to date last) time that a woman has scored in Formula 1. The relationship was due to continue in 1976 but Peterson became available and March preferred him. Zanon so Lombardi switched to RAM, although it was not a success. Peterson on the other hand did well and won the Italian GP that year. Zanon later provided money for Ronnie to rejoin Team Lotus in 1978, providing the money to pay Mario Andretti's salary.

After Peterson's death at Monza, Count Zanon began to support Michele Alboreto, and in 1981 organised for Michele to join Tyrrell, paying for the team's supply of Cosworth engines, and was delighted when Alboreto won the Las Vegas GP in Caesars Palace Grand Prix in 1982.

That year, the Banco Ambrosiano, Italy's second largest private bank, which had close ties with the Vatican, collapsed and, in the course of the years that followed, the Italian authorities investigated what had happened. In 1992, Zanon was one of 33 people convicted of fraud, although the sentence was overturned by the court of appeal in 1998. Zanon died in 2005, at the age of 78.

During his career, the family's banking business had grown significantly and in 1984 they acquired Morval Vonwiller, a boutique bank based in Milan, from Credito Romagnolo. This was relocated to Switzerland in 1989 and merged with an asset management company the family controlled. It opened offices in Geneva and Lugano, branches in Monaco and Georgetown in the Cayman Islands and a mutual fund headquartered in Luxembourg.

Few are aware that Count Zanon was also involved in getting Paolo Barilla into the Joest Porsche which won Le Mans in 1985 and later, in 1997, he helped Alboreto to get into the Joest-run TWR Porsche that won that race that year.

On top of that of all of this, he was at the centre of negotiating a settlement between Ayrton Senna and Toleman in 1984, when Ayrton wanted to leave to join Team Lotus. This resulted in Zanon buying Senna's Toleman contract, so that the Brazilian could move teams...

The F1 driver called Shane

In 1961, the Formula 1 World Championship kicked off in the middle of May, with the Monaco Grand Prix, with the first race with the new 1.5 litre engine regulations. A week later, there was the Dutch GP at Zandvoort but then there was a break of almost a month before the Belgian Grand Prix, which meant that the big F1 stars were looking for things to do.

Many of them went to the Nürburgring, to race in the 1,000 km and then headed back to Brands Hatch for the Silver City Trophy, which was scheduled to take place on Saturday, June 3. It was raining when practice began on the Thursday and it was not long before there was a big accident at Paddock Hill Bend, the treacherous first corner at the Kentish circuit. The youngster Shane Summers had crashed his Terry Bartram-run Cooper-Climax T53. The car hit the barriers at the exact point where there was a concrete wall protecting the tunnel that passes under the track from the paddock to the pits and the little-known 24-year-old was killed in the impact.

He was born in 1936 in the village of Rossett in Denbighshire. It was just a mile from the English border, just outside Chester. His family owned the John Summers Steelworks at Shotton, a few miles away on the River Dee. When he was only four years old, his father Spencer was elected as a Conservative MP for Northampton in a by-election, and so the family moved to south. Spencer Summers was a man who was obviously rated by the Prime Minister Winston Churchill, as he was soon put in charge of the regional organisation at the Minister of Supply, under Lord Beaverbrook, ensuring that the army had all that was required. It was an important job. Later, when the war came to an end, he was named Secretary for Overseas Trade, although he would hold that role for only a few weeks before the general election which shook things up as the Labour Party won the vote and Clement Attlee became the Prime

Minister. Summers lost his Northampton seat to Labour. He would return to the House of Commons four years later after being nominated as the Conservative candidate for Aylesbury, after the previous incumbent retired. It was a safe seat and he would hold it until his own retirement in 1970. He was content to remain a backbencher as he was again busy running the family firm. He was knighted in 1956.

One of Spencer's roles in the post-war period was as chairman of the Outward Bound Trust, which opened an international network of schools aiming to develop character, leadership and a sense of service through challenging outdoor activities. Shane travelled the world to instruct at Outward Bound schools in Malaysia and Africa.

When he returned to Britain, he decided that he wanted to go racing and acquired a swoopy Lotus 15 sports car from an old school friend. This was prepared by Terry Bartram and Summers enjoyed much success that year. The pair then decided to acquire a new Cooper F1 car to race in 1961. He showed promise in the UK and aboard with a front row starting position in the Großer Preis von Wien at Aspern in Austria, but he retired from the race with a suspension failure. He went up against the big stars of the day in the Aintree 200 in April and finished 12th in a field of 28. He then finished fourth in the London Trophy at Crystal Palace. His sixth race that summer was at Brands Hatch and there the story ended before it had really begun.

That year, there was a second British F1 driver called Summers, also driving a Cooper, but Chris Summers was no relation to Shane, although this did cause some confusion…

A most unusual event

The Dutch Grand Prix of 1961 was not really a gripper. The season, which had begun a week earlier in Monaco, marked the start of a new Formula 1, with the engines having been downsized from 2.5-litres to 1.5-litres.

The British teams had been opposed to the new regulations but Enzo Ferrari was in favour because his team had struggled to beat the British with the old machinery and there was basically nothing to lose with a complete rethink. Of course, he had the added knowledge that Ferrari had developed a successful engine for the 1.5-litre Formula 2 in the late 1950s. For the 1960 Formula 2 season, Carlo Chiti, Ferrari's chief designer, laid out a completely new rear-engined car, powered by the F2 Ferrari Dino V6. This had its first run at Solitude in July 1960 and beat all the factory Porsches on their home ground.

This chassis would become the basis of the 1961 F1 car, while Chiti had some new ideas for the engine as well, widening the V-angle from 65 to 120-degrees. This not only increased the power by around 10 hp, but also made the engine lighter and with a lower centre of gravity. While the British manufacturers were working on V8 engines – and running behind schedule – Chiti's F1 version of the F2 car with the new engine configuration proved to be much more powerful than its rivals. The cars were heavier and their handling was not as good, but they were much faster in a straight line.

The first race of the new formula had been in Monaco where Stirling Moss was able to beat Ferrari on a track where the handling was more important than the power. A week later in Holland it was a rather different story as Ferrari dominated practice, taking the whole front row with Phil Hill on pole from his team-mates Wolfgang Von Trips and Ritchie Ginther. Stirling Moss's Rob Walker Lotus and Graham Hill's BRM shared the second row. Von Trips led from the start while Graham Hill made a good start to head Phil Hill for a while before being overtaken by the American and by Jim Clark. Hill fell back to fight with Moss and Ginther with the Ferrari driver getting ahead, although he went wide on the last lap, which allowed Moss to grab fourth. But it has been a Ferrari walkover, with Von Trips followed hom by Phil Hill and then a gap of 12 secs to Clark and further nine seconds back to Moss, who finished a tenth ahead of Ginther.

It had not been a great event, except for the Ferrari fans in the dunes that day. However, as they all headed home, few of them had realised that the race had a unique place in Formula 1 history, at least up to that point. After 75 laps of racing – 195 miles – all 15 starters had finished the race – and no-one had even been into the pits. No-one had ever seen such reliability in F1 before. That achievement would not be matched again for 44 years and that was a bit of a cheat because the United States GP at Indianapolis in June 2005 featured only six starters – and all made it to the finish. Three months later F1 did it properly and all 20 starters at the Italian GP at Monza made it to the finish, headed by the McLaren of Juan-Pablo Montoya, ahead of the Renaults of Fernando Alonso and Giancarlo Fisichella.

A quiet force from Japan

Formula 1 is a world that boasts a lot of fixers and consultants, and more than a few wannabes as well, hoping to swim in the money that sloshes around the sport, in order to grab a taste of the big bucks for themselves. They duck and they weave and they have even been known to speak with forked tongues.

But beneath the surface of this world, there are a number of real power-brokers, who make things happen – but are happy to stay out of the limelight. Not being in the news is a badge of honour.

Japan's Masaru Unno, who died early in 2019, was one of them. He was well-connected, smart and very successful – and he was someone who even Bernie Ecclestone listened to when it came to matters in Asia – and specifically in Japan. Born in Toba, not far from Suzuka, in 1941, Unno grew up in post-war Japan as the country was rebuilding after the devastation of the war. The initial rebuilding came in Japan where factories had to be rebuilt and companies given new direction. That was effectively completed by 1955 and then Japan turned to rapid expansion of its export business, which led to an economic boom that saw the country's GDP rise from $91 billion to $1 trillion in 15 years. It was a way to show the world that Japan was a global player.

Unno studied at Hitotsubashi University, one of the most prestigious universities in Japan, best-known for its economics and business faculties. After graduating, he joined the exciting Honda company, an upstart motorcycle firm with unusual ideas and ambitions to enter the world's car markets. Honda's move into cars began in 1963 with launch of the T360 mini pick-up truck, which was quickly followed by the S500 sports car. From these humble beginning Honda Motor grew. Unno was employed in Honda's export department, setting up subsidiaries in different countries as the company grew and, in doing so, became a close collaborator with the company boss Soichiro Honda, who would remain a major player in the company until his death in 1991, although he officially retired from the business in the early 1970s.

Unno was sent off to France to become Vice-President of Honda France and, in 1974, was then told to establish a Honda subsidiary in Switzerland and became its first President. It was in this capacity that he went to Monaco in 1977 and watched the Grand Prix in the company of former Honda F1 boss Yoshio Nakamura and 1964 Formula 1 World Champion John Surtees. He was enthralled by what he saw. His passion gradually became a   and ultimately he left Honda to set up his own   s in Europe representing firms, importing, exporting and distributing new technology, sporting goods, television rights for sporting events and promotional products.

In this role he played a key role in negotiations to establish a Japanese GP in the 1980s at the Honda-owned Suzuka circuit. He was also soon negotiating TV rights deals for F1 in Asia, employing a number of people to help him, including a youngster called Craig Pollock, who would later set up British American Racing. As a promoter of the Japanese GP, he was given a seat on the F1 Commission for many years, although he spent much of his time at homes he owned in Europe, notably his own vineyard in the Côte de Nuits in Burgundy, in the appellation of Gevrey-Chambertin. He was also an accomplished pilot and hang-glider flyer.

A star that dimmed early

So, Charles Leclerc has signed a five-year deal to stay at Ferrari – and people still don't know how to say his name properly. This was not helped by the fact that his management decided that it was too difficult to stop Anglophones saying Lecl-ERK and so began telling people that this was how one should pronounce it. This is not correct.

In French the c at the end of Leclerc is not pronounced and so if you are going to get the name correct, you need to call him Charles Lecl-AIR. Or, you can do what some in the F1 media do and call him Chuck Lecluck.

And, no, he's not related to General Philippe Leclerc, the man who led the troops liberating Paris in 1944. Nor is he related to Edouard Leclerc who opened his first supermarket in Brittany in 1949, since when the E.Leclerc has grown into one of France's major retailers.

In fact, it is a fairly common name in France, derived from the profession of being a clerk, or a scribe. It has a number of variations, including Leclerc, Le Clerc and LeClerc and even Leclercq. In translation it would be similar to Schrieber, or Schriever from German, Clark or Clarke in English and Klerk in Dutch.

When you use the correct pronunciation, one finds that Charles is not the first Lecl-AIR in Formula 1 as Michel Leclère was also a driver back in the 1970s, although he arrived in the sport at a time when there were so many talented Frenchmen that not all could make it at the top.

Leclère came from the town of Mantes-la-Jolie, the first major town you come to when you leave Paris, going to the east, down the Seine Valley towards Rouen. Like many of his generation, he started relatively late, as he was attending a business school. He was 22, and still a student, when he embarked on a season in the Renault Gordini Coupe de France in 1968, at the wheel of a Renault 8 Gordini. The following year, he was runner-up and then switched to the single-seater Formula France (later to become Formula Renault) in 1970, driving a privately-run Alpine-Renault, tuned by his brother Jean-Louis. He won the first Formula Renault title in 1971 and moved up to Formula 3 in 1972, which he won at his first attempt in a factory Alpine and so moved up into Formula 2 in 1973, teamed with Patrick Tambay and Jean-Pierre Jabouille, racing the Elf 2 chassis. He finished sixth in 1974 and was runner-up to Jacques Laffite in 1975, winning three races and added two further victories in 1976. By then, however, he had made his F1 debut with a third Elf-supported Tyrrell in the United States in 1975, alongside Jody Scheckter and Patrick Depailler. He then signed to drive for the Wolf Williams team, driving a Hesketh, but lost his drive to Arturo Merzario, because he had backing from Marlboro Italy. He switched to sports car racing with a Gitanes-sponsored Mirage and would also later race sports cars in America.

In 1979, he was mentioned as a possible replacement for Patrick Depailler at Ligier after the latter had broken his legs in a hang-glider crash, but the drive went to Jacky Ickx instead. Leclère then decided to retire from racing and settled down to become a driver coach, with his ML Pilotage Concept company. He has since studied naturopathy and is now an expert practitioner.

Black gold

They call it "black gold" and oil's unique position as a portable, energy-dense power source has made it one of the world's most important commodities in the last 150 years, particularly since the invention of the internal combustion energy, but even before that, when oil was used for lighting and power-generation.

To put that into some kind of perspective, the US oil magnate John D Rockefeller was the country's first billionaire, with a fortune that amounted to more than two percent of the US economy in 1913, when it was estimated to be worth as much as $900 million, which translates, so they say, into $21 billion today. Others put the figure at over $300 billion, based on the two percent of the country's GDP today. At the turn of the century, Rockefeller controlled around 90 percent of the oil business in the US. Yes, that really does say 90 percent.

However, in 1911, the US Supreme Court decided that Rockefeller was too powerful and must break up his company. The result was that his empire was divided into 33 different companies, largely geographical. This did not stop them acquiring one another as time went by. Thus Standard Oil of New Jersey became the world's largest oil company in 1954 and began marketing its products under the Esso name, coming from the initials of Standard Oil. This led to disputes with other Standard Oil offshoots and so it changed its name to Exxon in 1972.

One of its rivals was the Standard Oil Company of New York – which became known as Socony. The firm adopted the name to Socony Mobil Oil in 1955 and 11 years later transformed itself into Mobil Oil. Seven year later, it dropped Oil from the name and became Mobil. Then in 1988 it was taken over and by its sibling and rival Exxon, to create the modern ExxonMobil.

Perhaps one should add a little more detail to understand just how powerful Rockefeller was in his day. Standard Oil of California, another of the 33 offshoots, became known as Socal, but this was not really snappy enough and so it began marketing its products under the Chevron name. Along the way Chevron gobbled up Standard Oil of Kentucky, Gulf, Texaco and Unocal.

And then there was Standard Oil of Indiana, which chose the Amoco brand in 1925 before being bought by BP in 1998, where it was merged with Sohio, which grew out of Standard Oil Ohio, giving BP a solid presence in the US markets.

And, finally, there was the Ohio Oil Company, another Standard Oil orphan, which changed its name to Marathon and relocated to Houston, Texas, in 1990.

Today, the US firms have slipped down the ladder of the biggest oil companies in the world as other firms have developed, notably in China, Saudi Arabia, Russia and China, but they continue to turn over hundreds of billions per year... with profits each year in tens of billions.

In December 2016, Red Bull Racing established a partnership with ExxonMobil, to use Esso fuel and Mobil oils in Formula 1. A Formula 1 sponsorship is peanuts when you look at such numbers…

F1 is also playing a major role in creating ever more efficient engines, aiming to help reduce global emissions and to extend the world's oil resources until someone can work out how to power everything by other means...

A story about rubber

Tyres can create negative publicity for rubber companies involved in Formula 1. In the days where there was competition, races could be won or lost by one tyre company or the other, but with a single supplier, tyres are only really mentioned when things go wrong. No-one says "my tyres were fantastic today", they say "I managed to make my tyres do what I wanted". However, the F1 association makes a tyre company seem a little more glamorous, and allows them to sell more expensive premium tyres, because consumers think the tyres are a little sexier. Well, that's the theory...

Today, Pirelli seems happy enough to use F1 to show that it is capable of making very specific tyres, which do what F1 wants them to do. Having said that, Pirelli has only won 223 victories, even with its unique supplier status since 2011. This still a long way behind Goodyear, which was in F1 nonstop between 1964 and 1998, winning 368 races.

As of 2019, only nine companies have competed in F1: Avon, Bridgestone, Continental, Dunlop, Englebert, Firestone, Goodyear, Michelin and Pirelli. They have come and gone at various times, with only Goodyear making one appearance, albeit from 1964 right up until 1998… The American firm had tyres in 494 races and won 368 of them, although for 113 races it was the single supplier. Pirelli has competed in just 378 Grands Prix and has won 223 times (as of the end of 2019) but 179 of those victories have come as the single supplier. All of the companies except Avon have managed to win races, but Michelin always had opposition, although the French firm won 102 of its 215 races. Dunlop was the same, with 83 wins from its 175 starts. Bridgestone, on the other hand, won 175 times, but 116 of these victories were as the sole supplier.

Today, Bridgestone and Michelin are competing to be the biggest tyre firm in the world, with Goodyear and Continental a long way behind, competing for the third spot. A way behind them are Pirelli, Sumitomo (Dunlop) and Hankook are quibbling over fifth place.

The irony of all this is that Goodyear is a little like the modern firm Tesla, as it has absolutely nothing to do with the man after whom it is named.

Charles Goodyear was a chemist who, in 1844, discovered how to manufacture stable, hardened yet pliable rubber by treating it with sulphur at high temperatures. He patented his invention, but never made a fortune, largely because the patents were challenged as there were others who claimed to have done the same thing before him. A lot of years were spent fighting legal actions and Goodyear died, penniless, in 1860 at the age of only 59, shortly after he heard of the death of his daughter.

It was nearly 40 years before the company bearing his name was started in 1898 by Frank and Charles Seiberling of Akron, Ohio. They decided that the rubber business was a good idea. They looked for a name and concluded that Goodyear deserved better and so started a company with his name and began to sell stock. The new automobile enabled the firm to become the world's largest tyre company by 1916 although the Seiberlings would be kicked out of their own business in 1921 during a financial crisis with bankers handing over the management of the business to others.

One can only wonder what Charles Goodyear would have made of the company's record in F1.

Peru's F1 driver

What's the most famous thing one can think of that comes from Peru?

Those of a certain age will say "Paddington Bear", who arrived at Paddington Station after stowing away on a ship from "Darkest Peru", and has now become an icon of marketing types, making lots of people very rich, including the Clarkson family, as in Jeremy Clarkson, who made a fortune manufacturing Paddington teddy bears. While Clarkson is famous in the automotive world, he doesn't really make it in Formula 1, as his occasional interventions are rarely anything positive for the sport.

For F1 fans, the answer to this question should be Jorge Koechlin von Stein. Now, I am sure that some are currently saying: "What?" or "There's never been a Peruvian Formula 1 driver" and things like that, but in fact the Koechlin family has a lengthy history in Grand Prix racing, which dates back to the very early days of the automobile.

The family can trace its roots back to the 15th century to the town of Stein am Rhein in Switzerland, although the name spread from there to Zurich, where one branch of the family developed; and also to Mulhouse in France, where the Koechlin's became textile manufacturers and later local politicians. The family would later produce Paul Koechlin, the winner of the 1895 Paris-Bordeaux-Paris race although, to be fair to Emile Levassor, he finished 11 hours ahead of Koechlin but his automobile had only two seats and the race was supposed to be for four-seaters.

In any case, Jorge's great-great grandfather left Mulhouse to work for a textile business that had been set up in Jung-Bunzlau in Bohemia (now the Czech Republic) and he settled there. When his family grew up, one of his sons decided to emigrate to Peru in 1852. Today, there are more than 300 Peruvian Koechlins.

Jorge was born in the coastal town of Huacho in 1950, where his branch of the family owned a fishery. He was one of eight children. Later they moved to a large farm near the Peruvian capital of Lima. For reasons that are not entirely obvious, Jorge's dream was to become a racing driver. He started competing at 21 and two years later, without much in the way of money, he headed to Britain to race Formula Fords, as many South Americans did in that era. He started out with a Merlyn chassis but then found work as a factory driver with Elden, a small car manufacturer based at Wrotham Hill, near Brands Hatch. This led to him making his Formula 3 debut with Elden in the autumn of 1974.

He switched to Formula Renault Europe in 1975, racing a works Lola run by Mader Racing. It was not a great success and he struggled for money in 1976, competing in a few sports car races, but then reappeared in 1982 having found funding to take part in the Aurora Formula One Championship in Britain, driving a Team Peru Williams FW07. His best result was second behind Jim Crawford. He tried to race in CART after that but there was not enough funding.

Back in Peru, he would purchase the Spanish-language Automundo magazine in 1990 and set about building up a business, expanding it into TV and producing a weekly show in Spanish for ESPN, while also doing F1 commentary work for various channels in Latin America. He continued to race in local races from time to time, winning the Gran Premio Nacional de Carreteras Camino del Inca in 1985.

While he continued with his career in the media, his brothers had embarked on interesting careers as well. Jose created a eco-friendly hotel chain called Inkaterra, while also working in films promoting the Amazon basin, notably Werner Herzog's Aguirre, The Wrath of God and Fitzcarraldo. His brother Pedro started his own airline called Wayraperú before standing for President of Peru, on an environmentalist ticket.

Jorge has also now turned to politics and was a candidate for the Partido Popular Cristiano in the upcoming Congressional elections in January 2020.

A man called boss

Hugo Ferdinand Boss was born in Metzingen, a small town to the south of Stuttgart in what was then the kingdom of Württemberg. It was July 1885 and Hugo was the last of five children born to the couple.

Sadly, Hugo was the only male survivor and thus became the heir to the family shop in Metzingen, where Heinrich Boss and his wife Luise Münzenmayer sold lingerie and linens. Hugo went through the local schools and then at 14, began an apprenticeship as a merchant in the nearby town of Bad Urach.

After three years, and another two when he was away doing his compulsory military service, he returned home in 1905 and soon took over managing the business. Nothing much changed until 1914 when he was called up and served in the German Army as a corporal throughout the war.

In the chaos of post-war Germany, Boss went home to Metzingen but it was still not until 1924, when he was 39 years of age, that he took the decision to set up his own factory, with the backing from two local entrepreneurs. The business began with just 20 seamstresses. One of the firm's first big commissions came in 1925 from Rudolf Born, a Munich-based textile distributor. The order included a significant number of brown shirts for the Nazi Party, which was regrouping after the failed Munich Beer Hall Putsch at the end of 1923. Its leader Adolf Hitler was then in prison but was released just before Christmas in 1925 and soon convinced the Bavarian authorities to lift a ban on his party. It was reformed and began to grow. Hugo Boss provided the uniforms.

The economic situation was very difficult at the time and, by 1931, Boss was effectively bankrupt. That year Boss became a member of the Nazi Party and as a consequence of this decision received more orders from the party, which helped to rebuild the business. As the 1930s went on and the Nazis became more powerful, Boss got more and more orders, including uniforms for the Wehrmacht (German army), the Waffen-SS, the Hitler Youth, the Post Office and the national railway employees.

When World War II broke out, he expanded the business to meet the demand for more uniforms and took on 140 forced labourers, almost all of them women. The firm treated them much better than many other companies but when the Allies arrived in Metzingen in April 1945 Boss was classified as "incriminated", fined 100,000 Reichsmarks and stripped off his right to vote. He appealed against the sentence and was later reclassified as a "follower," who had worked with the Nazi regime but had not been actively engaged in the politics.

The Hugo Boss company continued to manufacture uniforms, working with the French occupation forces and then with the Red Cross.

Hugo died in 1948, at the age of 63 and the business passed into the hands of his daughter's husband Eugen Holy. It remained a relatively small business but, in the 1950s, it diversified and began to manufacture business suits. These became increasingly popular in the 1960s, but it was not until Holy's sons Jochen and Uwe took over the business in 1969 that things really began to move as they decided to switch the company's focus to producing ready-to-wear suits for men, following the lead set by Yves Saint Laurent with his launch of Rive Gauche at the end of 1966.

To promote this business they decided to focus on male sports and began sponsoring activities in motor sport and later expanded into golf, tennis and sailing. Growth was rapid and Boss entered the US market in 1976.

Five years later, Boss entered F1 as a sponsor of McLaren. It would remain a backer of the team for the next 33 years until the decision was taken in 2014 to switch to Mercedes F1. That deal lasted for just two seasons and Hugo Boss took the decision to begin an association as an official partner of Formula E.

The Holy brothers decided to float the company at the end of 1985 and went off to start another fashion business. By 1990, Hugo Boss had come under the control of the Japanese company Leyton House, ran by Akira Akagi, who was running his own Formula 1 team at that time. However, this lasted just a year before Akagi ran into legal trouble at home and 77.5 percent of the company was sold to the Italian textile group Marzotto.

This also had strong links with motorsport as brothers Vittorio and Giannino Marzotto both had raced Ferraris in the 1950s. The business was effectively run by the Marzotto family until 2007 when 82 percent of the business was acquired by the British private equity firm Permira, which grew the business considerably in the course of the next eight years before it began divesting itself of the shares in 2015, when Marzotto began upping its shareholding once again. The majority of the company's shares, however, are publicly-traded.

What if? (part 1)

Sébastien Loeb is something of a force of nature. He has won nine World Championship titles and, to date, 79 WRC victories, the most recent being the Rallye de Catalunya in 2018. What is most remarkable about the driver from Alsace is that he didn't win his first World Championship until he was 30.

Loeb's climb to success was by no means meteoric, beginning when he got his driving licence at 18, and he bought a Renault Super 5 GT Turbo, with money from his grandmother, and rapidly lost interest in gymnastics, in which he had previously competed. He was soon racing his Renault in illegal street races, while studying to be an electrician. He was talented but somehow did not impress the judges in the Rallye Jeunes FFSA competition in 1995 and 1996, which he failed to win on both occasions. Rally raid competitor Dominique Heintz, who owned a garage in the region, read that Loeb had set the fastest times in the competition but had not been selected, and decided that he would set up a team for Loeb, with a friend called Rémi Mammosser. The team was called Ambition Sport Auto and it bought a Peugeot 106 Rallye for Loeb to drive. They won their class first time out on a regional rally. The first season ended up with a lowly ninth place in the Volant Peugeot series but the team partners mortgaged their houses to get Loeb a Citroën Saxo Kit Car for the Trophée Citroën in 1998. Sebastian won three times but still finished only sixth in the championship. He won the series the following year and then moved through the French national gravel rally championship in 2000, winning the 2WD class. He had finally done enough to be hired by Citroën in 2001, to compete in the inaugural FIA Super 1600 Drivers Cup and the French Rally Championship. He won both and finished second when given the chance to drive a factory Citroën Xsara WRC on the San Remo Rally. That got him into the factory team in 2002 and his first victory followed in Germany that year. He was runner up in the World Championship in 2003 before finally winning his first title in 2004.

What is often forgotten about Loeb is that he is an all-rounder and raced for Pescarolo Sport at Le Mans, finishing second in 2006. He won the Race of Champions three times, in 2003, 2005 and 2008 and, in December 2007, was given the chance to drive a Renault F1 car at Paul Ricard. He would do a second F1 test in 2008, this time with Red Bull Racing and there were serious discussions about a possible driver with Scuderia Toro Rosso in 2009, alongside Sébastien Buemi, although in the end it was concluded that he had not done sufficient circuit racing to warrant a superlicence.

In addition to his other exploits, he won the X Games in 2012 and won the Pikes Peak hillclimb in a Peugeot 208 T16 prototype. He then moved on to racing for Citroën in the new FIA World Touring Car Championship in 2014, won two races and finished third in the standings. He later tried the World Rallycross Championship, racing for Team Peugeot-Hansen and most recently has been competing in the Dakar.

One can only speculate how he would have done in F1…

What if? (part 2)

Yannick Dalmas was one of those drivers who seemed to be on their way to stardom in Formula 1, but circumstances worked against him.

When he was a child, he lived in the village of Le Beausset. His father renovated old cars and played football with motorcycles – a sport known as motoball. When Yannick was nine, the drinks magnate Paul Ricard began to construct a racing circuit on the scrubby plateau above the village. Naturally, he attended all the big events after it opened and even took part in classic car display when he was 11, as a passenger in a Model T Ford. The duo bumped into François Cevert in the paddock and Dalmas remembers that this was the moment when he decided he wanted to be a Formula 1 driver.

He started out in motocross but suffered so many injuries that he decided to try cars and entered the 1980 Marlboro Cherche un Pilote competition. He failed to win that year and again in 1981 but in 1982 he was finally victorious (there were around 1,000 contestants each year). He won a fully-funded Formula Renault drive in 1983 with the celebrated ORECA team. He finished third in his rookie year and won in 1984 and, in his first year in Formula 3 in 1985, was runner-up to his team-mate Pierre-Henri Raphanel. He won the title in 1986 with six wins, moved into Formula 3000 with ORECA in 1987 and won races in Pau and Jarama and finished fifth in the title. By then, everyone had heard of Yannick Dalmas. He made his debut in F1 with Larrousse at the Mexican Grand Prix that year – and was signed to drive for the team in 1988. The car was not very competitive but he did a better job than his experienced team-mate Philippe Alliot and came close to scoring points on two occasions, but then, at the end of the year, he was struck down by an attack of the rare Legionnaires Disease.

Dalmas returned to F1 at the start of the 1989 season but was not fully recovered. By the mid-season he was dropped by Larrousse. He found a seat with AGS but this was the era of pre-qualifying in F1 and there was really nothing he could do. In 1990, he managed to qualify a few times, his best result being ninth place.

It was, he concluded, a pointless exercise to try to race in F1 without a decent car and so he took up the offer of a factory drive with the Peugeot sportscar team in 1991. Paired with Keke Rosberg, he won the races at Magny-Cours and in Mexico City and then in 1992, teamed with Derek Warwick, he won the World Endurance Championship title and with Mark Blundell, joining them, they won the Le Mans 24 Hours. He finished second at Le Mans in 1993, sharing with Thierry Boutsen and Teo Fabi, but when Peugeot quit, he joined a Porsche team, funded by Jochen Dauer, and won Le Mans again, racing a street-legal version of the Porsche 962, with Hurley Haywood and Mauro Baldi. He tried to return to F1 with Larrousse for a couple of races in 1994 but the team was not competitive. Back at Le Mans, however, he won his third victory a McLaren which he shared with JJ Lehto and Masanori Sekiya. He tried DTM and raced IndyCars but it was in sports cars where he enjoyed the most success winning the Sebring 12 Hours in a Ferrari 333SP. He would move on to BMW in 1999 and won Le Mans a fourth time in a BMW V12 LMR with Pierluigi Martini and Jo Winkelhock.

He was then 37 years old and decided that it was time to retire as a driver but began to work as a driver consultant and ambassador for manufacturers and sponsors.

In recent years, Yannick has been the FIA driver steward for the World Endurance Championship, with occasional appearances at F1 races as well.

One can only wonder what would have happened but for the Legionnaires Disease.

The story of Arthur Legat

Arthur Legat is not a name that most Formula 1 fans will have ever heard, but he holds a unique place in the sport. He was the oldest ever F1 debutant, a record that is unlikely to ever be beaten as he was 53 years old at the time – and it has been quite a while since there was an F1 driver of that age…

When one looks at his record in Formula 1 in 1952 and 1953, it may look like Legat was not a great talent. He was more than a minute off the pace of pole position man Alberto Ascari at Spa in 1952, although, to be fair, Stirling Moss was half a minute off Ascari's pace that day, driving an ERA, Peter Collins was two seconds slower than Moss in an HWM and Prince Bira was 51 seconds off the pace in a Simca Gordini.

Machinery was important, even in those days.

A year later Legat returned with the Veritas and was slightly slower, although his appearance that day makes him the third oldest man to have started a Grand Prix…

What one needs to remember is not the machinery, but also Legat's age and the fact that he raced rarely. One might call him a gentleman racer, but that creates the wrong impression as Legat was not some rich aristocrat, out having fun, but rather a garage and breakdown recovery service owner, who liked to race when he had time and money.

He was born in Haine-Saint-Paul, a small town between Charleroi and Mons, in 1898. It was his home town and he died there in 1960. In those days, motor racing in Belgium was really only two circuit: Spa-Francorchamps and Chimay.

Legat made his debut in competition in 1923, initially as a sidecar passenger in motorcycle races but then in 1926 he raced a 1100 cc Amilcar CGS (Chassis Grand Sport) cyclecar at the new high-speed road circuit at Chimay, which hosted the first Grand Prix des Frontières that year. He did little else, competing in only a few local hillclimbs apart from his annual outing at Chimay.

Chimay was his circuit. For the race in 1931, he acquired a Bugatti Type 37A, which was a similar chassis to the famous T35B, but was fitted with a 1.5-litre engine for voiturette races. He used this to win the Grand Prix that year and again in 1932. He would later buy a T35B from Georges Bouriano, which he raced at Chimay for the first time in 1934 and finished second in 1937.

After the war, by which time he was in his late forties, Legat bought a Maserati 4CM and raced it at Chimay in 1949. Two years later, he acquired a German-built Veritas Meteor and raced the car at Chimay in 1952 and 1953. The decision to buy a Veritas allowed him to take part in the World Championship of 1952 when the series was run to Formula 2 regulations and so he entered his car in the Belgian Grand Prix, becoming the oldest F1 debutant ever, at the age of 53, in 1952. He finished 13th, five laps down, but had become a Formula 1 driver nonetheless.

He continued to race each year at Chimay until 1959... shortly before his death.

The story of Estéfano Nasif

One of the least-known of all Formula 1 drivers was Estéfano Nasif, who raced a privately-entered Maserati 250F in the Argentine Grand Prix of 1960. He later popped up again with the De Tomaso F1 car but failed to qualify for the Italian Grand Prix. On the face of it, he might not seem to have been much good, based on his results, but back home in Argentina, in his home town of Concepción, in the province of Tucuman, there is a racing circuit named in his honour, there's a school that bears his name and even one of the city's main streets is named after him.

Concepción is 750 miles to the north-west of Buenos Aires, at the foot of the Sierras Pampeanas, a range of mountains that run parallel to the Andes, rising up from the plains in the east.

Nasif Moisés Estéfano was born there in the late autumn of 1932. His father Jorge and mother Elia were both of Lebanese descent, there being a large community of Lebanese in the country – now numbering around 1.5 million – having left their homeland because of persecution by the Ottoman Turks.

Nasif was the second of five brothers but he dropped out of high school to help his father run the family business. In 1951, he learned to drive at the wheel of a Ford 40, which dated from the 1930s, and he had soon made his racing debut in a race in the local 9 de Julio Park in the city. He then had to stop his racing activities when he went off to complete two years of military service with the Argentine navy at Bahia Blanca, 950 miles from home.

When he returned home he went straight back to racing and scored his first win in August 1955 in a race in the town of Juan Batista Alberdi. He soon began to travel outside his own province to compete and scored his first national success in 1957 at the Autodromo in Buenos Aires.

Two years later would later make his debut in the Campeones de Fuerza Libre, Argentina's top racing category at the time, the championship being won that year by none other than José Froilán González.

Early in 1960, he made his F1 debut at the wheel of a privately-entered Maserati 250F, but finished 10 laps behind the winner in 14th place after a series of problems.

The following year he invested in a new car but it was never delivered. The money disappeared and he had to sit out the best part of three years before he could compete internationally again. He was offered a drive in the 1962 Italian GP by fellow countryman Alejandro de Tomaso but was unable to qualify the uncompetitive car.

Back home in Argentina, he entered the new Campeones de la Fórmula 1 Mecánica Argentina with a locally-built Loeffel-Chevrolet, constructed by Carlos Loeffel, a well-known racer and car builder in Argentina's famous road races in the Turismo Carretera category. Estéfano won the title in 1963 and 1964.

He was back in Europe in 1964 but only had enough money to buy an old Lotus 22 for Formula Junior races in Europe, although he did several GT events that year with more success. He returned home and after competing in the local single-seater series with some success, eventually concentrated on the Turismo Carretera.

He was killed in an accident in the autumn of 1973 at Aimogasta in the La Rioja province, not far from his home town, during an event called the Gran Premio de la Reconstrucción Nacional. His car suffered a mechanical failure in a fast corner and rolled a number of times. He was thrown from the vehicle when the seat belts failed and died of head injuries shortly after the accident.

In his career he competed in 101 races and won 21 of them, but perhaps it is his record of podiums that is more impressive, with 51 top three finishes.

A few names to play with

Even today, there are certain elements of British society who like to blame the Germans for everything. Given that it is now 75 years since the end of World War II, this does seem a little archaic. Still, without the Germans, Britain would likely not have the strong motorsport industry that exists today. Why so?

Well, Britain's post-war motor racing boom was based on the fact that the country had a huge number of airfields that has been built to defeat the Germans, which were deserted as soon as the war ended. Thus, circuits sprang up wherever the locals could sort out deals with the Air Ministry, or with the owners of the land on which the airfields had been built.

Thus without the Germans, there would never have been a racing circuit at Silverstone...

History is a fascinating thing and if one trawls back to medieval times, one can discover that Silva Tone derives from the Latin for Wood Town. This is logical because at the time the area was covered in the Forest of Whittlewood. Forests being good places to hide, there was a Benedictine priory built in the peace of the woods, named Luffield Abbey and not far from this was a chapel dedicated to St Thomas a Becket. There was also a Chapel Copse, a Wild Wood and some fairly worthless land called Maggot Moor.

King Henry VIII changed all that in 1542 when he seized all the land belonging to the monasteries and sold everything off after separating England from Papal authority and declaring himself the Supreme Head of the Church in England. The land of Luffield Abbey became Luffield Abbey Farm while the old abbey itself fell into ruin. Only the chapel survived but this was turned into a private residence. The forest was gradually being cut down over the centuries and, by the early 19th Century, not much woodland was left.

It was at this point that (take a deep breath) Richard Temple-Nugent-Brydges-Chandos-Grenville, the 1st Duke of Buckingham and Chandos, arrived on the scene. He felt the need for a grand tree-lined carriage drive from Stowe House to Silverstone village, as befits a man with such a long name, and so acquired the necessary land, leaving Luffield Abbey Farm to continue its quiet existence.

Little really changed until 1940 when civil servants in camouflaged Morris Tens were spotted in the area, looking for possible sites for airfields. Wild Wood, up near Chapel Copse would have to go. They couldn't find any trace of Luffield

Abbey but reported that the St Thomas a Becket Chapel would have to be demolished (although the stones were numbered and removed to a farm, 50 miles away). The duke's tree-lined avenue fell victim as well, although a section of it did survive, as the principal road through the airfield (minus the trees, of course). It was decided that the site would suit a Class A aerodrome design, with three converging concrete runways in a triangular pattern. The longest runway was aligned southwest to northeast to allow aircraft to take off and land into the prevailing winds.

The other two runways were for days when the wind blew from other directions. They were all joined by a perimeter track that curved gently, to allow bombers to manoeuvre. Once the plans were completed, the construction company Mowlem moved in and work began, with the runways being laid and the buildings, which were pre-fabricated – to standard designs – hurriedly put up. The work was completed early in 1943 and Operational Training Unit 17 moved in. The base was to be used for teaching new crews to fly the Wellington bomber and 54 planes were supplied, many of them having previously been used in bombing raids over Germany. There were a lot of accidents, with 124 airmen killed in training. In that period, RAF Silverstone housed 2,300 RAF and Women's Auxiliary Air Force (WAAF) staff. And then, very rapidly, the war ended and the base was shut down.

Silverstone resident Maurice Geoghegan was delighted at this development and, in the summer of 1946, he took his new Frazer-Nash sports car out on the old airbase. There were, he discovered plenty of different possible layouts to try. The RAF did not have the staff to put guards on every old airfield and so it was left open to the public. Not long afterwards, Geoghegan went to the Shelsley Walsh Hillclimb and met with some pals in the Mitre Oak public house in Ombersley and discussed Silverstone. Consequently 11 Frazer Nashes and a Bugatti turned up at Silverstone not long afterwards. They had a completely illegal race, which involved some unusual risks: one of the party ran over a garden fork which had been left on the ground and was lucky to escape with only a grazed arm and, so legend has it, Geoghegan hit a sheep which had wandered on to one of the runways.

The rest is history.

An unexpected twist

Raul de Mesquita Boesel was a lucky man. Born into a wealthy and well-connected family in Curitiba, Brazil, he was one of four brothers who grew up in a world of equestrian competition. When he was a teenager, Raul twice won the Paraná state show jumping championship but at the age of 16 he discovered motor racing, after going to a local kart track with a friend. He liked the look of it and a year later had won his first karting championship in Curitiba.

The family insisted that he finish his studies so he did not make his car racing debut until he was 20, when he began racing in the national stock car championship. He finished fourth in his debut year and it was clear that he talent to go a long way. So he headed off to Europe to race Formula Ford 1600s and immediately won nine of his 27 races, although he finished runner-up in both of the two British FF1600 championships. This was good enough to attract the attention of the British Formula 3 teams and in 1981 he joined Murray Taylor Racing. He finished third in his first season and earned a test with McLaren. His ambitions were helped by the fact that Brazilian President João Figueiredo was a family friend and helped to organise sponsorship from the government-owned Instituto Brasileiro do Café (IBC), advertising Cafe do Brasil. This helped him to get a drive for 1982 with the Rothmans March F1 team.

It was not a great car and, as the season went on, Boesel struggled to qualify for races. He looked for a better option in 1983 with his coffee money being boosted by some backing from Embratur, the national tourist board. There were not many options but Ligier had been a winner in 1981 and Boesel hoped that the team could rise once again. The problem was that Ligier was short of cash after the withdrawal of Talbot and the cars that were built for 1983 were in reality revamped 1982 cars, modified to replace the Matra V12 with the Cosworth V8. Ligier was working on a Renault turbo deal for 1984 but until that happened the team had to compete against teams using turbo engines. Once again Boesel failed to scored a point, although he did manage a seventh place.

With no real options in Formula 1 in 1984, he went home to Brazil and joined the INI Competicion team, driving a Berta-Volkswagen in the Codasur Formula 2 series in Latin America. He won a race but decided to move to the United States in 1985, to drive for Dick Simon in CART. He scored some promising results in 1986 as he used the experience gained in his rookie year, but no top drives were available and so he took the offer of a drive with Tom Walkinshaw's Silk Cut Jaguar sports car team. In 1987, he became the first and (to date) only South American to win the FIA World Endurance Championship, taking his Silk Cut Jaguar to five wins in 10 races. The following year, teamed with John Nielsen and Martin Brundle he won the Daytona 24 Hours. Another stint in CART proved frustrating, although he finished third in the Indy 500 in 1989 and so he returned to sports cars in 1991 with the Bud Light Jaguar and finished runner-up at Le Mans. In the years that followed, he finished second in CART races on five occasions but could never win a race and decided in 1998 to return home to Brazil where he raced in the national stock car championship until his retirement in 2006. After he finished racing, he decided to try a new career as an international DJ, based in Miami, but performing all over the world.

A long time in the F1 game

A lot of folk think that fashion magnate Lawrence Stroll has bought a Formula 1 team just because of his son Lance. But if you take a wander back in history, you find that Lawrence has been supporting Formula 1 teams since long before Lance was born. It is a story that goes back to the 1980s when Stroll and his business partner Silas Chou sold their European licences to sell Ralph Lauren/Polo clothing and bought the rights to the Tommy Hilfiger brand. As part of their plan to expand the businesses, they did a deal to use both the Pepe Jeans and Tommy Hilfiger brands to sponsor Team Lotus, which had just been taken over by Peter Collins and Peter Wright, after the Chapman family decided it was time to get out of Formula 1. Stroll would remain a sponsor until the end of 1994 when the team collapsed. It was four years before Hilfiger returned to Formula 1 as a sponsor of Ferrari, the plan being to open a chain of Hilfiger stores in Italy. Lance Stroll was born that same year.

The Hilfiger-Ferrari sponsorship led to another deal with Stroll and Chou buying the British jeweler Asprey & Garrard in 2000 when the Brunei Investment Group sold the firm after Prince Jefri Bolkiah, the Sultan of Brunei's playboy brother, ran the company into trouble. Both companies had been Ferrari sponsors… The upshot of this was that Stroll became close to Ferrari boss Jean Todt, which probably explains why Lance was a member of the Ferrari Driver Academy from the age of nine onwards.

Asprey was not a great success for Stroll and Chou. They invested a great deal but sales did not develop as much as they had expected and they decided to sell in 2006 to private equity firms. That same year, the duo sold their shares in Hilfiger for an impressive $1.6 billion and turned their attention to another brand that they had acquired in 2003, Michael Kors. This led to a very successful IPO in 2011, before Stroll and Chou exited the fashion business in 2014. Stroll has since concentrated on his son's racing career, taking him to Williams, buying the troubled Force India and taking over Aston Martin, in order to turn his team into a factory operation.

Along the way, Stroll has bought a few impressive "toys", including in 1999 the Mont Tremblant racing circuit in Canada, which was rebuilt under the guidance of circuit designer Alan Wilson. In 2013, he added a rare 1967 Ferrari to his impressive car collection, paying a rumoured $27.5 million for the car.

A huge legacy

Aristocrats are a funny lot. Lavish wealth apparently does that to some people. Take a look around at some of the more eccentric ones and you will find those who had zebras trained to pull their carriages around London; those who had pianos installed in their Rolls-Royces; or who arrived at dinner parties, riding on the back of a bear. And of course there were those who built strange things, such as underwater ballrooms... Others were less eccentric and being so-called "sportsmen" became motorsport administrators.

The people who were involved with the Association Internationale des Automobile Clubs Reconnus (AIACR), the forerunner of the Fédération Internationale de l'Automobile (FIA) were all European aristocrats: barons, counts, viscounts and even princes. They regularly had a "de" between their name and surname, indicating that they had large estates somewhere or other (or, at least, used to). In fact, it was not until 1965 that someone with a relatively normal name arrived to head the organisation: Wilfred Andrews, the first British FIA President. Most of those mentioned about never needed to worry about such things as work, and took on their roles because that was what people in their position did. This is why such roles were (and remain) unpaid. The people doing them didn't need money.

They tended not to be celebrated competitors.

However, there are exceptions to every rule and Francis Richard Henry Penn Curzon was definitely that. He was President of the British Racing Drivers' Club for many years and represented Great Britain in the Commission Sportive Internationale (CSI), a division of the FIA which was delegated the organisation of automobile racing as long ago as 1922. In the end he would become a Vice-President of the CSI.

So what, you might ask, did he do that was so good for motorsport? Well, where should we begin? Perhaps we should explain who he was. He was born into one of Britain's most famous families, descended from Admiral Lord Howe, a distinguished naval officer, who became the First Lord of the Admiralty, whose only daughter married into the Curzon family, which was a clan that could trace its noble roots back to the 1600s.

Curzon's father married one of the daughters of the 7th Duke of Marlborough and thus, in addition to his string of minor titles, was also a cousin of Winston

Churchill and, naturally, related to the Viceroy of India – the Marquess Curzon of Kedleston.

Educated at Eton, he was interested in cars from the very beginning and in 1898, at the age of 14, went off to France for a summer holiday job, working as a mechanic in a French garage, learning about cars and how to speak French. After Eton, he went to Christ Church College, Oxford, served with distinction in World War I, joining the Royal Navy and seeing action in the Dardanelles campaign as a gunnery officer aboard HMS Queen Elizabeth before becoming the commanding officer of a battalion of the Royal Naval Reserve Division on the Western Front.

After the war – at the time he was known as Viscount Curzon – he stood for election as a Conservative candidate to become the Member of Parliament for Battersea South in London and held the seat for 11 years before moving to the House of Lords when he inherited the title Earl Howe when his father died.

Being a rich young man with not much to do, he got himself into trouble from time to time as an enthusiastic motorist and so, in 1928 – at the age of 44 – he decided that he would start motor racing at the wheel of a Bugatti T43. His first major event was the Ulster Tourist Trophy of 1928, on the Ards circuit. He had a huge lead by the halfway stage when his fuel tank began to leak and he had to retire. Having shown his ability, and having money to buy the best machinery, including a Mercedes-Benz SSK which had previously been raced by Rudi Caracciola, and a celebrated 1927 Delage, he began to enjoy good results. His biggest claim to fame came in 1931 when sharing an Alfa Romeo with Sir Henry Birkin he won the Le Mans 24 Hours. In his first year in competition, he co-founded the British Racing Drivers' Club, with Dudley Benjafield and became its president in 1929.

He was soon racing in Grands Prix, winning a number of events in Europe and at home. He had some pretty exciting escapes, including flying into the trees at Monza. He moved on to ERAs in the late 1930s, hurt himself quite badly in a crash at Brooklands in 1937 but returned to action to compete against the mighty AutoUnions and Mercedes GP cars in the Donington Grand Prix. At the end of 1938 – when he was 54 – he decided to retire from the sport and lead a less dangerous life…

War then broke out and he was back in action with the Royal Naval Reserve, ending the war as a Commodore of Atlantic Convoys.

It was after the war that his role in motorsport became important. At the time, Britain had no racing circuits. Brooklands had been ruined during the war when some of the banking was demolished and Donington had been turned into an army camp. Racers had nowhere to race. As President of the new 500 Club, he played a vital role in convincing the government of the day that it would be a good idea to use airfields as motor racing venues. Along with the aforementioned Mr Andrews, Howe played a key role in securing the use of RAF Silverstone and helped to organise the first British Grand Prix in 1948. Under his leadership, the BRDC developed from being a private dining club into a high-profile motorsport association and race promoter.

On top of all of this, he was one of the first drivers to race with a crash helmet, a decision that he believed saved his life on no fewer than three occasions. Others began to follow suit.

His children grew up surrounded by the sport and his daughter Lady Sarah Curzon married Piers Courage, the F1 dr ver. Another daughter Lady Georgina married Home Kidson, another racing driver, who the brother of Glen Kidson, a celebrated racer and aviator.

Earl Howe died in 1964, at the age of 80, leaving a hell of a legacy…

Confusions

The official posters for the French Grand Prix are more than a little confusing. If you take a look at the 1968 version from Rouen, it clearly says that the race was the "1er Grand Prix de France". If you check the 1969 poster, when the race was held at Clermont-Ferrand, it is billed as the "2ème Grand Prix de France".

But how can that be when we all know – or at least have been told many times – that the French GP in the world's oldest motor race, dating back to 1906? Things get rather more confusing when you look at the poster of the 1975 race, held at the Circuit Paul Ricard. It clearly states that the race is the "61ème Grand Prix de France". Sure enough, if you check 1976, the race is billed as the 62nd Grand Prix. So did they hold 60 Grands Prix between 1968 and 1975?

There is another problem. If the first Grand Prix was held in 1906 and one adds 69 years, logically, one should have the 70th Grand Prix in 1975.

Now we know that there were two World Wars which ought to mean that there were no races between 1914 and 1918 and again between 1939 and 1945. But that's not right either because that would mean 12 missing races (five plus seven) and so the 1975 race ought to have been the 58th… But that's wrong too because there was a famous Grand Prix in 1914 when Georges Boillot fought Mercedes in his Peugeot at Lyon. Ah, but in 1955, you might say, the Grand Prix was cancelled following the Le Mans disaster. So add one and take another away and the 1975 should still be the 58th, not the 61st.

But then, when you think about it, after World War I the Grand Prix was not revived until 1921 (when Jimmy Murphy won for Duesenberg), so one must deduct two more from the total. And after World War II, the first Grand Prix in France was not until 1947, so another two must be knocked off the total. So you get 58 minus four which means that the 1975 race ought to have been the 54th Grand Prix, not the 61st.

Oh, wait a minute, there was no race between 1909 and 1911, so that's another three to knock off the total, which means the 1975 race ought to have been the 51st. So how on earth have the French managed to come up with 61 races?

Merde, ces Français sont compliqués…

There is, of course, an explanation for all of this. The French GP really was the world's oldest motor race, but it is also true that the first French GP did not take place until 1968. How so? Because before 1968 the race was known as the Grand Prix de l'Automobile Club de France.

It was all the fault of President Charles de Gaulle. After the liberation of Paris in 1945, his provisional government issued Ordinance 45-1922 declaring that all sporting French organisations must be authorised to continue in their roles by the Minister of Education. De Gaulle wanted the country's sporting administrators to be strong and independent of politics and business interests. In this respect, the ACF was not in a very strong position because of its relationships with the country's automobile manufacturers. To resolve the problem the ACF established the Fédération Française du Sport Automobile (FFSA) in 1952, to comply with new French laws. The first FFSA President was Augustin Pérouse, who also happened to be the President of the ACF. This comfy arrangement continued into the 1960s by which time FFSA members were increasingly frustrated by the situation. It was a time of change in France, with increased opposition to traditional institutions. This would lead to the civil unrest in May 1968.

In the motorsport world, the rebellion came a little earlier with the FFSA applying to be given the sporting power by the FIA, to replace the ACF. The FIA did not want to get involved in the domestic affairs of its members and ruled that autumn that it would not change existing arrangements, unless asked to do so by the ACF. However, the FFSA had the support of manufacturers, race organisers, entrants, drivers and, most importantly, politicians. The French government, represented by the Minister of Youth and Sports, François Missoffe, a former French Ambassador in Japan, invited the FIA to have discussions about the matter and a compromise was reached with the ACF giving up its sporting power in a seemingly generous fashion, when in fact it had been forced to do so…

Thus the 1968 Grand Prix was no longer the Grand Prix de l'ACF and so was the first French GP, as the posters state. However, after a while, the difference ceased to matter and so the FFSA went back to using the numbering system that had previously existed.

However, this system can only be described as odd because, in the 1920s, in order to emphasize France's position as the cradle of motorsport, it was decided that the big annual races organised by the ACF between 1895 and 1905, latterly known as the Gordon Bennett Cup, should be deemed to have been Grands Prix de l'ACF. Thus, they declared that the 1st Grand Prix de l'ACF had actually been the ninth... The new first race having been the 1895 Paris-Bordeaux-Paris event.

This was a rather daft idea given that the ACF was not established until late in 1895, after the Paris-Bordeaux-Paris had taken place.

But, hey, Nicolas Chauvin was an apocryphal French figure from Napoleonic times, who legend suggests was a nationalist zealot to such an extent that his name passed into the language as "chauvinism"...

A passionate engineer

No-one really knows why Geoffrey Taylor decided to name his first racing special after the shortened version of the western Canadian province of Alberta, but the car was called an Alta. Perhaps it was a wistful thing because the cars were built in the safe and comfortable world of Surbiton, in the suburbs of London, half an hour by train from Waterloo, while Alberta was a more rugged and exciting world. Whatever the case, Alta was the name he chose – because he liked the sound of it.

Tayler's father was a consulting mechanical engineer who originated from Salford, a town to the east of Manchester that had been engulfed by the booming population during the industrial revolution. The young family left Salford in the late 1890s and by the time Geoffrey was born, had settled in the pleasant seaside town of St Annes on Sea, to the south of Blackpool. Not long afterwards they moved south and settled in a large house on Coombe Lane in Norbiton, Surrey, not far from Kingston-on-Thames.

Geoffrey was too young to fight in World War I and, in the mid-1920s, he began providing special GT (Geoffrey Taylor) kits for the light sports cars manufactured by ABC Motors Ltd, which was based in nearby Hersham. He machined these himself working on a small lathe in the disused stables behind the family house. ABC stopped making cars in 1927 and the 24-year-old Taylor decided on an ambitious project to built has own sports cars. He was keen on the Riley Nine, which had come out the previous year, but felt that he could improve upon it and using his own rudimentary equipment designed and built an all-alloy 1.1-litre twin-cam engine, hand-filing components and fitting the motor into an ABC chassis frame. His goal was to produce a small, light and low sports car. The car was finished and registered by the end of 1928, and made its competition debut on the London-Land's End Trial at Easter 1930, and he then took part in a variety of different events in the course of the next couple of years, impressing observers and creating interest in the vehicle.

He registered the Alta Car and Engineering Company Ltd at the start of 1931 and set about creating a factory on a piece of land that he had acquired in Tolworth, right next to the then new A3 Kingston by-pass. Unimpressed by what the builders were offering to do, Taylor bought the necessary supplies and equipment and built the factory with his own hands at far less cost and much more quickly. By April that year, he was ready to start manufacturing copies of his original car, modified to make production easier. He commissioned Rubery Owen to build him steel chassis frames and fitted them with his own engines and transmissions, while also experimenting with supercharging to increase the horsepower available. The engines were developed with a new slimmer car in 1937, commissioned by Philip Jucker who sadly crashed it on its debut on the seafront at Douglas on the Isle of Man and was killed. But with drivers such as Peter Whitehead, Taylor was able to show the potential of the design and by 1939 the cars were winning national races.

The war then intervened and Taylor had to switch his business to government work but in 1945 he began making plans to build a Grand Prix car, while also making light alloy cylinder heads for Austin 7s. In the years that followed Alta produced supercharged 1.5-litre versions of the engine to be raced in both Formula 1 and normally-aspirated units for Formula 2. There were a string of good results with John Heath, George Abecassis and Geoffrey Crossley driving. There were requests for road-going versions of the cars, but Taylor was never very interested and, in 1950, he had three Alta F1 cars racing and was supplying his engines to Heath's Hersham and Walton Motors (HWM). The HWM-Altas were most competitive with Stirling Moss finishing third place in Bari and Johnny Claes winning the Formula 2 Grand Prix des Frontières at Chimay.

The Alta racing cars were gradually abandoned but the engine business boomed with Coopers, HWMs and Emerysons, including Moss winning the London Trophy at Crystal Palace in a Cooper-Alta. Competition became more intense, but in 1955 Alta agreed a deal with Connaught Engineering to supply engines and Alta scored its best result with Tony Brooks winning the non-championship F1 Syracuse GP, while drivers such as Les Leston, Archie Scott-Brown and Jack Fairman and Stuart Lewis-Evans all achieved good results with the engines.

Gradually, however, the demand reduced as new options came on to the market and Taylor's health became a problem. In the end he decided to close down the business and retired to the country, settling in Midhurst in Sussex. His engines continued to be raced until the end of 1960, while the 29 cars that he built are now all collectors' items.

Sadly, his health did not improve and he died at 63 in the autumn of 1966.

His son Michael tried to revive the Alta name in the 1970s but that was not a success.

The little-known story of Honda

Rice polishing is an odd industry. You take kernels of rice and polish them in machines so that the original brown rice turns white, becomes more attractive, more digestible and easier to cook. Many think this also has a more delicate flavour. However, the polishing process removes many of the good things, which is why health-foody folk prefer brown rice.

In the early years of the 20th Century in Japan, some of the rice-polishing machines that were used were driven by petrol engines and, as a toddler, Soichiro Honda's favourite pastime was to visit local rice-polishing mill to watch such an engine operating. He was so small that his grandfather had to carry him most of the way, but he loved the machine and the noise and smells it produced.

Honda's father Gihei was a blacksmith but as people turned away from horses as their means of transport, he turned his efforts to repairing bicycles and so Soichiro grew up surrounded by machinery and happy to tinker with them. He was disinterested in schooling but was thrilled to see occasional cars when they passed through the village of Komyo, 10 miles to the north of Hamamatsu in the Shizuoka province, between Toyota and Nagoya. From a young age, Honda was someone who knew what he wanted and at 10 he borrowed one of the bicycles in his father's workshops and cycled 20 miles to watch the demonstration of a flying machine, piloted by the visiting American Art Smith. Soichiro did not have the money to buy a ticket and so climbed a tree and watched the demonstration, returning home in awe of a machine that could fly.

He left school at 15 and saw an advertisement for an automobile servicing company called Tokyo Art Shokai, which was basically little more than a garage in the Yushima district, to the north of the city centre. While he was there the region was hit by the Great Kanto Earthquake in September 1923 which killed around 140,000 people, the damage being done not only by the quake but also by fires that raged through the city and a tsunami that swept away coastal villages. The earthquake nearly put Art Shokai out of business but its owner Yuzo

Sakakibara and his brother Shin'ichi kept on a couple of apprentice mechanics, Honda being one of them. They started rebuilding the business and decided to build a racing car to advertise the firm. They found an old Daimler engine and fitted a chassis to it, but the result was not very good and so they tried again with a Curtiss OX-5 V8 aircraft engine. This was fitted into the chassis from an old Mitchell automobile.

At the end of 1924, Shin'ichi with Honda as his riding mechanic, won the Fifth Japan Automobile Competition. A few months later Honda received a call up for military service, but was found to be colour blind and so did not have to go into the army and returned to finish his apprenticeship. After six years working with Art Shokai, he asked Yuzo Sakakibara if he could open his own branch of Art Shokai in Hamamatsu. He was then 25 but the business quickly gained an impressive reputation. Honda earned a great deal of money and began to build his own Hamamatsu racing car, powered by a supercharged Ford engine. This was quite successful, but at the opening race of the new Tamagawa Speedway, a three-quarter mile oval, built near Yokohama in 1936, disaster struck. There were a total of 24 cars entered and a big crowd turned up to watch. Honda was leading when close to the finish, he collided with a slow-moving car that pulled out of the pits in front of him. The Hamamatsu was launched into a series of rolls and Honda and his brother Benjiro were thrown out. Soichiro broke his wrist and dislocated his shoulder, in addition to suffering facial injuries, while Benjiro fractured his spine.

Although he took part in another race that autumn, Soichiro was convinced by his family that it was time to stop racing... or at least driving. His passion for the sport drove him to enter F1 when the company began building cars in the 1960s an to enter Formula 1 almost immediately...

The Italian who never worked at Ferrari

Some Formula 1 engineers never get the recognition they deserve. In part it is down to timing, in part because some don't care and in part because F1 did not have the same profile as it does today.

One such man was Italy's Giulio Alfieri. Unlike most Italians in Formula 1, Alfieri never worked for Ferrari.

Born in Parma in the summer of 1924, he excelled in school and won a place to study mechanical engineering at the Politecnico di Milano. He graduated in the summer of 1948, and soon began working at the Piaggio-owned Cantiere Navale Reuniti shipyard in Genoa, developing steam turbine engines. It was not really his thing and eight months later he moved to Innocenti in Milan, where he developed Pierluigi Torre's Lambretta engine in an effort to break speed records. After four years, he was head-hunted by Maserati and started working at Modena in August 1953.

By then Gioachino Colombo had finished the design of the 2.5-litre straight-six that Maserati had conceived for the new Formula 1 regulations, due to begin in 1954. The rest of the car stilled needed to be designed and manufactured. Colombo left Maserati in November that year, before the 250F prototype had run and Alfieri and Vittorio Bellentani took over the role. They had the prototype running at the Modena Autodrome in November but it was damaged during the first test when another car spun into it. It was thus a real struggle to finish two new cars (plus all the customer work with older machinery) in time to get everything shipped out to Argentina on Boxing Day. They worked through Christmas Day to get everything done.

The race was scheduled for January 17 at the Autodromo in Buenos Aires but the team had serious problems with overheating, as the cars had only run in cold European winter weather. There were a series of engine failures and eventually it was concluded that the best option was to run the 250Fs on castor oil, because it works better than petroleum-derived products at high temperatures – although only for relatively short periods. Maserati members scoured the city's pharmacies buying 60 half-litre bottles of the medicinal oil. As dawn broke on race day, they started testing and continued for as long as possible before the race.

It all held together and Fangio won the race. He would win again at S,pa in June but then left Maserati to drive for Mercedes. Later that summer factory driver Onofre Marimon was killed at the German GP, an accident which upset Alfieri so much that afterwards he never attended another F1 race, working on the cars in practice but then going home on race morning.

At the end of that season, Bellentani departed to join Ferrari and so Alfieri took over as technical director for all Maserati projects, including F1, sports cars and road cars. Mercedes was dominant in F1 and so Alfieri decided to try some new ideas, including a streamlined version of the 250F, which he had actually tested in a wind tunnel at the Politecnico di Milano. For 1956 there was a completed revised car, which was lighter and stiffer with plans for a new V12 to replace Colombo's straight-six, which had been heavily-developed. Stirling Moss won for Maserati at Monaco and Monza and that attracted Fangio back to Modena for 1957, when he won four races and Maserati won the World Championship.

The bad news was that late in 1955, Argentine President Juan Perón was overthrown in a coup d'état. At the time Maserati's owner Adolfo Orsi had a deal with Perón for a large order of machine tools, paid for in wheat. The new government stopped the deal and Orsi found himself in serious debt. The company was put into administration by the Credito Italiano bank, although

Orsi stayed in charge and remained a shareholder. This meant that the racing had to stop. The V12 was raced by Jean Behra at Monza and then set aside. The 250Fs were sold to customers.

In the years that followed, Alfieri built the Maserati 3500 GT and the celebrated Maserati Birdcage for sports car racing, while also developing engines for road cars such as the Maserati Merak, but the company did not have the money to compete in F1, although Alfieri experimented with engines for the 1.5-litre formula, which were raced by customers. The programme was cancelled in 1964 after the announcement of the new 3-litre F1 rules for 1966. Cooper asked Maserati to design an engine for the new formula and Alfieri revived the V12 and Maserati won in Mexico in 1966 thanks to John Surtees and then again in South Africa in 1967 with Pedro Rodriguez driving, but Repco was dominant and the car company was still struggling and had no money to develop the engines. In 1968, Orsi decided to sell. Argentine Alejandro de Tomaso wanted to buy the business but Alfieri opposed the deal and in 1969 the company ended up in the hands of France's Citroën. The Maserati engines were used in Ligier sports cars but by 1975, the firm was bankrupt again. This time it was bought by de Tomaso and Alfieri was promptly fired by the new owner. Alfieri became president of Honda Italia for a while and then joined designed motorcycle engines for Laverda before joining Lamborghini from 1979 until his retirement in 1987.

The adventures of "Dédé la Sardine"

There are some people who lead such extraordinary lives that one doubts the veracity of their tales. And yet when you delve into the stories, you find that they are true – or at least you cannot prove that they are not.

The story of André Guelfi is unbelievable – but most of it seems to be true. It is a tale which winds its way back to the port city of Mazagan (now El Jadida), 65 miles south-west of Casablanca, in Morocco, in 1919. Guelfi's father was a Corsican who, after a long history in the French military, became the harbour master of Mazagan, Morocco at that time being a French protectorate. André's mother was Spanish but with roots in Turkey. She was a professional pianist and so André grew up speaking French, Spanish and the local Arabic dialect.

He was by nature an entrepreneur and was already making money at the age of 10 by driving tourists along the Plage Haouzia, an eight-mile beach, in a car modified so he could reach the pedals. At 16, he left school and found a job as a messenger boy in a local bank. He discovered a dossier relating to unpaid debts and proposed to the bank manager that he collect the money, in exchange for 15 percent of the money. He made enough to invest in a sardine fishing business, run by his uncle. Although war broke out when he was 19, Morocco was not greatly involved until the end of 1942 when Allied forces arrived and drove out the Vichy French. Dédé joined the army and was despatched to Italy. The ship was sunk on the way. He returned to Morocco and was posted as a driver with General de Gaulle's Bureau Central de Renseignements et d'Action (BCRA), involved in covert activities in Italy. This gave him a taste for speed and adventure.

When the war in Europe was over, he volunteered to go to Indochina and join the so-called Commando Conus, a select Free French airborne unit, under the command of Captain Adrien Conus. Although based in Saigon, the unit saw action against the Viet-Minh at Tay-Ninh and then in special missions in Laos. In between these adventures, Guelfi found time to open a garage in Saigon before returning to Morocco in 1946.

His love life was, by all accounts, as adventurous as his career. He fled Morocco in 1947 to avoid an undesirable marriage, settled in Paris, bought a bar and began to indulge in his two new passions: flying and motor racing.

He started out in competition with a Delahaye and then switched to a Jaguar. He then returned to Morocco and began to build up the sardine business, introducing refrigerated factory ships and earning himself a fortune – and the nickname "Dédé La Sardine". In order to achieve his financial success, he developed a close relationship with the powerful politician Mohamed Oufkir. Money was suddenly not a problem and he rose to prominence in North African races, sharing victory with Jean Behra in a factory Gordini in the Casablanca 12 Hours. The then finished sixth at Le Mans, sharing a Gordini with Jacky Pollet. He was Moroccan champion in 1955 but then made little impact until 1958 when he finished second in the Prix de Paris at Montlhéry, at the wheel of a Cooper F2 car. It was no surprise that he was invited to take part in the inaugural Moroccan Grand Prix that autumn, at the wheel of an F2 Cooper. He finished last but had become a Grand Prix driver. His racing career would continue on and off until the late 1960s but his life changed dramatically in 1960 when his business was effectively wiped out by the Agadir earthquake. He decided that it would be better to start his new business further south, in the newly-independent Mauretania. He quickly made friends with President Moktar Ould Daddah until the latter discovered that Guelfi was paying "commissions" to the minister of finance. Guelfi left the country in a hurry...

Back in Morocco, all was well for a while but there was then a coup d'état against King Hassan II. Guelfi's friend Oufkir was executed and his family imprisoned. Guelfi was hounded by the new regime, which demanded that he handed over a plane that Guelfi owned.

In the end he blew it up and departed Morocco.

He settled in France again, divorced his wife and soon married the niece of President Georges Pompidou. By doing so, he became the co-owner of 45 percent of a company that owned 128 buildings in the centre of Paris. A year later, he bought control of the business by acquiring a further six percent. He began building up a real estate business and soon money was rolling in again. He bought himself a huge mansion in Lausanne and purchased a private jet, which he flew himself. He then acquired the Le Coq Sportif sportswear company and was soon involved in business dealings with FIFA and the International Olympic Committee, becoming an advisor to Juan Antonio Samaranch, the President of the International Olympic Committee.

He played an important role as "a consultant", doing deals to ensure that Russia won the 1980 Olympic Games, a deal which won him a lot of friends in high places in Eastern Europe. He became increasingly involved in doing government-level deals and earning commissions. Well-connected with Elf, its first boss Pierre Guillaumat having been involved with Guelfi in the BCRA, he began acting as an intermediary for the oil company and made his Swiss companies and bank accounts available to pay "retro-commissions" to Elf executives. He was at the centre of the celebrated Elf Scandal in 1994 and spent 36 days on remand in the La Santé prison in Paris, where he met the colourful entrepreneur/singer/politician Bernard Tapie.

He agreed to finance the extraordinary Tapie to get back on his feet and in the years that followed he paid Tapie a total of €14 million as he fought a long legal battle with the French government. Tapie eventually won but the loans were never repaid which caused great bitterness.

He was released from jail and would later leave Switzerland and sell his property there after the Swiss agreed to work with the French in the Elf investigation. In 2003, he was finally sentenced to a suspended three year sentence and a large fine. He was also involved in a long battle with Elf over $30 million in commissions which came from deals between the French and German governments over the sale of the Leuna refinery.

He moved to the island of Saint-Barthélemy in the Caribbean.

Early in 2016 his name popped up again with numerous references in the Panama Papers…

He died later that year, just after his 97th birthday.

A sleepy place

You may not have heard of the Duchy of Saxe-Meiningen, a relatively minor region in what would eventually become Germany. It is centred on the town of Meiningen, in what is today known as Thuringia but was previously in East Germany. The ruling family of the duchy made little impact until 1818 when Her Royal Higness Princess Adelheid von Sachsen-Meiningen was selected to become the wife of William, Duke of Clarence and St Andrews, the third son of King George III. There seemed little chance that he would become king until 1817 when his elder brother George's daughter Princess Charlotte of Wales died. George had no other legitimate children but there was still Prince Frederick, Duke of York and Albany, George III's second son, although he also had no heirs. George duly became King George IV when his father died in 1820. Seven years later Frederick died at the age of 63. William then 62 became the heir to the throne. Adelheid (by then renamed Adelaide to sound less German) was 35. Three years later, George IV died and William became William IV and Adelaide became the Queen Consort of England. She was popular with the British as she was relatively young, modest, dignified and generous.

In the years that followed, Edward Wakefield and others established the South Australian Association, aiming to set up a freely-settled and British-planned colony on the southern coast of Australia, with the citizens coming from the home country. Wakefield wanted to call the colony's capital city Wellington, after the celebrated general who had helped get the colony agreed, but King William felt it would be more agreeable (for him) if the new city was named after his wife. The city was established at the end of December in 1836.

Colonel William Light designed the new city, using a grid layout, with wide boulevards and public squares, with a swathe of parkland ringing the whole place. It was a pleasant place and, as it allowed complete religious freedom, it developed into a city with a large number of churches and so became known as the City of Churches. It had a reputation of being a big country town rather than a buzzing metropolis and was regarded by other Australian cities as being rather sleepy and dull. It was a reputation that the city sought to change in the early 1980s. The locals were keen to make a big impact with the sesquicentenary celebrations in 1986 and set up a Jubilee 150 Board to consider ways to use the event as a way to gain international recognition for the city.

No-one had considered anything radical until a Christmas in 1982 when entrepreneur and motor racing amateur Bill O'Gorman was at a corporate party and the discussion turned to what the city should do for its jubilee in 1986. He joked that it would probably be celebrated with "sewing and knitting" but was then asked what he suggested. His reply was simple: a Formula 1 Grand Prix.

When he thought about it later, he liked the idea, wrote to the South Australian Premier John Bannon and suggested the idea. Bannon saw the opportunity and after South Australia's Vern Schuppan won Le Mans in 1983 there was a celebratory dinner at which Bannon announced plans for a race. The key was to get the locals enthusiastic, without stirring up too much resistance to the idea. Once a plan was formulated, O'Gorman and Mal Hemmerling, a former director of the South Australia cabinet office who was taken on as executive director of the project, flew to London to meet with Bernie Ecclestone. It was May 1984 and Ecclestone showed little interest in the idea, although he noted the fact that a senior government official was involved. A few weeks later, at the British GP, O'Gorman met him again. The Dallas Grand Prix had been a disaster and Bernie was interested in Australia. They struck a deal a few weeks later with the first race scheduled for November 1985. There was not much time but the government made it happen, with laws being changed and the circuit being modified to reduce the disruption in the city by having the pits inside the Victoria Park racecourse. A new section of road had to be laid to cross the racecourse in two places. The pits were a temporary structure which could be disassembled each year.

The first event was deigned to be an end-of-season party for Formula 1 and it established the city as a place that F1 enjoyed going. The slogan beamed around the world was "Adelaide Alive" and suddenly it was.

The second race featured the incredible World Championship showdown between Nigel Mansell, Nelson Piquet and Alain Prost which featured Mansell's hopes exploding when a tyre blew and the championship outsider Prost scored an amazing victory to snatch the title. In the end Adelaide hosted the Grand Prix for 10 years but Ecclestone had already made a deal with Ron Walker in Melbourne to switch the race to Melbourne as soon as Bannon was no longer Premier and couldn't extend the contract further. That happened in 1992 after the collapse of the state bank. Ecclestone and Walker did a deal with Victorian State Premier for a race in Melbourne in 1996.

The government of South Australia sold its equipment to Melbourne…

If you go down to the woods today

Duke Karl Eugen von Württemberg had a couple of passions in life. He liked women and had a string of mistresses, producing 11 illegitimate children with no fewer than eight different ladies. Born in 1728, he succeeded his father as the ruler of Württemberg in 1737, when he was just nine years of age. He married at 20 and the new couple went to Paris for their honeymoon where he was impressed by the Château de Versailles and its contents. He ended up making four other visits to Paris during his lifetime, buying things for his castles. Building castles was really his biggest weakness. In fact, he built so many that the duchy struggled to pay for all of them. He had an extensive library and was passionate about opera, but it was building castles that really got him excited. That and his mistresses, of course. His wife left him after eight years and he ended up without a legitimate heir, the duchy going to his younger brother when he died in 1793.

Thirty years before his death he felt the need for a hunting lodge and summer residence and ordered a new castle to be constructed to the west of Stuttgart, close to the road to Leonberg, in a forest known as Glemswald. He had already built a castle, known as the Bärenschlössle (the Bear Castle) close by but wasn't grand enough for the extravagant Duke and so a new palace, designed in late Rococo style, was built just up the road. This featured a wide tree-lined avenue that went in a straight line for a modest eight miles until it arrived at Schloss Ludwigsburg, which boasted only 452 rooms. The new castle was named Schloss Solitude, the Duke choosing the name because it was meant to be a refuge where he could relax and reflect on life, with only a huge staff of servants present, to keep him fed and watered. The problem was that with so many palaces to choose from (and mistresses to be entertained), Duke Karl Eugen rarely had time to visit all his castles and a year after it was completed he decided to set up an elite military academy inside the castle. The most famous student being Friedrich Schiller, the celebrated playright, poet and philosopher. After the Duke died, the school was closed down and gradually the castle fell into disrepair and was abandoned.

Early in the Twentieth Century, with the arrival of the automobile, Schloss Solitude became the finishing point for a hillclimb course from Stuttgart. This continued until 1925 when it was decided to lay out a proper circuit 13.8-miles long to the south of the castle. The roads were narrow with no run-off at all and for much of its history Solitude was run only for motorcycles. Later this would shortened to become a very fast seven miles.

The track hosted the German Motorcycle Grand Prix on seven occasions between 1952 and 1964, sharing the race with Hockenheim every other year. It was upgraded in 1957 and in 1960 it hosted a Formula 2 race, which was won by Wolfgang Von Trips in a Ferrari. It was by then a huge event with crowds estimated to be in the region of 290,000. The circuit was also used by NSU, Mercedes-Benz and Porsche as a test track. It had the reputation of being a sort of mini-Nürburgring and was popular with the drivers.

The first Solitude F1 Grand Prix took place in 1961, with the race being won by Innes Ireland in a Lotus after a thrilling battle with Jo Bonnier's Porsche. A year later Dan Gurney led Bonnier in a Porsche 1-2, while Jack Brabham and Jim Clark rounded off the track's F1 history in 1963 and 1964. The circuit switched back to Formula 2 in 1965, with victory going to Chris Amon in a Lola but then the track fell victim to concerns about safety not only for the drivers but for spectators as well. One can still drive around the old track, as the roads still exist but there is little evidence of the old circuit, except the old scoring tower...

Norman wisdom

The city of Caen sits nine miles inland from the sea, on the Orne river, in lower Normandy. It has long been a river port where ships are better protected than at Ouistreham, the village where the Orne flows out into the English Channel. Overlooking the town of Caen are the remains of a once-mighty castle, one of the largest medieval fortresses in Europe. Nearby are the abbeys of Saint-Etienne and Sainte-Trinité. All were built (or at least started) by William the Bastard, the illegitimate son of Robert le Magnifique, Duke of Normandy.

It took William some years to secure control of the duchy and to build himself a castle, but he then turned to other matters and in 1066 set sail with an army to claim the kingdom of England and thus was able to change his nickname to William the Conqueror, which was less of a burden for the poor fellow. Apart from William, Caen is celebrated for its stone, which is pleasant to the eye and easy to work with and thousands of tons of it were shipped to England to build the cathedrals at Canterbury and Norwich, the Abbey of Westminster and even parts of the Tower of London.

When William died in 1087, he was buried in the Abbey of Saint-Etienne where his tomb remains to this day, although the locals don't mention that the grave was desecrated several times and all that is really there is a thigh bone. After William, Caen returned to being a backwater until it was decided to build a canal alongside the Orne, to allow bigger ships to reach the town. This coincided with the arrival of the railways, while the earth dug for the canal was used to aid the construction of a hippodrome on the flat lands to the west of the town, known as La Prairie, originally a marsh that had been drained in medieval times. Caen became a more important port with trains running from the quayside all the way to the Gare Saint-Lazare in Paris, where the citizens were happy to eat fresh fish rushed each morning from the port.

Caen was never much of a tourist destination, as the visitors went to the sandy beaches at nearby Cabourg and Deauville, but it remained a busy town with a coastal paddle steamer service that went across the Seine estuary to Le Havre, carrying both goods and passengers in the days before the automobile made it easier to get about. There was also a freight service across the Channel to Newhaven, at least for a time.

In an effort to attract visitors, the hippodrome was joined by a velodrome and in the early years of the 20th Century, it was decided to host automobile races. These were given the title Coupe de Normandie and took place on a triangular road circuit to the west of the town, running up the main road to Bayeux and then back by way of Tilly-sur-Seulles. The earliest races were amateur affairs for wealthy locals, but in 1909 and 1910, Peugeot voiturettes dominated, with victories going to the redoubtable Georges Boillot and to Jules Goux.

It was not until 1944 that Caen was thrust on to the world stage when around 80 percent of the town was literally blown to bits by Allied bombers which dropped 2,000 tons of bombs on the city one night in July 1944, as a prelude to an armoured assault the following day to drive out the Germans. Nine thousand buildings were completely destroyed that night with another 650 badly damaged. Only 2,000 remained. The Allied push was successful but there was little left in Caen but rubble. It took almost two years just to clear this away. The city's reconstruction would not be finished until the early 1960s.

Much of the local population lived in wooden huts while the work was done. One of the first tasks was to rebuild the roads and the local mayor Yves Guillou pushed for a new network of wider boulevards, rather than trying to rebuild the original streets. Once this was done and work began on the buildings, it struck the mayor that it might be a good idea to host motor races on his new roads, in order to show the world that Caen was still open for business. The local branch of the Automobile Club de l'Ouest thought this to be a splendid idea and, in 1952, a temporary street circuit was laid out around the hippodrome on La Prairie and the first Grand Prix de Caen was held for Formula 2 cars. There was a decent entry with 16 cars, including a quartet of works Gordinis, a couple of private Ferraris, and even two HWMs sent out from England. The big names of French racing were there and Maurice Trintignant beat his team-mate Jean Behra to victory. It was a great success.

The ACO then suggested that the 1953 race should be for Le Mans sports cars and 16 cars arrived with a battle for victory going to the little-known Pierre de

Chancel, a garage owner from Paris who drove his own Panhard, beating René Bonnet in his DB.

It was then decided that the 1954 race should be for Formula 1 cars and 10 Grand Prix cars arrived for the 3rd Grand Prix de Caen. The entry might have been small but there was some quality in the field with Trintignant's Scuderia Ferrari 625 beating Stirling Moss in a factory Maserati 250F. The fourth Grand Prix de Caen was not until 1956, because the 1955 race was cancelled in the wake of the Le Mans disaster but on a damp track Harry Schell drove his Maserati 250F to victory over André Simon's Gordini.

In 1957, Guillou had a stroke and handed over the role of mayor to his deputy Henri-François Buot. The race was timed to be between the British GP and the race in Germany and while Maserati declined to attend, Jean Behra was permitted to find a ride elsewhere and convinced BRM to loan him a pair of BRM P25s which needed development. Behra won the race by more than a lap, ahead of Roy Salvadori in a Cooper-Climax T43.

A year later, it was decided to hold the race on Sunday, July 20, at the start of the French holiday season. The only problem was that the British Grand Prix was scheduled for the previous day, which made life pretty interesting for nine of the 12 drivers taking part, as they had to get themselves and their cars (in most cases) from Silverstone to Caen overnight. The race was scheduled for the late afternoon to give the late arrivals time to practice in the morning. The Grand Prix was a straight fight between Moss in a Cooper and Behra in a BRM with Jo Bonnier and Bruce Halford chasing in Maseratis. In the end Behra's car broke down, leaving Moss to win the race.

Early in 1959 Guillou stood down as mayor and was replaced by Jean-Marie Louvel, not a man who saw the value of motor racing. The race died.

A most unusual life

Racing drivers come from many different and varied backgrounds but few of them are involved in "the arts". There are not many writers, dancers or painters who have raced and while some drivers have been very good musicians, the average F1 driver seems to be more attuned to machines than to ethereal matters. Strangely, Leslie Marr's family background came from the world of engineering. His grandfather was Sir James Marr, a celebrated shipbuilder who ran the Joseph Thompson and Sir James Laing shipyards, the Sunderland Forge & Engineering Company, which fitted out new ships, the Silver Line shipping firm and the Wolsingham Steel Foundry. He began running the Thompson shipyard in 1908 after the early death of Robert Thompson and was raised to a baronetcy in 1919 for services to the government during WW1.

His son John was also an engineer, working in the family businesses, while also being in the Territorial Army. He was called up in 1914 and served as the commander of the Durham Heavy Battery on the Western Front until 1917 when he was recalled to work at the Admiralty. After the war, he married May Thompson, the daughter of Robert Thompson and Leslie was born two years later. Sadly, John would die of pneumoria at the age of 53, when Leslie was only nine. A year later Sir, James died as well, leaving Leslie as the 2nd Baronet with a considerable fortune awaiting him when he was 21. His mother May was a character, sent to a finishing school in Belgium. She graced the ballrooms of St. Moritz and bobsleighed with a Russian Prince, while also visiting Egypt with her parents. She was one of the first women in the north of England to own her own automobiles and looked after them herself. These included a Darracq and later a Fiat. During the war, she served in the Red Cross but was also a very good shot and opened a rifle range to train soldiers. After his father's death, his mother struggled to cope and ended up spending some time in a psychiatric hospital in Kent. Her brother Stanley made a big impact with his wild nature and driving escapades.

Leslie was sent away to school in Shrewsbury in his teens and then went to Pembroke College, Cambridge, where he studied engineering. He graduated in 1942 and was then called up into the Royal Air Force Technical Branch (Radar), initially at the Yatesbury radar school and then at Dollarbeg Castle in Dollar, Scotland before being sent to Islay in the Hebrides. He was then posted back to a more lively station at Beachy Head where V1 and V2 rockets were being fired all the time and he had several near-misses. He was then despatched to Egypt where he was put in charge of a top secret Air Ministry Experimental Station (AMES) around the Middle East. It was during this time that he began to paint seriously before he was posted back to Egypt and then to the Isle of Wight by the end of the war.

He then decided that he wanted to pursue art, rather than going into shipbuilding. He returned to London and attended the Heatherley School of Fine Art in Pimlico and then moved on to the Borough Polytechnic, where he studied under David Bomberg and was one of the founders of the Borough Group of artists, which held exhibitions in a large room above a bookshop. This included Cliff Holden, Edna Mann, Dorothy Mead, Peter Richmond, Dennis Creffield and Dinora Mendelson, Bomberg's step-daughter, who Marr married in June 1948. They separated after only a couple of years and he moved to Shropshire to paint landscapes. He felt the urge to buy himself a racing car and acquired a Connaught A-type with which he competed in British races that summer, finishing third in the United States Air Force Trophy at Snetterton the following summer, behind Tony Rolt and Bob Gerard. In 1954 he raced in the British GP and finished 13th, but he was a long way off the pace.

The following year he bought a new streamlined Connaught B-Type and won a race at Davidstow in Cornwall, although he was happy to admit that the competition was weak. A second appearance in the British GP later that summer saw him spin off after a brake failure. That autumn, he shipped the car to New Zealand and went out to take part in the annual races there. He finished third in the Lady Wigram Trophy.

In the final round at Invercargill, he was hit in the face by a stone and spun into a ditch, wrecking the car. He decided that enough was enough. He returned to Europe and focussed on his painting, but still returned to New Zealand later to paint.

He remarried in 1962 having met his second wife who was working as a mechanic in a garage. They had two daughters. They lived in a thatched cottage on Exmoor in North Devon from 1963 until 1969 and Marr then turned his attention to pottery, moving to Norfolk where he built a large kiln and opened a gallery.

He began visiting Scotland on a regular basis and bought a house in Glencoe in 1973. He tried his hand at photography as well and, in the late 1970s, published a book about church architecture. The couple moved to the island of Arran in 1983, where they remained until 1991, before returning to Norfolk. His marriage broke down although he married for a third time in 2002.

He is styled Sir Leslie Marr, 2nd Baronet but has never used the title.

The risk taker

In 1979, the Monaco Grand Prix – the seventh round of the World Championship – took place on Sunday May 27. Going into the Monaco weekend, Ferrari's Jody Scheckter led the World Championship with 25 points, but he had won only one race. Ligier's Jacques Laffite, who had won the first two races of the year, had 24, while Carlos Reutemann (Team Lotus) was third, despite not having won a race. He had 21 points. Ferrari's Gilles Villeneuve was next with 20 points, having won twice. He was equal on points to Ligier's Patrick Depailler who had won in Spain. The title was wide open…

Scheckter won that weekend and stayed ahead, increasing his total to 30 points, because the points system allowed only the best four results from the first seven races, despite being structured 9-6-4-3-2-1 for the top six. They were all still in the hunt but there was then a five-week break before the French GP at Dijon on July 1.

The weekend after Monaco was a long weekend in France, with the three-day Pentecôte holiday. There was little for the F1 drivers to do. Formula 2 took place at Pau and there was the annual Nürburgring 1,000 km sports car race in Germany, but for the F1 drivers it was time off. Patrick Depailler decided to go home to his native Puy-de-Dôme département, the area around the city of Clermont-Ferrand, which features a string of picturesque volcanic craters, cones and domes. His plan was to go and jump off the side of a mountain, strapped to a hang-glider, and see how long he could keep the device in the air, looking for thermals and updrafts in the airflows around the mountains. It is a pastime that requires not only skill and courage but also experience. And it's dangerous because flying with the wind can often bring surprises.

Depailler was not a man who worried much about risk. He smoked like a chimney, he had raced motorcycles in his wild youth, he still liked to ride them, and he loved to scuba-dive. And, of course, he was a Formula 1 driver... which meant that he had a contract stating he wasn't supposed to do these things.

But he found it hard to live without the thrill of such activities. This had been illustrated a few years earlier when Ken Tyrrell agreed to run the young Elf protégé in a third car for the French GP at Depailler's home circuit of Clermont-Ferrand, alongside Jackie Stewart and François Cevert. Tyrrell was impressed and so in 1973 offered Patrick the chance to race in the Canadian and United States GPs at the end of the season. Ten days before the Mosport race, he crashed a trials bike and broke his leg. The opportunity was lost. But Tyrrell took him on for 1974, having lost Stewart to retirement and Cevert to a crash at Watkins Glen. Paired with Jody Scheckter, he showed his speed, taking pole position in Sweden that year and finishing second to his team-mate. That year he also won the European Formula 2 title, winning four of the nine races he took part in. He would score 14 podiums in the years that followed, racing the Tyrrell six-wheeler in 1976 and 1977, before he finally won his first F1 victory at Monaco in 1978. He finished fifth in the World Championship that year and then agreed to join Ligier, which was expanding to two cars and switching from Matra engines to Cosworths. Designer Gérard Ducarouge designed the beautiful JS11 and the team began to the season with three wins in the first five races: two for Laffite and one for Depailler. Both drivers were obviously in the running for the title...

This seems not have been a consideration when Depailler launched himself into the air on Sunday, June 3, headed his hang-glider away from the mountain and began to look for thermals. He looped around and flew close to a cliff, where one can often find air moving upwards, but then an unexpected gust pushed the hang-glider into the cliff face and it tumbled to the rocky ground below. He survived but had hurt both of his legs and a wrist in his fall. His friends called for help and a medical helicopter was despatched by the Protection Civile service. He was put on to a stretcher and winched away, being flown to the main hospital in Clermont-Ferrand. He had multiple fractures of his right tibia and fibula and a broken right wrist – and his left ankle and foot had both been damaged badly. Surgeons completed a lengthy operation to try to put the bones back in place, but they warned that he would probably need more surgery. For some time, there was still a risk that they might need to amputate. Guy Ligier recognised that Depailler was gone and so signed Jacky Ickx for the rest of the year and began talking to France's next rising star Didier Pironi about a drive for 1980.

Depailler was not a good patient and as things were healing in August he managed to fall out of his hospital bed and re-break his leg. It was not until November that he knew for sure that he would be able to race again, thanks to a series of operations conducted by Professor Emile Letournel, the head of orthopaedic surgery at the Centre Médico-Chirurgical de la Porte de Choisy in Paris.

He managed to convince Alfa Romeo to sign him for 1980 but in the early part of the year, he was still in pain and not fully mobile. The car was fast – which was demonstrated when he qualified third at Long Beach, the fourth race of the year – but not at all reliable. He was soon back on the pace and often beating his team-mate Bruno Giacomelli in qualifying. But then the team went testing in Hockenheim in the week before the German GP. On August 1 the Alfa Romeo suffered a suspension failure in the high-speed Ostkurve at around 175 mph. There was no catchfencing in place and the car hit the barriers. Depailler did not survive. He is buried in the cemetery of his home village of Crevant-Laveine, in the land of the volcanoes of the Puy-de-Dôme.

An unlikely tale

In the early 1930s, AD (Anton) Hildebrand was in his mid-twenties and working as a writer of radio plays with the Algemene Vereniging Radio Omroep (AVRO), the public radio service of the Netherlands. In 1935, he published a book for children about a fictional brown bear called Bolke de Beer, who escaped from a zoo and went to live in a forest near Apeldoorn, with a group of animal friends. The book was a huge success and in the years that followed (despite the war), Hildebrand wrote a further nine books about Bolke. Later the stories would become a television series with puppets. Bolke was one of a number of different animal characters that Hildebrand wrote series about during his lifetime.

His son Tonio, who was born before the first Bolke book was published, benefited from his father's wealth. He raced with some success in the 1950s and 1960s on the Dutch national scene and became something of a celebrity with a life of seemingly unlimited money, fast cars, beautiful women and wild adventures, with a group of friends that included circus performer turned TV personality Bas van Toor, comedians Rijk de Gooyer and Appie Bueno de Mesquita and the singer Willy Alberti. Tonio carefully cultivated his image sporting a large moustache and always smoking a fat Havana cigar. In 1979, he agreed to sponsor Michael Bleekemolen in a Lotus B team, which would be run by BS Fabrications, using the old Lotus 79 chassis, which had won the title in 1978 with Mario Andretti. Team Lotus would move on to a new Lotus 81.

At the time, Bleekemolen was 29 but had shown promise in Formula Vee and in European Formula 3 that year in a factory Chevron, winning several heats and taking overall victory at Enna. He had finished fifth in the championship, which was won by fellow Dutchman Jan Lammers. He was a man in a hurry because there was not much money available in the Netherlands and he was in competition with Lammers, Arie Luyendyk and Huub Rothengatter. That summer he did a couple of Formula 2 races with a Fred Opert Chevron and tried to break into Formula 1 with an ATS. The previous year he had tried to qualify for the Dutch GP with a RAM March but had failed and with ATS it was a similar story, although he did make it into the race at Watkins Glen, where he retired with an oil leak.

That autumn, the deal with Lotus was agreed and everything seemed to be in place and over the Christmas period Bleekemolen went off for a skiing holiday. While he was away, the FIA issued an entry list for the World Championship. Bleekemolen read about it in a German motorsport magazine and was upset to see that not only was he not there, but also there was no sign of the team either.

It emerged that the Dutch motorsport federation had failed to do the necessary paperwork. A late application was made but it was turned down by the federation because there was no shortage of cars and it did not want there to be pre-qualifying. As a result, Bleekemolen had to give up the plans and raced instead in Formula 3, where he joined Roger Heavens Racing and finished a distant runner-up to Alain Prost. But the money for F1 was no longer there. Hildebrand ran into trouble with the Dutch tax authorities and skipped the country, escaping to Belgium. He would later spend six months in prison in Holland.

Bleekemolen had another chance in 1981 when he was named as a full-time driver in the British Formula 3 Championship by Barron Racing, which had a Ralt-Toyota. His results were disappointing and after six races he was replaced by a young Brazilian called Roberto Moreno.

Bleekemolen drifted away from single-seaters and spent many years racing in Renault one-make championships.

The adventures of Bob Sparshott

To the north of Saint Albans in Hertfordhsire, the B651 passes through the quaint half-timbered village of Wheathampstead, dips down and crosses the River Lea and then climbs uphill to the Mid Herts Golf Course, one of the oldest in England, dating back to 1892. It then reaches the village of Gustard Wood, which boasts the inevitable pub, The Cross Keys, and of course the local church.

It was in this idyllic English setting that Ernie and Ethel Sparshott settled and where their son Robert was born in 1944. Ernie was a carpenter but as the work reduced, he turned his hands to construction work. Robert soon became known as Bob, went to the local school in Harpenden and then spent time at Hatfield College before getting a job with a little-known company called Lotus Components in Cheshunt in 1962, when he was 17 years old. After a while, he was switched to the Lotus service department which was then operating out of a hangar at Panshanger Aerodrome, between Hatfield and Welwyn. Lotus boss Colin Chapman was already into flying at that point and his Piper Comanche was based at Panshanger. Chapman and Jim Clark would often pass through on their way to foreign races.

Young Bob Sparshott wanted to be in the racing side business and in 1964 he switched across to Team Lotus, working under the celebrated Bob Dance. They were assigned to the Lotus Cortina Racing Team in the United States, where three cars were sent to take part in the 1964 United States Road Racing Championship (USRRC). As the pair were based in the States, Lotus called them up to help with Clark's car at the Indy 500 that year, and were back again at Indy in 1965 – when Clark won the race.

For 1966 Sparshott returned home to England and began working with the Lotus Formula 2 team as mechanic to Graham Hill. He then moved into F1 in 1968, to work with Hill. Graham would win the title that year, but the team lost Jim Clark in a Formula 2 accident in Hockenheim. At the end of the year, Sparshott decided it was time to lead a quieter life and set up his own fabrication business in Luton, not far from his home village. He formed a partnership with John Woodington, working for a number of F1 teams, and the business was named BS Fabrications. It was very successful as there were plenty of small F1 teams in that era.

In 1972, Sparshott agreed to run a March 722 Formula 2 with a Formula 1 engine for Mike Beuttler in selected events. This was called a March 721G and was sufficiently competitive that March built similar versions for the factory team. That year, the team also ran American Brett Lunger in Formula 2 under the Space Racing banner.

The second BS Fabrications venture into Formula 1 came in 1976 when Henri Pescarolo's sponsor Norev bought a Surtees TS19 and asked Sparshott to run the car for him, alongside the factory entries of Alan Jones (Durex) and Lunger (Chesterfield). The programme began at Monaco where Pescarolo failed to qualify but the Frenchman went on to start seven races and managed to finish five of them, his best result being a ninth place at the Austrian GP. Vittorio Brambilla then arrived at Surtees with money from Beta for 1977 and so Lunger asked BS Fabrications to run him in Chesterfield-sponsored March 761. After a few races, it was decided to switch to a McLaren M23 and that arrangement continued into 1978 with an upgrade in the mid-season to a newer McLaren M26. This left the M23 available and Sparshott offered the drive to the young Nelson Piquet for the Austrian, Dutch and Italian Grands Prix. In the end Piquet did a one-off race with Ensign in Germany before joining BS Fabrications for the planned three races.

For 1979, there was a plan to run a Lotus B team, using the all-conquering Lotus 79, while the factory would move on to the new Lotus 80. The original idea was to run two cars for Rupert Keegan and Michael Bleekemolen but the project disappeared because Keegan didn't have the money and Bleekemolen didn't have the right paperwork. That winter, Sparshott became involved in the creation of the Chaparral 2K Indycar, which John Barnard and Gordon Kimball were busily designing for Jim Hall in England, and which Barnard insisted be built in the UK. The car was very successful although Hall was unimpressed by the cost involved. In the end, two cars and a third set of parts were completed and shipped off to the United States where Al Unser Sr ended the season with a victory in Phoenix. In 1980, Johnny Rutherford took over and took the car to victory in the Indy 500 and went on to win the title.

After the Lotus B Team project failed, BS Fabrications began to work on a project to build a chassis for Argentine Ricardo Zunino. The team ran Zunino briefly in British Formula 1 but it all fell apart because of uncertainty surrounding the Argentine GP. As a result, BS Fabrications closed down in January 1980. The factory was used to build the Toleman TG280 with which Brian Henton and Derek Warwick finished 1-2 in the European F2 Championship that year.

Sparshott would later start a new operations called BS Automotive and won the Formula 3000 title with Christian Danner in 1985. Bob retired from racing in 1988 but went on running a company called Sparshott Technologies Ltd, making components for racing teams.

A strange F1 career

Of all the Formula 1 drivers in history, Jean Lucas probably had the strangest debut in the sport. He made just one appearance, at the Italian Grand Prix in 1955, standing in for Robert Manzon.

Why? Because Lucas was the team manager of Equipe Gordini and Manzon, by all accounts, threw a wobbly and refused to drive what was a very difficult car on the new high banking at the Autodromo Nazionale. Gordini had spent plenty of money to get there and so Lucas stepped in to drive the car...

His F1 career lasted seven laps before the Gordini broke down.

To be fair, Lucas was no slouch in a racing car. He had been racing since 1949 and had scored a number of impressive results in sports car events, winning some major events.

Born in 1917 in Le Mans, the city famed for endurance racing, Lucas's racing career did not begin until after World War II, but which time he was 28. He took part in some local rallying events and then was entered to race a Ferrari 166MM in the Le Mans 24 Hours, partnered by the pseudonymous "Ferret", the shipping magnate Pierre Louis-Dreyfus who usually raced under the name of "Heldé" (which in French is a verbal version of his LD initials). In other words, it was in effect a factory Ferrari entry, alongside the lead car, driven by Luigi Chinetti and Lord Selsdon. The car was entered by Jean-Arthur Plisson, Chinetti's partner in Ferrari's Paris agency. It was a difficult weekend as Lucas damaged the car avoiding a child who had wandered on to the circuit during the practice session. The repairs were finished just before the start but the race ended in retirement. Chinetti and Selsdon won the race.

Lucas obviously impressed Chinetti because three weeks later the two shared a 166MM to win the Spa 24. The following year at Le Mans, Lucas was paired with Selsdon, but they failed to finish. Later that summer Chinetti and Lucas won the 12 Hours of Paris at Montlhéry.

After that Lucas was less involved, went to live in Morocco and created a sardine fishing business, following in the footsteps of his friend André Guelfi. He won the Rallye du Maroc in 1951 in a Ferrari 212 and then, in 1952, he and Chinetti went to Mexico and finished third on the Carrera Panamericana, as always with Ferrari.

It was then that he was offered the role of team manager of Ecurie Gordini and, although still close to Chinetti, he took the opportunity and later had a similar role with Monomill, a racing business established by another friend René Bonnet.

With a number of his racing friends, he established the Ecurie Los Amigos to race as and when they could.

In 1956, he finished second in the Paris 1000 with Harry Schell, and then tried single-seaters again to finish fifth in the Grand Prix de Caen. In 1957, he tried a Cooper Formula 2 car and finished second at Reims. That year he also scored his best result at Le Mans, driving a Equipe Los Amigos Jaguar D-Type, which he shared with "Mary", the French industrialist Jean-Marie Brussin, a synthetic diamond manufacturer. They finished third.

This meant that he was invited to race in the 1957 Moroccan Grand Prix, a non-championship Formula 1 race. He crashed his Maserati 250F at high speed on the Ain-Diab circuit in Casablanca and suffered serious head injuries. He retired soon afterwards, aware that he could no longer race. He bought a bar in Paris, called the Bar de l'Action, located at the top end of the Avenue d'Iéna, close to the Arc de Triomphe. This was managed by Harry Schell's wife Monique and became a meeting point for the motorsport folk in Paris, notably Schlesser, Jean Behra, André Simon, Amédée Gordini, Henri Greder, Jose Rosinski and any foreign drivers who happened to be in town.

In the same period, Lucas tried his hand at journalism, writing articles for an automobile magazine called Moteurs.

It was in the Bar de l'Action that Lucas and Gérard "Jabby" Crombac decided to establish a monthly magazine called Sport-Auto, at the start of 1962. Four years later they launched a second racing title called Champion.

In those exciting years, Crombac and Lucas helped Jean Bernigaud to establish the Ecole de Pilotage at Magny-Cours, which would become the famous Winfield School. They were also involved in establishing the Volant Shell and the Ford Jeunesse competitions, which helped to grow interest in racing in France and played an important role in developing France's famous generation of racing drivers in the 1960s and 1970s. In the same era, Jim Clark was living in Paris and was regularly to be found at the Sport-Auto offices where they had access to the latest English racing magazines. He also managed the careers of Schell and Jo Schlesser.

In 1976, Lucas decided to leave the magazine to Crombac and move to the west coast. He set up his own monthly devoted to his other passion, horses. He would later become the director of the regional daily newspaper L'Eclair de Nantes. He retired to live on the Ile de Ré, an island off the coast, where he settled in the town of St-Martin-de-Ré until his death in 2003.

How to lose at musical chairs

In the 19th Century, the village of Cascais became a favourite place for the Portuguese royal family to go bathing. The locals soon built a railway to the pleasant fishing village and it became a fashionable place to go. The penultimate stop on the railway was in Estoril, which was then little more than scrubland, but very rapidly a series of mansions were built. The overthrow of the monarchy in 1910 led to a republic being declared but plans continued to develop in the area, leading to the construction of the Hotel Palacio in 1928. When it opened, it hosted Nobuhito, Prince Takamatsu, the brother of the Japan's Emperor Hirohito, for his honeymoon.

During World War II, Portugal was a neutral country. Its ruler Antonio do Oliveira Salazar was anti-communist, but he didn't like the nationalism he saw in the Axis countries. The result of this was that the country became a hub of international espionage and intrigue. Intelligence agents on both sides rubbed shoulders and hundreds of locals worked for one side or the other, gathering whatever information they could. Among those who passed through was Commander Ian Fleming, a British officer attached to the Naval Intelligence Division, who was en route to the United States. He claimed that he lost money at the casino, playing chemin de fer with the chief German agent in Portugal. In the 1950s, Fleming wrote a book called Casino Royale inspired by his adventures, introducing the character James Bond. In 1969, the Palacio would be used to film scenes in the James Bond movie On Her Majesty's Secret Service. By then, Estoril was famed as a place where exiled royals settled. These included the exiled heir to the Spanish throne, the Infante Juan, Count of Barcelona; there was also Umberto II of Italy, Carol II of Romania and Miklos Horthy, the regent of Hungary. The Duke of Windsor (the former King Edward VIII of England) also spent time there after he escaped the Nazi invasion of France in 1940.

The Portuguese dictator Antonio de Oliveira Salazar was also fond of the place, had a house there and ordered the construction of the coast road from Cascais to Lisbon to speed up access.

At the start of the 1970s, the mega-wealthy heiress Fernanda Pires da Silva, owner of the Grão Pará group decided to fund the construction of a racing circuit on the rocky plateau behind the town of Estoril. This opened in 1972, with the first international event being the Grande Premio do Estoril a non-championship Formula 2 race in October 1973, which was won by the factory March of Jean-Pierre Jarier. The second race had to be cancelled because of a military coup in early 1974 that overthrew the country's ruling party and so the first European Formula 2 Championship race did not take place until early in 1975 when Jacques Laffite won in his Elf-sponsored Martini MK16. The championship returned in 1976 and 1977 with René Arnoux winning the first race and Didier Pironi the second. There was also a sports car race called the Grande Premio Costa del Sol, which was won by the Alfa Romeo T33 of Arturo Merzario.

Then things went quiet as the country was in political turmoil and it was not until 1980 that the new President of the Automovel Club de Portugal, Cesar Torres, began to push for a Grand Prix. As South Africa was also in trouble because of its apartheid policies, the F1 teams were looking for somewhere to test with money being found to pay for some renovation work, Estoril became the primary testing venue of the sport. This led in 1984 to the track being granted the final round of the World Championship, with Alain Prost and Niki Lauda battling for the title, with the Frenchman winning the race but Lauda's second place giving him the Drivers' title – by just half a point.

In 1985, the race was scheduled for April. It was raining but Ayrton Senna scored his first F1 victory, driving for Team Lotus.

The race then went back to September and became a favourite race at the end of the European season. The track tended to promote close racing and the weather was usually good although, as Estoril is only a few miles from the westernmost point of Europe, it tended to be affected by stiff breezes and rain storms coming off the Atlantic Ocean. A bigger problem, however, was the attitude of the locals. Torres was by then a big player at the FIA and was Max Mosley's deputy, and while Bernie Ecclestone was always pushing for better facilities, the Portuguese seemed to think that they had a right to a Grand Prix. It was one of F1's favourite events, but nothing was happening. In 1996 there was a strong hint that Portugal should watch out when Malaysian Prime Minister Mahathir Mohamad paid a visit to watch the Grand Prix at Estoril.

In the end, Ecclestone ran out of patience and the race was not included in the calendar for 1997. This convinced the Portuguese government to come up with money, but the disappearance that year of Torres, who died of cancer, meant that the country's influence in the F1 disappeared. The government bought control of the track to try to speed up improvements but nothing was done in time for 1998 and the upgrading was not completed until February 2000. By then, F1 had begun to embark on its global expansion.

There was no room for the race with the Malaysian GP having joined the schedule, and the revival of the United States GP. The music has stopped and there were not enough chairs left...

A missed opportunity

The French Grand Prix was always an itinerant event. The venue changed from year to year, the race often being used as a political tool to keep the different regions happy. In the early years after World War I, the European nations began building huge speedways to match the British and the Americans, who had built Brooklands and Indianapolis in 1907 and 1908. The Italians built Monza, the Spanish Sitges-Terramar and the French somehow managed to build two speedways: Montlhéry to the south of Paris and Miramas, on the plain of the River Rhône, near Marseille.

The autodrome at Montlhéry was built on a wooded plateau. It is a steep climb up from the valley below and there is only one access road, although down below the circuit is a major junction where the RN104, the outer ring road of Paris, and the RN20, which was once the main road to Orléans, Toulouse and Spain, meet. This is just 16 miles from the centre of Paris.

Once there was a tram that ran to the nearby village of Marcoussis, built to carry fruit and vegetables from the farms to the market at Les Halles. When the speedway was built this was still in operation and allowed huge crowds to get out to the facility.

The track was built entirely with private money. It is a 1.5-mile high-banked oval with straights of around 180 metres in length and then huge banking at each end, which gets to 49.3-degrees (yes, you did read that correctly). It was built from concrete. It cost a fortune and the track struggled financially from the very start. The construction of the road circuit that goes from the oval out into the woods and back again cost so much that the track ended up in administration. But, Montlhéry was the closest thing the French GP had to a home before World War II, hosting races in 1925, 1927, 1931 and from 1933 to 1937. Reims hosted the race for four consecutive years between 1958 and 1961 but it was not until the 1980s that the race had its first long-term contracts, primarily with Paul Ricard from 1985 until 1990. And then, of course, Magny-Cours from 1991 to 2008.

When the money ran out in the late 1930s, Montlhéry was acquired (cheaply) by the French government and large sections of the estate were transformed into a military camp. This was used by the Germans as an internment camp. By the end of the war, the entire property was in a mess. The new government had more important things to worry about and agreed to lease the speedway to the Union Technique de l'Automobile et du Cycle (UTAC) on condition that the organisation repaired and maintained the facility and ran motor races. It took two years to get the track operational again and even then the concrete was becoming a problem as bumps had developed where the concrete sections met one another.

The track faded from the international scene and there were a series of nasty accidents leading to the deaths of Guy Mairesse, Louis Rosier and several others. In 1964, there was an even worse crash when two drivers and three marshals were killed in a single incident. But the circuit continued to host French Formula 3 races until 1989. The concrete might have made the track difficult, but it also made it strong.

The FIA President at the time was mercurial Frenchman Jean-Marie Balestre, a man who was keen to keep France at the top of motorsport as a time when British influence in F1 was growing more and more. At that point, there were still several French F1 teams and a string of French drivers.

It is a little-known fact that Balestre dreamed of bringing the French GP back to Paris, and came up with an imaginative project of using Montlhéry. That might sound completely bonkers given the nature of the track, but his idea was to revive the facility by converting the banking into grandstand seating and creating a modern road circuit in the old infield, using some of the forest sections as well. It was a brilliant idea, but the government of François Mitterrand was not interested. It had a project to rebuild Magny-Cours and use F1 to boost the economy of the Nièvre region where the President and some of his closest allies were strong.

There were also problems with cutting down trees and there remained the thorny question of access. Perhaps with government backing it might have been possible…

Montlhéry lost its racing licence in 2004, although UTAC continues to use the facilities for its testing programmes.

How not to build a brand

Property development is a risky business but there are big rewards at the end if things go well. However it requires money to buy properties and to fund construction or refurbishment. In order to raise the money required, a lot of property developers look for someone willing to lend them money. The only problem with this is that they usually require some form of security before taking a risk. Lenders may be satisfied with the property being used as collateral in such circumstances but many prefer the promise of cash. So, it is generally a business for those who have money.

Japan's Akira Akagi was fortunate in that his father had already built a property development company called Kenzai before he joined the firm, after studying business administration at university. His background is rather unclear with several birth dates and suggestions that he was Korean, which is something best left unsaid in Japanese business circles. At some point, he also spent time in England, living in the London suburb of Leyton (near the Olympic Park in Stratford). When he returned to Japan, Akagi took over Kenzai and soon began expanding the empire. He created a holding company called Marusho Kosan, which dealt with real estate, leasing and property management. Japanese property was booming at the time, and Akagi then decided to create a lifestyle brand, similar in concept to Virgin, which Richard Branson built up a few years earlier. His idea was for the brand to be active in many different businesses expanding the portfolio into restaurants and clubs, retail, travel, sportswear and even the record business. The name he chose was Leyton House because he wanted a cosmopolitan-sounding name, something which was considered to very cool in Japan at the time. For his branding, he chose a vivid aquamarine blue colour and decided to use motor racing to brand the brand.

Akagi was very keen on racing and had, supposedly, done some rallycross in his youth. He met an up-and-coming racing driver called Akira Hagiwara and decided that he would take him to F1 and the first Leyton House racing car was a Mercedes 190 touring car which was entered in the Japan national series. Sadly, Hagiwara was killed very early on after he crashed while testing at Sugo. Akagi then decided to look internationally and found a deal to fund Italian racing entrepreneur Cesare Gariboldi's Formula 3000 team, known as Genoa Racing, with a young Italian driver called Ivan Capelli. Ivan won the International Formula 3000 title that year and Leyton House money took him to Formula 1 in 1987 with March Racing. At the same time Akagi sponsored Kazuyoshi Hoshino in Japanese Formula 3000 and he finished runner-up in the title.

In 1988, Akagi bought into the March F1 team and a year later took control of the whole business, including all of March's racing assets, including the wind tunnel and the Formula 3000 operations. It was all going rather well. Akagi even bought the German fashion house Hugo Boss.

Then the Japanese property market collapsed and soon a number of scandals began to emerge. At the same time, Adrian Newey's CG901 chassis proved to be a very sensitive car, difficult to set up. There was no money to do development and the team decided to dump the young designer.

As things developed in Japan, the focus was on Fuji Bank, which had issued fake deposit receipts to 23 of its clients, so that they could use these as collateral for loans. These entrepreneurs borrowed a total of $1.9 billion from 16 finance companies. When this came to light, the bank dismissed four employees. Police later arrested two of them along with two of the businessmen involved: Akira Akagi and Masato Yajima of Marusho Kosan.

In jail, pending a trial, Akagi was in no position to fund an F1 team. He sold it to a consortium of interested parties but the team had disappeared by 1993.

Akagi remained in prison for some time but later emerged and went back to doing business, although with less ambitious goals and with more sensible funding options. He also kept a lower profile. He died in August 2018.

A grisly tale

Formula 1 in the early 1970s was extremely dangerous. The cars had become faster and faster but the circuit and car safety was not keeping pace with development, despite the safety campaigns initiated by Jackie Stewart and the Grand Prix Drivers Association (GPDA). Watkins Glen in New York was a particular problem and following François Cevert's death, there at the end of 1973, the GPDA complained about the state of the steel barriers. Two weeks before the 1974 race, Denny Hulme, the president of the GPDA warned track officials that the barriers needed to be moved back in a number of places.

Cevert had literally been cut in half by the barriers when his car landed upside-down on top of them, and the drivers wanted action. But nothing was done. That year the sport had already lost Peter Revson, killed in April while testing at Kyalami. In Jarama soon afterwards Arturo Merzario's Williams went over the barriers but luckily he was unhurt and no-one else was injured. In Germany both Mike Hailwood and Howden Ganley crashed and each suffered serious leg or foot injuries.

At the end of the year, the F1 circus took off to North America for the last two races: at Mosport Park in Canada and then two weeks later at Watkins Glen, where the World Championship would be decided between Emerson Fittipaldi of Team Lotus, Ferrari's Clay Regazzoni and, with an outside chance, Tyrrell's Jody Scheckter.

It was a clear warm day one the Sunday in Watkins Glen and there was a crowd of 105,000 to see the title decider. It was the first anniversary of Cevert's death, as the Frenchman had been killed in practice the previous year. At the start of the race pole position man Carlos Reutemann took the lead for Brabham, chased by James Hunt's Hesketh, Carlos Pace in the second Brabham and Niki Lauda's Ferrari. The title contenders were all behind the Austrian but Regazzoni was dropping away from the fight with a damper problem.

On the 10th lap, Helmuth Koinigg, the 25-year-old Austrian driver who had made a big impression when he finished 10th in Canada for Surtees on his F1 debut, crashed at the southern end of the circuit, in the corner known as The Toe, understeering off the track because of a slow puncture. The car went through two rows of catchfencing and then hit the three-layer steel barrier head-on. The impact was such that the bottom layer gave way. The middle rail did not give way and the car passed beneath it. Koinigg was decapitated, his body remaining in the cockpit, but his head, still encased in his helmet, ended up on the gearbox at the back of the car. In those days there were different ideas about accidents, and as the marshals realized that there was nothing that they could do, they placed a tarpaulin over the car and the race went on… The news reached the Surtees pit 25 minutes after the crash and Big John withdrew the second car, being driven by Jose Dolhem, as a mark of respect.

There were plenty of theories about what had happened but it was clear that the posts that secured the barriers had stayed in place and had not lifted out of the ground. Others suggested that the securing bolts used to secure the metals rails to the were fitted without vital large-diameter washers that help to spread the loads when there is an impact, which meant that the bolts were torn through the wood, which allowed the bottom rail to move.

It was against this background that the Spanish GP in April 1975 took part only after the drivers went on strike and refused to practice because they found that the barriers were not properly bolted together. Teams helped marshals fix the barriers overnight but the drivers were still not convinced and only backed down when they were threatened with legal action and threats that the local police would seize the cars. Even then, the World Champion Emerson Fittipaldi refused to start the race. The race was stopped after 29 of the 75 laps after Rolf Stommelen suffered a rear wing on his Embassy Hill and crashed over the crash barriers. Five spectators were killed and Stommelen suffered a broken leg, cracked ribs and a broken wrist.

Koinigg is buried Vienna's Heitzing cemetery, not far from the Schönbrunn Palace.

Where titles are decided

The 2020 season is the 70th anniversary of Formula 1 and, at the time of writing, a total of 29 different venues have hosted the race at which the World Championship was decided. And you might be hard-pressed to guess which venue has had the most title showdowns. It depends, to some extent, on the calendar but there have been seasons in which one driver was incredibly dominant and so the title has been done in the summer.

Some venues are a little bit dodgy in that in 1955 there wasn't really a championship decider because, when the British GP took place in July, Fangio did not know he had won the title. Prior to the race at Aintree, the French GP had been called off and subsequently the Grands Prix in Germany, Switzerland and Spain were all cancelled, which meant that by the time F1 got to Monza, two months later, Fangio had a big enough points advantage over Stirling Moss to have secured the title. And, one can argue that having a championship showdown in 1970 was not really correct as Jochen Rindt had been killed at Monza and so could not fight for the title. Jacky Ickx (Ferrari) was still in a position to overtake Rindt with three races remaining. He won in Canada, but Emerson Fittipaldi's victories for Team Lotus in the US put paid to his chances, not that he would have wanted to take the title in that way. The other factor that changed things was the scoring system, which was complicated in some years, with only a certain number of scores counting in each half-season…

The answer to the question is the Autodromo Nazionale at Monza, which saw the World Championship decided there on no fewer than 12 occasions. However, as F1 became increasingly global, the race ceased to be one of the last races (today it is the 15th of 22 races) and so it hasn't hosted a title deciding race since 1979.

The second most frequent venue for the World Championship deciding race has been Suzuka in Japan where, since the 1980s, there have been 10 title showdowns in Japan, and much post-race celebrating in the once-famous Log Cabin karaoke hut. These included the infamous title won by Senna in 1990 by driving Alain Prost off the road, which was in truth, simply revenge for what Prost had done to him the previous year. But these days times have changed and Suzuka has not hosted a showdown since Sebastian Vettel won his second title in 2011, almost a decade ago.

There is then a big gap back to the venues that have hosted five title deciders: Mexico City and Interlagos. Mexico held three in the 1960s, including John Surtees's last-minute victory in 1964. It was a three-way fight that year between Graham Hill (39 points), John Surtees (34) and Jim Clark (30). It looked simple enough for Hill but a collision with Lorenzo Bandini left Clark in a position to take the crown. On the penultimate lap, his engine failed, leaving Hill as World Champion until Ferrari switched second-placed Bandini with third-placed Surtees on the last lap – and so Surtees won… by a point. In the modern era, Mexico has added two further title-deciders thanks to Lewis Hamilton in 2017 and 2018.

Interlagos was where Jenson Button won his title in 2009 but it will always be remembered for the 2008 race when the title was decided after the chequered flag when Felipe Massa had won the race (and seemingly the title) until Lewis

Hamilton overtook fifth-placed Timo Glock in the final corners to get the place he needed to take the title... Wow!

Abu Dhabi has hosted four title deciders, all in the modern era, with Vettel winning a four-way showdown in 2010 and Hamilton in 2016 trying everything to stop Nico Rosberg winning the title, backing up the field hoping that his team-mate would tangle with other cars.

Hamilton was not the type to drive another racer off the road to win, which is not something one can say about Michael Schumacher, who took Damon Hill off in 1994 in Adelaide, and tried to do the same to Jacques Villeneuve in Jerez three years later. Adelaide has hosted three title deciding races including the amazing race in 1986 when Prost came from nowhere to take the title after Nigel Mansell suffered a tyre failure and Nelson Piquet was called in to check his rubber...

There were three championships settled at the Nürburgring in the 1950s and 1960s but that was only really possible if a driver had been really dominant, as happened with Alberto Ascari in 1952, Juan Manuel Fangio in 1957 and Clark in 1965.

Watkins Glen in the US was where three titles were decided while Austin in Texas has recently hosted two showdowns in 2015 and 2019. Double showdown status also goes to Estoril in Portugal, where Niki Lauda won the title by half a point in 1984 and where Prost wrapped up his successful 1993 campaign. Hungary was twice a showdown venue when Mansell and Schumacher had dominant seasons, while Las Vegas's two deciders were because it was the last race of the year in 1981 and 1982.

The others, for the record, were Aida (1995), Ain-Diab (1958), Brands Hatch (1985), Bremgarten (1954), Buddh International (2013) East London (1962), Fuji (1976), Jerez (1997), Kyalami (1983), Magny-Cours (2002), Montreal (1980), Osterreichring (1971), Pedralbes (1951), Porto (1960), Sebring (1959), Aintree (1955), and Spa (2004).

A power behind the scenes

With one or two notable exceptions, one doesn't hear much about the race promoters in the world of Formula 1. They are often government types, who know how to work the system and who understand that one has to be careful when dealing with public money.

At the end of the day, however, their job is to create value from the events and while not all Grands Prix promotions company can be profitable given the costs involved and the fees that must be paid, the benefits from an event comes in a less tangible form: as global recognition for a city or region; as tax revenues from the new visitors that the event draws to the region, not just in terms of spectators but also in visitors who hear about the place because of F1 and decide to visit. In many respects it is a thankless task, as there are always folk standing on the sidelines shouting that the event is not worth the money spent. When all is said and done, an F1 race has value if one makes use of it correctly. Those who do it right create races that stay on the calendar for years. Those who do it wrong last a few years and then slide away.

Australia's celebrated race promoter was Ron Walker, who died in 2018 at the age of 78. Walker was a fixer who knew people in sport, politics and business. He made things happen. But he couldn't do everything himself and behind him, as deputy chairman from 2006 until 2015, was John Harnden.

Harnden is a civil engineer, a graduate of the University of Adelaide in South Australia. He joined the well-known Kinhill Engineers in 1986 and very quickly became involved with Formula 1, beginning as a manager of engineering projects on the Adelaide street circuit. In 1990, he was named as track manager, overseeing the construction of the circuit each year and making sure that everything was as it should be. This was so successful that he was then sent off to develop other new tracks, working on the Zhuhai International circuit in China, on a Malaysian project for a Formula 1 race that didn't happen and doing a study for a street race in Buenos Aires, Argentina.

When the Australian Grand Prix left Adelaide to move to Melbourne, Harnden was on Ron Walker's shopping list and did much of the work to set up the Albert Park event, including some of the circuit design. After the new race kicked off successfully, he was appointed deputy to chief executive Judith Griggs and he then took over from her when she departed Melbourne in 1998 to return to Europe to work for Paddy McNally's Allsport Management.

When he took over the role, Harnden was only 32 and was clearly a man with a big future. Four years later, he was plucked out of the Grand Prix to become head the organisation to put together the Commonwealth Games in Melbourne in 2006. He was then named deputy chairman of the Grand Prix Corporation, while also running the theme park firm Village Roadshow from 2007 until 2010. His next role was as head of South Australian cricket and was then appointed as the chairman of the organising committee for the 2015 Cricket World Cup.

He became chairman of the Australian Grand Prix Corporation that same year as Walker was very ill with cancer. He served in the role until September 2019 when the government of Victoria appointed him CEO of the Melbourne and Olympics Parks Trust, the body which oversees sporting facilities in the city and runs the Australian Open tennis competition.

He was replaced at the Grand Prix Corporation by Paul Little, the founder and managing director of transport and logistics group Toll Holdings, who is also a former chairman of Essendon Football Club and has been chair of Visit Victoria, the state's tourism and events organisation. One of Harnden's last deals was to secure a new contract for the Grand Prix, until after the 2025 event.

A lad from Coventry

John Judd was born in Kidderminster in 1942, but grew up in Coventry, the centre of the British motor industry, even after being heavily bombed during World War II. When he left school, he started applying for apprenticeships with some of the local companies but was rejected by Jaguar and then by Coventry Climax. Fortunately, the latter had second thoughts and took on Judd as an apprentice, sending him to study at the local technical college before assigning him to work on the company's Formula 1 programme, with the celebrated engine designers Wally Hassan, Harry Mundy and Claude Bailey, who were then developing the 1.5-litre Climax FWMV V8, working with Cooper driver Jack Brabham, who had won the World Championship in 1959 and 1960.

Brabham had a variety of businesses, one of which Jack Brabham Conversions, based in Woking, which installed Climax engines in road cars, and Brabham Racing Developments (BRD) which manufactured the first Brabham Formula Junior racing cars.

The first Brabham F1 car – the BT3 - arrived in the middle of 1962 and the relationship with Coventry Climax – and with Judd – continued. With new three-litre rules coming for 1966, which the FIA announced in November 1963, Brabham began to look around for other options. There was also the new Tasman Series in Australia and New Zealand which had a 2.5-litre engine formula, which kicked off in January 1964. Brabham asked the Australian components company Repco to develop a Tasman engine for him and together they chose an Oldsmobile block as the starting point.

At around the same time, the Swiss F1 journalist Jabby Crombac was contacted by Yoshio Nakamura of Honda and asked to suggest a team to run a Honda engine in Formula 2. Jabby then approached Brabham and asked if he was interested. Black Jack was always interested in free engines but was also always looking for an advantage. Honda seemed like a good gamble. Brabham and Nakamura met in October 1964 in Paris and five months later two Honda engines appeared at the Brabham factory, with two engineers who spoke no English at all. The results were poor and so at the end of 1965 Brabham went to

Japan to meet Nakamura and told them that he needed a new engine. At the start of 1966 totally new engines appeared at the factory, designed by Tadashi Kume himself. That year Brabham and Denny Hulme won all the championship races bar one.

By then Brabham has won another F1 World Championship as well, thanks to his friends at Repco. In Early in 1965, after Coventry Climax announced it was quitting racing at the end of the season, Brabham suggested an F1 engine, based on an Oldsmobile block. Repco liked the idea and despatched Phil Irving to Britain to work with Jack on the design of the new "Australian" power unit. The small size of the engine meant that it could be used with the existing chassis but most importantly it was light, powerful and reliable. Brabham was ready for 1966 when most of his rivals were not. Judd was recruited to help the programme and in 1966 and 1967 Brabhams won two consecutive Drivers' and Constructors' Championships.

Importantly, Brabham also met an important young engineer from Japan, who turned up to help the Formula 2 development programme: Nobuhiko Kawamoto, who spoke good English. He and Brabham became firm friends.

During 1967, Repco discussed doing its own purpose-built 3-litre engine but the Ford Cosworth DFV, which had just arrived in F1 was so good that Repco decided that it would not be worth the risk.

Brabham did a deal to use DFVs in Formula 1 and Jack Brabham Conversions switched to become a Cosworth-tuning business. At the end of 1969, intending to retire and to sign Jochen Rindt to replace him, Brabham sold his shares in the business to his partner Ron Tauranac. Then in October Lotus boss Colin Chapman made Rindt a big financial offer to keep him for another year. Brabham could not compete financially and so decided to stay on for one final season as an F1 driver. The various companies were reorganised with Jack Brabham Conversions becoming Engine Developments and Brabham Racing Developments (BRD) changing its name to Motor Racing Developments (MRD). Brabham kept his shares in the engine business but left it to Judd to run. In the years that followed, Engine Developments prepared Cosworth engines for teams Williams, Lotus, Fittipaldi, Arrows and other F1 teams.

In the late 1970s, the business expanded to include Cosworth DFX Indycar engines, but then Honda's Nobuhiko Kawamoto, by then head of Honda Research & Development, suggested to Brabham that Engine Developments develop a new Honda F2 engines that would be used by Tauranac's new business Ralt. The Ralt-Honda F2 cars were very successful and won the European Championship in 1981 with Geoff Lees and then with Jonathan Palmer in 1983 and again in 1984 with Mike Thackwell.

The cancellation of Formula 2 at the end of 1984, saw Judd continuing to work with Honda but he also built the first engine of his own design: the Judd AV, a turbocharged V8 which first appeared in 1986 with a Galles Racing entry for Geoffrey Brabham (Jack's son), with an engine which was initially badged as a Brabham Honda. It became a Judd in 1987 and Brabham scored several podium finishes and in 1988 in Pocono, Bobby Rahal gave Judd its first Indycar victory.

By then, however, Engine Developments was involved in F1, using a variant of the AV, badged as the Judd CV which he supplied to Williams, Ligier and March. This continued to be used by various teams until the end of 1992, but in 1991 Judd unveiled a new V10, which would be used by Scuderia Italia in a Dallara-designed car.

During 1992, Judd agreed to work with Yamaha, which was struggling to build competitive engines for Jordan Grand Prix. Judd and Yamaha worked together to produce the OX10 family of engines for 1993, 1994 and 1995 and in 1996 built the OX11, a new generation V10. This was not very reliable but Mika Salo finished fifth on two occasions in a Tyrrell-Yamaha. Tom Walkinshaw spotted the potential and in 1997 he put together a package with World Champion Damon Hill and Pedro Diniz, using Arrows-Yamahas and Bridgestone tyres. Hill came close to winning in Budapest that summer...

But Walkinshaw had bigger ambitions and, in 1998, put together a deal to run its own engines (which were basically Hart V10s). Judd continued to develop his V10 that year and in 1999, but there were no customers.

And Judd turned his attention to sports cars and touring cars.

The other Peter Jackson

There are lots of Peter Jacksons in the world. Most folk these days will instantly think of the New Zealand film director, famed for his Lord of the Rings and Hobbit trilogies. However, there have been plenty of other Peter Jacksons who achieved success. There was, for example, the British cigarette maker who began operating at the start of the Twentieth Century and became best known for his du Maurier brand. After a series of takeovers, the company became part of British American Tobacco and began producing Peter Jackson-branded cigarettes in Canada and Australia. The brand even sponsored some celebrated Nissans in the Australian Touring Car Championship in the mid-1980s, being very competitive in the hands of drivers such as Glenn Seton and "Farmer George" Fury.

There was also an Australian fashion designer called Peter Jackson. It started in 1948 as a barber shop on Little Bourke Street in Melbourne. It began to sell ties and gradually moved into menswear and today is a fashion brand with outlets across Australia. There is a British academic of the same name, who is an expert in the medieval crusades. Another Peter Jackson is a British High Court judge, who had been in the papers for a number of his rulings. There was a famous boxer with the same name, a heavyweight from the Danish West Indies, now known as the US Virgin Islands. There have been a lot of footballers with the same name and fiction writers such as Stephen King and Michael Crichton have both used the name in their books. Oh, and Ernest Hemingway used to go by the name of Peter Jackson when he was trying to avoid being noticed (which, by all accounts, was not very often).

So, to be quite honest, it's quite a common name.

However, there are not many folk in the world who have heard of the Peter Jackson who was the force behind a once-celebrated motor racing company called Specialised Mouldings. Jackson started out as a humble upholsterer in the suburbs of South London. In the late 1950s, he was asked to fit out glass-reinforced plastic (GRP) Triumph Adventurer motorcycle sidecars. As a result, he became interested in the possibilities of fibreglass and found a backer to build miniature plastic Vanwall pedal cars for children. It was the time when the pedal car business was switching from metal to plastic and Jackson saw an opportunity to challenge companies such as Triang, which dominated the market. The prototype model was exhibited at the International Plastics Exhibition at Olympia in June 1959, but soon afterwards his partner pulled out, leaving Jackson without money to go forward. However, the pedal car had come to the attention of Eric Broadley of Lola, who asked him whether it was possible to make similar bodies for proper cars. Broadley lent him money and gave him moulds that Maurice Gomm had used to create aluminium panels for the Lola Mk 1 and work began in a basement beneath a shop in Thornton Heath. Peter's brother David joined the business, which they called Specialist Mouldings.

Soon Jackson approached the Cooper Car company and began working with them as well, and soon there was a huge demand for his fibreglass bodies. As business expanded, the firm relocated in 1960 to a better facility in Crystal Palace. Seven years, later the whole company moved to a new purpose-built factory in Huntingdon – not far from Lola. Arch Motors, a tubular chassis maker set up in Tottenham by Bob Robinson and Ted Young moved in next door and the two companies often worked together manufacturing chassis and bodies for all manner of racing teams, including several F1 operations.

Jackson realised that Specialised Mouldings could get more business if it provided additional services, including aerodynamic testing before his bodies were manufactured. At the time aerodynamics was becoming important. Over in the United States, Jim Hall was developing new aerodynamic ideas on his Chaparral sports cars, while Jerry Eisert was experimenting with his Harrison Special Indycars, which featured concepts by Shawn Buckley, who as a PhD student at the University of California, Berkeley, a couple of years later began researching under-car aerodynamics.

Later, as a mechanical engineering professor at MIT, Buckley would be briefly involved with Team Lotus as it developed ground-effect for F1. In Britain, Professor John Stollery, a former de Havilland engineer who worked in the aeronautics department at Imperial College London, was looking at similar concepts, while BRM's Tony Rudd sent his bright new assistant Peter Wright to work with Barnes Wallace, the famous inventor of the bouncing bomb, used by the Dambusters in World War II, to develop new ideas about under-car aerodynamics. Wright was soon busy in the Imperial College wind tunnel in London looking at new concepts.

But at the end of 1969, Rudd left BRM and Wright departed soon afterwards, having been offered an interesting role by Jackson to design, commission and operate a quarter-scale wind tunnel for racing car development. Once the tunnel was running, Wright worked with March's Robin Herd to create some of the aerodynamic surfaces for the March 701. And then in 1974 he went back to Team Lotus. The rest is history...

As for Specialised Mouldings, it moved away from motorsport as teams developed their own in-house wind tunnels and composite facilities, although as recently as 1991 built the Jordan 191 bodywork. The facilities were later taken over by Paxford Composites.

From small acorns

Henry Ford's first manufacturing plant outside the United States was opened in 1911, using an old carriage works at Old Trafford in Manchester, England, with the parts for the Model T Ford being imported from the United States, using the famous Manchester Ship Canal, and being assembled when they arrived. The site was close to the then new stadium used by Manchester United...

Once the cars were finished, they were whisked away by delivery companies that transported them to garages, dealers and customers across the country. There was plenty of opportunity and so, in 1926, Edward Toleman decided to set up a delivery company, to transport Ford around the country. Soon afterwards Ford decided to move its operations to Dagenham, Essex, on the River Thames, where there was more space available and it was easier to access by water.

Toleman decided it was best to relocate his business to stick with Ford. The business grew and in the 1950s was taken over by Edward's son Albert, by then it had 400 trucks and 2,000 employees and was delivering a million cars a year in the UK. People were used to seeing Toleman trucks on the roads. Albert Toleman fancied doing some rallying – and could afford to do it. Sadly, he died in 1966 at the age of only 56, leaving the business to his two sons Ted and Bob. Two years later, the firm hired a young entrepreneur called Alex Hawkridge, who soon began to find ways to make the company more and more money, primarily from helping Ford with storage for its body shells, by offering them a cheaper deal than existing storage facilities, yet giving Toleman a healthy profit. He then masterminded the purchase of a rival that was bigger than Toleman but had run into trouble. In the same period the firm began to get involved in motorsport sponsorship, initial on a small scale but gradually interest grew with Hawkridge and the Toleman brothers both trying racing. Bob became more and more involved as a driver in Formula Ford.

But then in the autumn of 1976 disaster struck. Bob was involved in a crash at Snetterton, suffered a fractured skull and was in a coma. He was transferred from Norwich General Hospital, to the specialist head injuries unit at Adenbrooke's Hospital in Cambridge, but died a couple of weeks later. It was a huge shock. But Ted and Hawkridge kept the racing going, running a team in Formula Ford 2000 for Rad Dougall and sponsoring various other drivers. They then decided to move to Formula 2 in 1978 with a March. It was not a success but for 1979 they did a deal with Ralt and Brian Hart and signed up Brian Henton alongside Dougall. Henton won twice and finished runner-up to Marc Surer, who was driving the leading factory March-BMW. It was then decided to build their own cars, designer by Rory Byrne, who had joined from Royale. Derek Warwick was taken on to partner Henton and the pair finished 1-2 in the European Formula 2 Championship, with sponsorship from BP and Pirelli. There was only one way to go after that. Toleman decided to go into Formula 1 with a turbocharged version of Brian Hart's F2 engine. The TG181 was a pretty poor car and neither Henton nor Warwick qualified until the Italian GP in the autumn. The second season was better but nothing special with Henton replaced by Italian Teo Fabi. It was not until the end of that year Byrne built the TG183, the first composite chassis, and things began to look up. By the end of 1983, Warwick and Bruno Giacomelli became regular points scorers. That was enough to convince Ayrton Senna to sign for the team in 1984 alongside Johnny Cecotto and the brilliant Brazilian scored three podiums. Cecotto was badly injured in crash in the mid-season and was replaced by Stefan Johansson, who finished fourth at Monza, where Senna was left on the bench, having decided to sign for Team Lotus in 1985, thus breaking his contract. It had been a promising year but the team ran into serious trouble that winter. There was no sponsorship and, more importantly, no tyre contract. Toleman had ditched Pirelli to join Michelin in 1984 but then Michelin pulled out and neither Pirelli nor Goodyear were interested in doing deals. The team missed the first three races but then Benetton agreed to take over the team and bought the Pirelli contract that Spirit Racing had had. In Germany Fabi put the car on pole around the new Nürburgring, a big surprise. At the end of the year, the team was bought from Toleman by Benetton…

It exists today, 34 years later, as Renault F1, having been owned by Benetton, then Renault, then a company called Genii Capital, during which it ran as Lotus, before being taken over again by Renault…

F1 comings and goings

Can you explain the significance of the following list? It begins – for this purpose – with Felipe Massa, followed by Fernando Alonso, Christian Klien and Nico Rosberg. Sebastian Vettel is on it, but Lewis Hamilton is not. Then there is Jaime Alguersuari, Jean-Eric Vergne and Esteban Gutierrez. Are you getting there? OK, it finishes off with Dany Kvyat, Max Verstappen, Lance Stroll, Charles Leclerc and Lando Norris? Some of the names might appear twice on the list and Alguersuari appears three times.

Give up yet?

Well, the explanation is pretty simple. Each one of these drivers listed was what the French would call the "benjamin" of Formula 1. The youngest driver who competed in each given year between 2002 until 2019. The ages differed by six years, with the oldest being Klien at 22 in 2005, the youngest Verstappen at 17 in 2015. The other teenagers were Stroll at 18 and Kvyat, Vettel and Alguersuari at 19. Massa, Leclerc and Rosberg were all 20, while Alonso, Gutierrez and Vergne were all 21.

If it proves anything, it is that if you want to get into F1 when very young, it's good to be a Red Bull driver.

When it comes to be being the oldest driver in a season in the same era, Michael Schumacher wins the game in five seasons, with his oldest season being in 2012 when he was 43. Kimi Räikkönen has been the old man of the grid since 2014, a period of seven years. He is now 41 and we will have to see if he goes further. Of the rest, Luca Badoer notched up 38 back in 2009. Olivier Panis did two seasons at 36 and 37. David Coulthard did one year at 37 while Mark Webber and Eddie Irvine were both 36. In recent teams as the grids have become younger, Räikkönen's 34 in 2014 was the youngest old bloke, which probably explains why he has stayed around so long.

From Bertie to Bond

Aston Martin is not new to Grand Prix racing. In fact, it has been involved with its own cars TWICE before: in the pre-World Championship era in 1922 and again in the World Championship itself, n 1959 and 1960.

The first foray began when Herbert "Bertie" Kensington-Moir drove an Aston Martin in the International 1500 Trophy on the Isle of Man in 1922. A month later, Aston's then owner Count Louis Zborowski and his chief engineer Clive Gallop raced Astons in the French GP at Strasbourg and, later in the year, there were three cars in the Junior Car Club 200 at Brooklands for Zborowski, Kensington-Moir and George Stead. The cars reappeared on occasion in 1923 but the company suffered a serious blow in 1924 when Zborowski was killed when his Mercedes hit a tree at Monza.

Aston Martin is also a company that has had a long history of financial difficulties, dating right back to the early years when Singer Motor Company dealers in Kensington, Robert Bamford and Lionel Martin, decided to fit a 1.4-litre Coventry Simplex engine into a 1908 Isotta Fraschini Tipo FENC chassis, derived from the cars that were built for the 1908 Grand Prix des Voiturettes at Dieppe.

Racing was always a core element for the company although after Zborowski Aston Martin was primarily involved in sports car racing. There were several financial crises along the way and, in 1946, the then owner Gordon Sutherland put an advertisement in The Times offering "a high class motor business" for sale. David Brown saw the advertisement and decided to see what it was all about. He was then 43 and already a very wealthy man. He had inherited David Brown & Sons, a transmission business which had been set up by his grandfather. He had built up the business – and diversified into the manufacture of tractors.

Brown visited Aston Martin's factory, the former Whitehead Aircraft works on Victoria Road, Feltham. He drove the prototype Atom and decided that he would buy the business. The deal, completed early in 1947, quickly resulted in a return to sporting activities with St John Horsfall and Leslie Johnson winning the Spa 24 Hours in an Aston Martin in the summer of 1948. By then, Brown had also acquired the Lagonda firm, which had a brand new 2.5-litre straight-six engine, which Brown felt would be perfect for his Aston Martins. Soon there was a factory team, trying to win the Le Mans 24 Hours. It took a long time but, in 1959, Aston Martin finally finished 1-2 in the celebrated French endurance event.

In the mid-1950s, a single-seater version of the DB3 was raced in Australia and New Zealand. In 1959, Brown decided to take Aston Martin into Formula 1 with the DBR4, a front-engined car designed by engineer Ted Cutting. The timing was awful, as Grand Prix racing was then switching to rear-engined cars and the front-engined Aston was just not competitive, despite the efforts of Roy Salvadori and Carroll Shelby. The cars were redesigned and lightened for 1960 and Salvadori was joined by Maurice Trintignant, but the performance did not improve and the company had little choice but to give up F1 at the end of the year.

Despite the setback, Aston Martin did well in that era, in part because of the firm's association with James Bond, which started in 1964 with the movie Goldfinger, which boosted sales of the DB5. In 1968, Brown was knighted for his services to the automotive industry.

And then Aston Martin hit trouble again… Brown sold the business in 1972 to Company Developments, an investment banking consortium, chaired by William Wilson, but the firm went into receivership just two years later.

And so it went on…

When Austin was a big player in F1

No-one ever remembers Ronnie Austin. There are various different versions of when the Concorde Agreement was signed, but what is on the record is that a key player in making it all happen was Ronnie Austin, a partner in the law firm Clifford Chance in Paris. He had been based in Paris for 11 years and was asked to take part in the talks on behalf of Renault.

It became necessary in December 1980 when Goodyear announced it was terminating its involvement in F1 because of the political battles between the governing body FISA (a part of the FIA) and the team organization FOCA.

Over a three-week period Austin, Max Mosley (representing the Formula One Constructors' Association) and Marco Piccinini (representing Ferrari and the other grandee teams – except Renault) met on a regular basis to go through terms that would be acceptable to all those involved. There was no FIA involvement in this part of the proceedings, but at a breakfast meeting in the Hotel de Crillon – the building next door to the FIA – F1 boss Bernie Ecclestone, Mosley and FISA President Balestre agreed on the basis of the deal. Balestre insisted that it be called the Concorde Agreement. The others did not care what it was called.

That was not early enough to save the South African GP. The promoters had been told that their race could only be given World Championship status if it was run in April and so the promoter decided to go ahead as a Formula Libre race, held on February 7 at Kyalami.

It was supposed to be the opening round of the 1981 championship and while it was supported by the FOCA teams, who mustered 19 cars: two each from Williams, Brabham, Lotus, McLaren, Tyrrell, Fittipaldi, Arrows and March, plus one car entries from ATS, Ensign and Theodore. The other teams (known as "the grandees") were aligned with the federation.

There was an announcement on March 5 that FISA and FOCA had reached an agreement, with a communiqué which revealed that there was a 93-page document that had been drafted and agreed on January 30. It did not mention whether the agreement had been signed. The signing date slipped back into March, but of the signatures were done by March 11, four days before the Long Beach Grand Prix. Although Ferrari raced in California, Enzo Ferrari did not sign the document until after the event.

At Long Beach there were 29 cars, with the addition of two cars apiece from Ferrari, Alfa Romeo, Renault, Ligier and Osella.

Balestre got his way with the name of the deal. The Concorde Agreement recognised the FIA as the owner of all commercial rights related to the Formula 1 World Championship, but gave the right to negotiate all commercials deals to FOCA – in exchange for a percentage of the profits. The teams agreed a scale of payments to share the revenues between them, but it all remained ultra-confidential, particularly the financial schedule (Schedule 10). The deal required the teams to appear and compete in every race and guaranteed their right to do so, so as to provide FOCA to sell the sport to TV companies.

So the Concorde Agreement was named after the Place de la Concorde, where the FIA had its headquarters, once part of the Automobile Club de France, which had acquired both number six and number eight and had integrated them into one building. They have since been separated again (to some extent), with the FIA leasing parts of number 8, including the entrance hall, which today houses the FIA Hall of Fame.

So it has nothing to do with the Anglo-French supersonic airliner that flew between 1976 and 2003. Concord in English and Concorde in French are basically synonymous, meaning agreement harmony and union. There is, of course, a certain irony given that one of the first battles in the American War of Independence took place at Concord, Massachusetts, in 1775, where assuredly there was little concord going on…

Goodyear, by the way, returned to F1 in June 1981, having achieved what it set out to do.

How not to double your money

Since 2016, Formula 1 has been listed on the NASDAQ stock exchange in New York. This means that it is a publicly-traded company and so in theory anyone can buy shares and become a co-owner in the business. In fact, it is listed on the NASDAQ and on the OTC exchanges, as there are actually three different classes of shares: there are Series A, Series B and Series C stock, with the ungainly ticker symbols of FWONA for Series A, FWONB for Series B and FWONK for Series C. The difference between them is that FWONA is on the NASDAQ and one vote equals one share; FWONB is on the OTC and one share equals 10 votes and FWONK (on the NASDAQ) means that there is no voting power, just money to be made.

So how did the super-secretive F1 world end up being listed on an American stock exchange, having to answer to the Securities and Exchange Commission (SEC)? Well, it involved some fancy footwork which amounted to a kind of reverse takeover. The already-listed Liberty Media bought a minority stake in the Formula One group holding company, known as Delta Topco, and then transformed itself into a new company called Formula One. This involved a lot of tidying up because F1 was not a transparent business, but there are still many confidential elements which have been carefully disguised in the numbers. On the day the purchase of Formula One was announced (September 7 2016), the company was worth $1.817 billion. Nine days later that had shot up to $2.320 billion, which meant that the business had theoretically added more than $500 million in value. In other words, the firm spent $1 billion and gained $500 million in additional value as a result of the deal. This was all done in parallel with Liberty's ownership of the Atlanta Braves baseball team and Sirius XM, the satellite radio group, each of which has its own stock, although they are all divisions of Liberty Media.

When the deal was first struck, Liberty Media offered the 10 Formula 1 teams the chance to buy 10 percent of the shares in FWONK. The goal, according to Chase Carey, was "to create much more of a long-term partnership, not a partnership that has a point in time where you go out and renegotiate the next eight-year partnership". Carey said that he wanted to create a situation in which there would be a shared vision of how to develop the sport and to share the benefits of working together.

There were 19 million shares set aside (worth just over $400 million) at the original sale price of $21.26. The teams had six months to accept the deal.

The shares did not include voting rights and none of the teams took up the opportunity, arguing that they should be given the shares and not have to pay for them.

Looking back, they might feel that they made a mistake as an investment of $40 million in 2016 would be worth around $90 million in early 2020, as the share price had risen to $47.

Who knows where it could be in the future?

Jolly old Cooper-Bristols

Talk to old F1 fans and they will wax lyrical about the jolly old Cooper-Bristols, which put Britain on the map (vaguely) in racing terms in the early 1950s, even if Ferrari dominated in Grand Prix racing. No-one ever mentions how it was the Bristol Aeroplane Company, famed for its multi-role Beaufighter, of which more then 5,500 were built during the war, acquired the design of its 2-cylinder engines. Nor do they mention the fact that the engine was designed by a German.

Rudolf Schleicher was actually born in Basel, Switzerland, in the summer of 1897, where his parents Rudolf and Clara owned a flooring business. When he was two, the family moved back to Munich where a new business was launched. Where his passion for engines came from is not clear, but his maternal grandfather Leonhardt Gürster was a master watchmaker and perhaps inspired the youngster in precision-engineering. While at school, he also drove trucks for his father's business before being called up to serve with a Bavarian motorised unit on the Western Front, largely providing the frontline troops with supplies. When the war ended, he won a place at the Technical University in Munich, studying mechanical engineering and, after graduating in 1922, he joined the Süddeutsche Bremsen-AG firm, which had taken over the remnants of BMW. The was manufacturing pneumatic brakes for Bavarian railways and had no use for the old BMW engine department, which was banned from making aero-engines under the terms of the Treaty of Versailles. So this was sold to Bayerische Flugzeugwerke AG, which was manufacturing industrial engines and farm equipment. BFW decided to rebrand itself BMW and went public the same year, planning to create a strong new business, based on motorcycle manufacturing.

The chief engineer Max Friz designed a 500cc boxer twin M2B33 engine, which went into the BMW R23 motorcycle, making its first appearance at the Berlin Motor Show in September 1923. Schleicher work not only on the design and development of the engine but was also the lead rider of the BMW factory team, scoring the firm's first sporting victory riding a prototype R32 on the ADAC Winter Rally in Garmisch-Partenkirchen, early in 1924. Friz was more interested in aero-engines and went back to them as soon as he was allowed and Schleicher was left in charge of the motorcycles. He developed the R37 for 1925 which doubled the power of the engine and would go on to win over 100 races. For the next few years, BMW dominated all 500cc racing in Germany. The R42 that followed was very popular, with 6,500 bikes sold, but Schleicher had bigger ambitions and was recruited by Horch in Zwickau, to be its head of engine testing, developing road car engines designed by Fritz Fiedler, who created a V12 for the Horch Type 600, a V8 for the Type 830 and a straight-eight for the Type 850 roadster.

By 1931, BMW was looking to build its own road cars and Schleicher was lured back to Munich. He designed the 2-litre straight-six M78 engine, which would be developed into the M328 used in the BMW 328, which was released in 1936. The engine was years ahead of its time, featuring aluminium-alloy cylinder heads fitted to a standard production cast-iron engine block because BMW insisted that the firm did not waste money on racing specials, so Schleicher, who had been join by Fiedler, built a car that could race and be used on the road.

The war saw Schleicher put in charge of BMW motorcycle production, the motorbikes being widely used by the military.

The BMW factories were, naturally, targets for the Allied bombers and, by the time the war ended, the BMW factory at Milbersthofen had been largely destroyed by bombing raids. Schleicher decided to leave to start his own business. The factory was to be demolished with anything useful being shipped back to the United States, as Bavaria was in the American Occupation Zone. It was at this point that Harold Aldington, who had run the AFN company before the war, selling BMW 328s, branded as Frazer Nash BMWs arrived on the scene, having flown from England in a Short Stirling heavy bomber. With the blessing of the War Reparations Board, Aldington turned up at Milbersthofen looking for plans, engines and any available staff. He was doing so on behalf of Bristol, which was planning to go into car manufacturing, as demand in the aircraft business was low and money was short, and had bought AFN as a starting point. Aldington met BMW's managing director Kurt Donath, who was trying to keep the company together, and bought the rights to manufacture three BMW models and the 328 engine. He also hired Fiedler. He flew home with rolls of drawings and a truck set off to England laden with 328 engines. Donath then turned to using the money raised to begin to manufacture pots and pans, agricultural equipment and bicycles.

As things began to return to normal, Schleicher's 328 engine proved to be the best-suited for racers and a string of BMW Specials began to appear in voiturette events. These became Formula 2 in 1948 and then in 1952, when it became clear that there were not enough engines for F1, the FIA decided to switch the World Championship to Formula 2 rules. The BMWs, Bristols and all the other engines based on Schliecher's 328 were all eligible for use in F1. Ferrari dominated but the 328 did a pretty decent job, given that the design was by then 15 years old…

As for Schleicher himself, he set up his own business called Schleicher Fahrzeugteile GmbH. Initially it did what was needed to survive, rebuilding engines and producing parts, but it gradually moved towards a core business of manufacturing camshafts. In the mid-1950s Schleicher was lured back to BMW as a consultant engineer for a number of years but his focus was on his own business, which he handed over to his sons during the 1960s.

He died in the autumn of 1989.

Le racing businessman

Carlo Alberto Pozzi was born in Paris in 1909 and was still a youngster when his father was killed at Verdun, during World War I. After the war, Pozzi was taken by an uncle to the new Montlhéry speedway near Paris and to his first automobile races. He was instantly hooked but racing cars were then wildly expensive and he did not have the money to take part.

When he was 21, he found a job at the Garage du Parc in the chic Neuilly-sur-Seine and began to sell automobiles to wealthy clients. Two years later, he opened his own garage in Saint-Maur-des-Fossés, in the south-eastern suburbs of Paris. He became a Ford dealer but also began selling secondhand luxury cars from companies such as Talbot, Delage, Delahaye and Hotchkiss. In 1936, he became a Delahaye dealer but then decamped to Mountauban, near Toulouse, where he started a charcoal business, later converting some cars to run on charcoal, as other fuel was scarce.

During that period, he created a very successful side business buying luxury and sporting cars, which had been left in the provinces. He drove them to Paris and sold them from premises in the 17th arrondissement. He acquired several racing cars during the war and, in 1946, he agreed to buy a pre-war Delahaye 135, but only after the owner had competed in the Nice GP. The owner then crashed the car in practice and offered the damaged vehicle to Pozzi before the race. He had the car repaired, drove it in the race and finished eighth, albeit many laps behind the winning Maserati of Gigi Villoresi. He then worked closely with Eugène Chaboud with an operation they called SFACS Ecurie France and helped him become French Champion in 1947. Pozzi preferred endurance events and in 1949 won the Grand Prix de l'ACF, which was held for sports cars that year. He also acquired a Talbot dealership in Paris and so when the World Championship began in 1950, he raced a Talbot-Lago T26C entered by Ecurie Charles Pozzi in the French GP at Reims. He finished sixth, having shared the car with Louis Rosier, after his works car broke down. He did not race again until 1953 when he took part in the Le Mans 24 Hours in a factory Talbot Lago T26GS, sharing with Pierre Levegh, finishing eighth.

In 1953 he began trading in Ferraris and quickly gained the confidence of Enzo Ferrari. He used the same tactics as he had in the war and would travel to Maranello about once a month and drive the new cars back to Paris, where they were sold. He did not become an official importer until 1969 when he took over the business, while also having concessions with Rolls Royce and with Chrysler. In the 1970s, he became a regular Ferrari entrant at Le Mans, while expanding the business from the main premises in Levallois-Perret to add agencies in Bayonne, Bordeaux, Lille, Lyon, Marseille, Nantes and Strasbourg. His business empire grew to become one of the most significant in France, until his death in 2001. The firm was later sold to Neubauer, a vast empire that sells 17 marques in France.

A man with big ideas

Hajime Tanaka has always been someone with grand ambitions. It has not always been easy, but he has achieved a great deal – and continues to work to do more.

Born in the Yamaguchi Prefecture, at the southern end of Japan's biggest island Honshu, in 1946, he grew up in shadow of Hiroshima, a city only 60 miles to the east. Several of his family were killed there the year before he was born when the world's first atomic bomb was dropped on the city. His family owned and ran the Tanaka Metal Company, which recycled scrap metal. It was one of the few Japanese companies that was in demand during and after the war, initially because of the need for steel during the war and then, when Japan was under US occupation, by the Americans, who wanted to dismantle Japan's many military bases. This led to the company working closely with the Americans and Tanaka grew up living in a world where there were strong American links. His father drove American cars and the family were used to American goods and culture. Although schooled entirely in Yamaguchi, he won a place to study economics at Japan's oldest academic institution, Keio University in Tokyo. He was a keen golfer and developed the ambition to build his own golf course. At the time golf was a sport that indicated wealth and success and the cost of joining a golf club was very high. He believed that he could soon turn a new facility into a very profitable business. After graduating, he drove around the Yamaguchi Prefecture looking for a suitable site and went to the Yamaguchi Bank and asked for a considerable loan. The bank, knowing that the family was to be relied upon, agreed and he spent $2.1 million in 1970 to buy the land at Nagato and then build a country club and golf course. By the time the work was done – and he did much of it by himself with bulldozers and excavators – he had revenues of $4.2 million as membership fees poured in. In 1972 he started work on another facility near his home town. That was finished in 1974 with a similar result. He opened a third course – which could be used day and night – at Shimonoseki. They were the three most popular and profitable golf courses in Japan, averaging 18,000 players per month.

He was rather at a loss for what to do after that. Money was pouring in as demand for golf grew and grew but he was not very interested in doing the same thing over and over again. The Yamaguchi Bank recommended that he take a break and travel the world to see if he could find inspiration for a new project.

He spent several months studying in the US and then went to Europe. As part of his trip, he went to see the Le Mans 24 Hours in 1986 and returned to Japan enthralled by motor racing and keen to become a racing driver. He was then 41 and had plenty of money. He bought himself a Honda Civic to race in a local championship and won the series at his first attempt in 1987. So he bought himself an F1 Tyrrell (it would end up being three) and he would take his cars out on different tracks around Japan. He also rode racing motorbikes and managed to have a number of serious accidents, breaking his collarbone badly twice while riding bikes and then smashing up one of his Tyrrells.

He concluded that opening an automobile country club was a great idea and decided that he would build his own circuit for Japan's super rich to use and for manufacturers to use for testing. He found a suitable piece of land in the neighbouring Okayama Prefecture and, having designed the track himself, began construction of Tanaka International. The plan included a plush clubhouse and a hotel on-site, in addition for plenty of garages in which the members could store their cars. He was able to sell 350 memberships at $100,000 each. He was printing money once again and quickly acquired an impressive car collection and the kind of contacts that come with such success.

So he set out to organise a Grand Prix at Tanaka International. The Okayama governor Shiro Nagano liked the idea as he was keen to promote the region as a tourist destination and high-technology centre, with its many pagodas, shrines and castles. The region also boasts the spectacular Seto Ohashi bridges – which span the islands of the Inland Sea - and links the island of Shikoku to the mainland. The problem was that the track was in a remote, densely-wooded and mountainous area, 12 miles for the nearest small town, along narrow roads. Ironically, the nearest town of any import was called Yunogo, which summed it up. Hotel accommodation was so scarce that F1 people had to travel 30 or

40 miles to get to the track and there was nothing for race fans. Tanaka was resourceful as ever arranging for fleets of buses to run up and down the access roads, ferrying people backwards and forwards.

Bernie Ecclestone liked Mr Tanaka's money and enthusiasm and it was agreed that the race would be called the Pacific Grand Prix. The first was in April 1994 and was won by Michael Schumacher, after Ayrton Senna's Williams was punted off at the first corner by Mika Häkkinen's McLaren.

The second race was scheduled for April 1995, but in January that year the Great Hanshin Earthquake destroyed much of the nearby city of Kobe, making it even more difficult for spectators to reach the track. The local authorities called off the race and rescheduled it for October, going back to back with the Japanese GP. Having achieved his ambition and having lost the support of the local government who felt that the experiment was not worth repeating, the race was stopped.

The company would go bankrupt in 2003 and was restructured. The circuit was renamed Okayama International Circuit, with the local government taking over control.

Tanaka had a new ambition, to own the commercial rights of an entire sport and founded the Japanese Billiard Council. This was followed by the International Billiard Council and, in late 2001, he organised the biggest ever billiard competition, attracting 729 contestants, battling for a prize fund of £1 million. The Tokyo 9 Ball International was a success for the players, but the media paid little attention. Billiards was not quite Formula 1.

He then hit on the idea of creating a floating sporting venue which could travel the world and host big events in different locations, thus generating revenues from the cities, in addition to the TV and sponsors. He began planning to build a ship with suitable sporting facilities.

While he was doing this, he stumbled upon new success when he asked the French fashion house Hermès to create a briefcase that he had designed. Jean-Louis Dumas, the boss of Hermès, though it was such a great design that the company agreed to put it into production as the so-called Mallette Tanaka. Soon after that he had a similar experience with the Finnish loudspeaker company Genelec, which created a very successful Tanaka line of speakers.

The ship project continued with his Ocean Silk Road Inc planning to build a liner called the Princess Kayuga, the largest ever cruise ship in the world. The 2009 recession stopped that programme and Tanaka spent the next four years working to redesign the Choshi City hospital, not far from Tokyo's Narita Airport.

In 2013, he relaunched the Princess Kayuga project with a new firm called Contents Network Inc. The ship design has grown to 500 metres in length, which is around 150 metres longer than the biggest existing liners. The ship will weigh 450,000 tons, which would be far and away the largest passenger ship ever built. The goal would be to create a ship with 3,610 suites, accommodating 8,400 passengers, with a crew of 4,000. This would include condominiums where wealthy people could live tax-free, cruising around the world. There would be three 1,200 room hotels offering suites and offices, around 50 different restaurants, a tax-free shopping mall, a sports stadium, a convention centre and a 2,000-seat concert hall with its own resident orchestra and conductor, allowing the ship to host world class events. There would naturally be a full-scale hospital, an art gallery and even an amusement park.

A floating city, in effect, taking world-class events, sports fixtures, conventions and exhibitions to different cities. A very big money-making machine…

Mr Tanaka is already considering building a fleet of tax-free floating cities.

The other Haas F1

It is rather an odd thing that the last two American Formula 1 teams that have raced (rather than just talking about going racing) were both owned by people called Haas – and they are completed unrelated to one another. Carl Haas was from Chicago, Illinois, Gene Haas from Youngstown, Ohio, a city between Pittsburgh and Cleveland.

Well, if truth be told Carl Haas wasn't really from Chicago. That is what he used to tell people and what appeared in his official biographies, but Carl Haas was born in Germany in 1929. If you look at stories about his life, it says that he was born in Chicago in 1930, but also that his father fled Germany to escape from Nazi persecution. Given that the Nazis did not come to power in Germany until 1933 the facts as presented just didn't add up…

Immigration records reveal that Carl moved to the United States with his family in March 1938, when he was just nine years old. They were Jewish and lived in Ludwigshafen am Rhein, where his father traded leather goods. It was a place where there was little discrimination. A Jewish resident was elected to the town council as early as 1860 and there were numerous Jewish-owned businesses and factories. But once the Nazis arrived, things changed. The Haas family got out just in time. In late 1938, the Ludwigshafen synagogue was burned and in the years that followed many of the Jewish population was sent to camps from which few returned.

Carl went to Hyde Park High School, Woodrow Wilson Junior and finally to the Illinois Institute of Technology. He then signed up to join a Ford Motor

Company management training programme. It was at this point that he went with a friend to the resort town of Elkhart Lake, 150 miles north of Chicago, to watch a street race that ran around the lake with the start-finish line on the waterfront opposite the celebrated Osthoff Resort. He was hooked and was soon racing an MG in local SCCA races. He was quite successful and so moved on to a Porsche Spyder and more exotic Ferraris and Jaguars. He began trading gearbox parts to help pay for his expensive new habit. As time went on, he began to import cars and components from Britain and by the early 1960s, had given up being a driver and turned to being a team owner and businessman. In 1967, he became the exclusive US importer for Lola Cars, a role he would hold for 36 years. He ran Lola teams in CanAm and Formula 5000 winning races and titles, notably in Formula 5000 with Brian Redman. This was followed by CanAm titles for Patrick Tambay in 1977, Alan Jones in 1978, Jacky Ickx in 1979 and Tambay again in 1980. He ran some sports cars but then decided to go into business with his old CanAm rival team owner Paul Newman (better known as a movie star) and the Newman Haas team won a string of titles with Mario and Michael Andretti, Nigel Mansell, Cristiano da Matta and, in the dying years of CART, four consecutive championships with Sebastien Bourdais.

In late 1984, Haas landed a big new sponsorship deal with Beatrice Companies Inc which agreed to finance not only the CART team but also a Formula 1 programme. Haas did a three-year deal to use Ford V6 turbos and signed up Jones. Formula One Race Car Engineering (FORCE) was set up in Britain and recruited some of the best-known names in the business including Teddy Mayer, Tyler Alexander, Neil Oatley, a young Ross Brawn and later an even younger Adrian Newey. The cars were called Lolas – it was good advertising for Haas – but were actually designed and built in the FORCE factory in Colnbrook. The engines were not ready for 1985 and so Haas ran Hart turbos, without much success. In July that year, James Dutt, the Beatrice CEO, was replaced by a new boss who was not into racing. The first car – designated a Beatrice Lola was launched that summer and Jones did a handful of races at the end the season. Jones was joined in 1986 by Patrick Tambay and the Ford engine arrived but Beatrice had withdrawn and although Haas tried to find the money to keep the team going, he failed and he sold the team to Bernie Ecclestone.

Haas went back to US racing and turned to race promotion at the Milwaukee Mile, Road America and in Houston. In 1994 he started a NASCAR Cup team with former Ford executive Michael Kranefuss and after selling out to CART rival Roger Penske went into partnership with Travis Carter to form another team which ran until the end of 2002.

In 1997, he split with Lola and for three years was the distributor of Swift cars but he then returned to Lola after the organisation was taken over by Martin Birrane.

Violently opposed to the rival Indy Racing League, Newman and Haas stayed until the end in CART in 2008. They finally switched to the IRL and won races with Graham Rahal and Justin Wilson but then Newman died at the end of the year. The team had a new partner by then in Mike Lanigan but won nothing in 2009, 2010 and 2011. Haas finally announced that he was stopping the team. Lanigan moved to join Rahal Letterman.

By then Haas had begun to suffer from Alzheimer's disease, from which he died in 2016.

The boy done good

Stefano Domenicali comes from the city of Imola, a fairly average little place, on the plains to the east of the Apennine mountains – the backbone of Italy. In the hills behind Imola, the Mille Miglia raced through the hills and in the 1950s the local council decided to try to boost the local economy by building a new road linking existing public highways which could be turned into a racing circuit. Construction began in March 1950 but it was not until 1954 that the first race took place. Keen to develop the idea, the track offered a large prize fund for a non-championship Formula 1 race in 1963. It was won by Jim Clark but Ferrari did not attend. A grandstand was built in 1965 and the Motorcycle World Championship paid its first visit in 1969. Money was found to build roads around the track and in the early Seventies it became a permanent closed circuit.

The son of a prominent local banker, Domenicali grew up as the circuit was becoming known internationally. This was largely thanks largely to another non-championship F1 race, known as the Gran Premio Dino Ferrari, which took place in September 1979 (being won by Niki Lauda in a Brabham-Alfa Romeo). This laid the groundwork for the one-off Italian GP in 1980, as Monza was closed for renovation work. After that, Imola joined the World Championship full-time with the San Marino Grand Prix, which began in 1981.

At the time, Stefano was still studying at the Liceo Scientifico di Imola, before moving on to study economics and business administration at the University of Bologna, the oldest university in the world. During his college years, the Ferrari-mad Domenicali often helped out at the circuit, doing whatever people wanted him to do, working as a pitlane marshal and in the media centre. He had decided by that point that he was not going to follow his father into finance and set his sights on getting a job at Ferrari. He sent in his CV to the company which was sufficiently impressed to hire him to work in the taxation department. It was a start.

Stefano's arrival at Maranello coincided with the firm finishing its upgrading work of the Mugello circuit, near Florence, which had been acquired as a test track in 1988. Ferrari needed someone to run events at the track and Domenicali earned himself a clerk of the course licence and between 1992 and 1994 he became the race director of Mugello, organising events including MotoGP and DTM.

In 1995, impressed at his skills, Ferrari put him in charge of human resources for Gestione Sportiva, Ferrari's competition department, and a year later was transferred into sponsorship liaison. Then, having a good grounding in the F1 business, he was named as the F1 team manager, a job he would hold for five years. After a season as the logistics manager, he was promoted to be the sporting director of the team in 2001, his role being to do all the necessary liaison with the FIA and the other teams and to know the rules inside out.

He did the job without drama and without rocking the boat and by November 2007 he was named to replace Jean Todt as the head of Gestione Sportiva, with Todt remaining the chief executive of the whole Ferrari company.

Stefano was then 42. The team won the Constructors' World Championship in his first year in charge, but it missed out on the Drivers' title in the exciting end-of-season showdown in Brazil. During his tenure, the team won 20 victories with Felipe Massa, Kimi Räikkönen and Fernando Alonso but there were no more championships and when the 2014 car arrived and was clearly not very competitive, Domenicali resigned, feeling that he had not achieved as much as he had hoped. Other, he hoped, could do better.

Later that year, thanks to his connections with Volkswagen's Luca de Meo, who had been a key Fiat executive before moving to the German firm, he was taken on by Audi as Vice President of New Business Initiatives, his job being to evaluate whether Audi should enter Formula 1 and if so, by which route be that taking over a team, working with an existing racing organisation or whether it would be best to start its own dedicated operation in Ingolstadt. The process took 16 months and then, early in 2016, he was named as the new chairman and CEO of Automobili Lamborghini.

The VW-owned supercar company, based in Bologna, was then selling 3,500 cars a year. Under Stefano's leadership, production has ramped up to 3,800 in 2017, 5,750 in 2018 and 8,205 in 2019, thanks largely to the launch of the Urus SUV with revenues rising from $1.25 billion in 2017 to $1.6 billion in 2018 and around $2 billion in 2019.

It is ironic that he has found success with Ferrari's rival, but his career still has a way to run yet...

The coin collector

Only one Canadian-built car has ever competed in the Formula 1 World Championship – and you can forget Walter Wolf Racing, which may have been entered on a Canadian licence but which designed and built its cars in Britain. The answer is the Stebro, driven by its designer (and builder) Peter Broeker.

By all accounts, Broeker is a bit of a mystery. However, we have reliable source of information, a short biography which appeared on the back of a self-published book called "Olympic Coins" in 1973. Broeker, you see, was a coin specialist in addition to his other skills, serving as president of the Montreal Numismatic Society and as chairman of the Canadian Numismatic Association.

He says that he was born in Hamilton, Ontario, a short distance from Niagara Falls, in 1926. Some sources suggest he was born in San Francisco, others say Germany and others say Pennsylvania. As there is no reason to suggest otherwise, his own story is probably the most reliable. He certainly travelled a great deal when he was young – hence his interest in coins – his father having businesses in different countries, including Argentina, Germany and the United States. Peter seems to have lived in several of these countries. He reportedly served with the US Army at the end of World War II, when he would have been 19, but then went on to study history and politics at college in Nashville, Tennessee, where he did his first races in stock cars.

He did not move back to Canada until 1952, opening a car repair business in Hamilton, not far from Niagara Falls, before relocating to Montreal in the late 1950s, opening the Strebro Garage with a colleague called John Stephens in 1959. This was basically a repair shop but they soon began to act as an agent for Judson superchargers, imported from Pennsylvania, before developing a business in stainless steel exhausts for mainly Italian cars.

Broeker began building his Stebro racing cars in 1960, using a BMC engine for the new Formula Junior in 1960. The front-engined Mark I Formula Junior was not very competitive and he built a Mark II, which was a rear-engined version of the car. The Mark III was a open-wheeler version of a Sadler sports car. None brought any real success. The Mark IV, built over the winter of 1962-63 was a space frame design, clothed in aluminium bodywork, fitted with a larger than normal fuel tank so that it would be able to be raced in longer events.

Broeker had the ambition to enter Formula 1 and did a deal with the Martin engine company in Britain to use an engine it was developing for the 1.5-litre rules. His goal was to build two cars and enter them for John Cannon and Ernie DeVos in the United States GP that autumn. He was granted an entry for Watkins Glen, presumably because the track thought a Canadian car might attract fans, but only one Mark IV was ready and the engines had not appeared. In desperation Broeker built up his own engine using a Ford 105E, as used in the Anglia, bored out to 1.5 litres, with as many tweaks as he had time to add. Cannon had gone off to race elsewhere and DeVos realised that the car was not going to be competitive and so Broeker decided to race himself. The car lasted only a few laps in qualifying before blowing an oil seal and spreading oil all over the track. He qualified last, 15 seconds off the pace and after a few laps in the race the car jammed in fourth gear, but Broeker refused to give up and ended the day seventh, just one place short of a point, although he finished 22 laps behind Graham Hill's BRM.

The Stebro thus became the first and only Canadian-built F1 car.

Broeker took a new Stebro Mark V to Europe to compete in F2 races the following summer, fitting the car with a more competitive Cosworth-tuned SCA engine, but the results were still not very good. He returned to Canada, developed the car more, fitted a better engine and went on to win a string of races in the years that followed, before rolling the car at Saint-Jovite in 1968, fortunately without injury. Rather than rebuild the car, he bought a Chevron, although this would be lost in a workshop fire.

He moved Stebro to a bigger facility in Pointe-Claire, near Montreal's Dorval Airport, but then decided to leave Quebec after the first separatist government was elected in 1976. He settled in Hawkesbury, Ontario, about 60 miles to the west of Montreal, just across the border. He still raced but fell victim to cancer, dying in Ottawa at the end of 1980, at the age of just 54.

Strebro died with him although the name would be revived 20 years later by a Swiss mechanic who started building exotic exhausts until the firm went out of business in 2013.

A year for the new boys

In 1989, Formula 1 found itself in a period of change. Many of the F1 drivers had been around for a few years. Things seemed rather stable. The big guns were Ayrton Senna, Alain Prost, Nigel Mansell and Nelson Piquet. Gerhard Berger scored the occasional victory. And then the F1 circus headed off to Brazil for the first race of 1989. Ferrari was in trouble, as the new 640 was so advanced that it was completely unreliable. The team could only run a few laps at a time before something went wrong. Qualifying in Rio produced a few surprises. Senna was on pole for McLaren-Honda but it was a surprise to see Riccardo Patrese second in his Williams-Renault. Berger was third for Ferrari with Thierry Boutsen fourth in the second Williams-Renault, Prost was fifth in his McLaren-Honda and Mansell was sixth in his Ferrari. It was all a little odd.

The race started with a bang, Berger made a great start and tried to pass Senna and Patrese into the first turn. Senna refused to give room. There was a collision and Patrese found himself in the lead. Mansell had expected to be out early but as the afternoon went on he found himself leading the race with the 640 running faultlessly. Everyone remembers Johnny Herbert's performance that day. He could barely walk, yet this pale pained figure not only out-qualified his more experienced Benetton team mate Alessandro Nannini but went on to finish fourth in the race. It was a great day for Mansell – although he cut his hands on the trophy – but it was Herbert who grabbed much of the attention. Fourth on his F1 debut. It was astonishing.

It was sad because no-one ever remembers who finished second and third that day. Prost was second but perhaps poor Mauricio Gugelmin deserved a little more recognition for his third place for Leyton House. He had a decent debut season in 1988 but nobody paid much attention to his first podium. There were just too many good storylines. There were a number of similar stories that year. In Monaco Stefano Modena took his Brabham to third place. Alex Caffi finished fourth in a Dallara. In Montreal Nicola Larini took the hopeless Osella to third place in the wet.

But the French GP was the race that revealed the new generation more than anywhere. Five drivers made their F1 debuts that day: Jean Alesi was called up by Tyrrell as Michele Alboreto could not stay on after the team did a deal with Camel. Eric Bernard replaced Yannick Dalmas at Larrousse, Martin Donnelly stepped in to replace Derek Warwick at Lotus after the latter crashed a kart (rather unwisely), while politics at Benetton saw Herbert dropped and Emanuele Pirro given the job. Finally, Bertrand Gachot made it through pre-qualifying for the first time with his Onyx. Bernard, Alesi and Gachot had already met at the track, six years earlier when all three were finalists in the Paul Ricard Elf Winfield racing school competition. Bernard had won that day. Two seasons later Bernard had won the French Formule Renault title with Alesi fifth. Two years after that the rivals fought over the French F3 title – Alesi had won. On the day of their F1 debuts, Alesi ran second and finished fourth. The others all impressed. In Germany a few weeks later, Pirro ran in third and so it went on. It was a year for the youngsters…

A country with a lively history

There was a time when the Agip name was everywhere in Formula 1. It was the fuel sponsor of Ferrari and the name was often to be seen on yellow trackside hoardings, with its six-legged fire-breathing black dog logo. It was as emblematic of Italy as Ferrari's prancing horse, Maserati's trident, the Lamborghini bull or the celebrated Martini stripes. Between 1974 and 1995, it was an integral part of the Ferrari story, before Shell took over. There were dalliances with other teams, notably Benetton, but then Agip faded from F1.

It is a story that began back to 1925 when Benito Mussolini seized power, changing his title from President of the Council of Ministers to Head of the Government on Christmas Eve 1925. He immediately began to enact nationalist and protectionist reforms in his role as "Il Duce", creating the machinery of a modern dictatorship, based on the promise of future national renewal. Rival political parties were banned, the press was manipulated to promote Fascist truth over anyone who criticised the regime and power was concentrated in the hands of the party. As part of this approach, Mussolini launched a national petroleum company. The Azienda Generale Italiana Petroli (AGIP) was the result. The company did well early on but the war left many of its facilities damaged or destroyed. The first post-war Prime Minister Alcide de Gasperi, leader of the Democrazia Cristiana party, asked Enrico Mattei to oversee the closing down of the business.

Mattei was the son of a carabiniere. He worked in the tannery business before the war, setting up a chemical company producing oil-based emulsifiers for the tanning and textile industries. When the war came, he joined a partisan group in the mountains around Perugia before moving to Milan to escape arrest. He was then put in charge of the Christian Democrat partisan forces, was caught in October 1944 and was lucky to escape two months later. When the fighting ended in 1945, he was appointed a member of the National Liberation Committee.

Rather than close down Agip, Mattei concluded it was better to rebuild and expand. De Gasperi agreed to support his efforts and this led to the establishment of Ente Nazionale Idrocarburi SpA (ENI) to combine all state-owned petroleum, gas and petrochemical companies into a single corporation, with Agip as one of the divisions. Mattei was put in charge and remained so, expanding the business from oil and gas to machinery manufacturing, textiles, finance and even acquired the newspaper Il Giorno.

But then in October 1962, he was killed when his Morane-Saulnier MS.760 Paris private plane came down in a storm, close to the village of Bascape, on approach to Milan's Linate Airport. The pilot Irnerio Bertuzzi, a celebrated war hero, and a Time-Life photographer called William McHale were also killed. A government inquiry concluded that the plane had crashed because of the storm, but there were suspicions that this was not the truth. There have been a number of investigations since which have proved conclusively that the plane was blown up, but no-one knows who was responsible. A French former secret agent Philippe Thyraud de Vosjoli claimed that the explosion was an operation conducted by the Service de Documentation Extérieure et de Contre-Espionnage (SDECE), France's secret service, while Tommaso Buscetta, an informer on the Italian mafia, said that it had been responsible.

In the years that followed under Eugenio Cefis, who was also accused of having been involved in the crash, ENI was used by the government as a holding company for different businesses, including more chemical companies and mineral firms. The decision to sponsor Ferrari in 1974 gave the firm enormous exposure and it expanded further, but it became increasingly unprofitable and had to reorganised in 1983 by Franco Reviglio. It was floated in 1992, although the government remained the primary shareholder. A year later, Agip was engulfed in the Tangentopoli corruption scandal, with the chairman Gabriele Cagliari admitting that he had bribed government officials. He was later found in his prison cell with a plastic bag wrapped around his head. This was ruled to be suicide, although there were a number of incongruous elements, including facial bruising, that did not quite fit the story.

After the scandal, Agip was put under the control of Franco Bernabei, who sold off more than 60 subsidiary companies, preparing it for full privatisation. This resulted in the loss of the Ferrari sponsorship contract as Shell was willing to pay twice as much. The IPO went ahead but by 2003 Agip had been reacquired by ENI, which although privatised as well, remains under the control of the Italian Ministry of Economy and Finance by virtue of shares it holds through the Cassa Depositi e Prestiti SpA investment vehicle.

Quite a family

In 1892, Tokujiro Ishibashi opened a tailor shop called Shimaya in the Honcho district of Kurume City, close to the port of Fukuoka, on the island of Kyushu, in south-western Japan. His children Jutaro and Shojiro were six and three at the time but as they grew up, they joined the family firm. In 1906, they took over the business at the ages of 20 and 17. They decided to reduce the tailoring and increase production of tabi, traditional Japanese footwear made from cloth. They invested in cutting and sewing machinery and, by 1916, had grown sufficiently to open a factory in the Arai-machi district. They then began to create rubber-soled tabi, called jikatabi, and expanded the sales across the whole of Japan with a company called Nihon Tabi. This was followed by diversification into athletic shoes in 1923 and in 1928 they opened a new factory in Fukuoka to manufacture shoes for sales all over the world. They had money to burn. They helped to establish the Kyushu Medical School, donating land and buildings and began collecting art, which would later form the celebrated Ishibashi Collection.

Shojiro also wanted to look at the tyre business and bought a tyre-making machine in 1929. Although the brothers had plenty of money behind them, it was a risky idea as the Japanese tyre industry was dominated by Dunlop (which had started in 1913) and Yokohama, which had begun in 1921.

Jutaro, who had by then changed his name to Tokujiro (their father's name), opposed the idea but Shojiro was sure it would work. This led to a split in 1931 with Tokujiro taking all the shares in the shoe business and Shojiro taking over the entire tyre business. The former would change the company name to Japan Rubber, while Shojiro played around with the English translation of the Ishibashi name – "ishi" meaning stone and "bashi" meaning bridge – and came up with Bridgestone. The Bridgestone company suffered after the war, initially having to manufacture bicycles to stay in business and in 1949 Shojiro provided the finance for the Tokyo Electric Car Company, which was set up from elements of the Tachikawa Aircraft Company Ltd. This soon became the Tama Electric Car Company but began to use gasoline engines created by Fuji Precision Industries. Shojiro acquired this firm and in 1952 transformed the business into the Prince Motor Company, which would later be merged into Nissan in 1966. Bridgestone went back into the tyre business in the early 1950s. As car sales boomed the company flourished.

The rivalry between the two brothers continued until 1958 when Tohijiro died. By then, Japan Rubber has changed its name again and had become the Asahi Shoe Company. Three years later – Shojiro decided to float the company and two years later he stood down and allowed his son Kanichiro to take over. He remained as chairman until 1973 and died in 1976 at the age of 87

In 1983, Bridgestone bought a Firestone factory in Tennessee and five years later acquired the whole Firestone company for $2.6 billion.

Bridgestone did not get involved in motor racing until 1963, battling with its rivals Dunlop and Yokohama, but the company long had the ambition to enter Grand Prix racing. The cost of the Firestone takeover meant that was impossible but in 1989 the firm began testing F1-spec tyres. Bridgestone finally entered F1 with Arrows in 1996 and after some impressive showings attracted McLaren and Benetton in 1998. It won its first World Championship with Mika Häkkinen.

The family remains both wealthy and powerful. Shojiro's daughter Yasuko Hatoyama married Iichirō Hatoyama, the son of Ichirō Hatoyama, who would became Prime Minister in the mid-1950s. Iichiro himself would become Foreign Minister in the 1970s.

Yasuko and Iichiro's son Yukio became Prime Minister in 2009, while his brother Kunio was a government minister several times, notably as Justice Minister and Minister of Internal Affairs and Communications.

Not bad for a family of shoemakers…

Another age

Life in Formula 1 was different back in 1969. Drivers did more than just Formula 1 races and their schedules were busy. On Saturday, September 20, for example, the F1 crowd raced at Mosport Park, where 24-year-old Jacky Ickx scored his second win in three races, beating his team boss Jack Brabham (43) with Jochen Rindt (27) third for Team Lotus. The circus then went off in different directions. Bruce McLaren, Denny Hulme, Jack Brabham and Jo Siffert headed for Michigan International Speedway, 370 miles to the west, by way of Toronto and Detroit. They were there to compete in the eighth round of the CanAm Challenge Cup, with Siffert driving a factory Porsche 917, McLaren and Hulme the McLaren M8, while Brabham had a Ford G7, entered by Agapiou Brothers Racing. McLaren won from Hulme, with Gurney in a third M8. Siffert was fourth a lap behind.

Others took off from Mosport going in the opposite direction, flying to Paris in order to take part in the Paris 1000 sports car race at Montlhéry. Matra had two factory cars on hand: a 650 for Jean-Pierre Beltoise (who had flown in from Canada) and a 630/650 for Pedro Rodriguez, who had raced one of Luigi Chinetti's North American Racing Team (NART) Ferraris at Mosport. They were paired with Henri Pescarolo and Brian Redman respectively. They were up against a field of Lola T70s, Ford GT40s and Porsche 908s but they finished 1-2 and then Beltoise and Rodriguez flew back across to New York and set off for Watkins Glen for the United States GP on October 5.

John Miles, Jochen Rindt, Piers Courage and Johnny Servoz-Gavin went even further, flying from Canada to Rome to take part in the XXI Gran Premio di Roma at the Autodromo Vallelunga, the seventh and final round of the European Trophy for F2 Drivers. Servoz-Gavin was there to wrap up the championship for Ken Tyrrell's Matra International. He had 31 points, while BMW's Hubert Hahne had 28 but things were complicated because only five scores counted and the

Frenchman has scored five times to Hahne's four. It meant that Servoz-Gavin was out for a victory. The Lotus team, run by Roy Winkelmann Racing had Rindt and Miles while Courage was at the wheel of a factory de Tomaso.

Servoz-Gavin won by a lap from Peter Westbury, driving a Brabham BT30, while Miles was third. Rindt and Courage retired. They were all soon on their way to Leonardo da Vinci International airport at Fiumicino to fly off to the United States.

The field was much the same as it had been in Canada with one or two changes among the privateers. BRM had run its third car for Bill Brack in Mosport but handed it over to George Eaton for Mosport. Miles had not gone back to the States as the four-wheel-drive Lotus 63 was going to be driven by Mario Andretti. He had been unable to race in Mosport because he was busy racing (and winning) with an STP Granatelli Hawk at Trenton in New Jersey. He had then flown out to California to race the same car on the dirt at the California State Fairgrounds in Sacramento, before flying back to join Team Lotus. Rodriguez was back in the NART Ferrari. The race was won by Rindt, chased home by Courage, with Surtees third for BRM.

And then they all went their separate ways again, the CanAm contingent heading to Laguna Seca for the Monterey Castrol GP where McLaren and Hulme scored another 1-2, Chuck Parsons for third in a Lola and Mario Andretti was fourth in an older Holman & Moody McLaren... And then it was on to Mexico City. Miles was back in action for Lotus as Andretti was away racing Indycars at Pacific Raceways in Kent, Washington...

It was another world.

A tale of fighter planes and vultures

Of all the names that Formula 1 cars have had, Klenk is perhaps the most onomatopoeic. It was the work of a German engineer-driver called Hans Klenk, who, at 32, had led an adventurous life before turning to racing cars in 1951, including having spent the war as a fighter pilot, flying Messerschmitt 109Es...

Born in the village of Künzelsau, to the north-east of Stuttgart, a few miles from Schwäbisch-Hall, in the autumn of 1919, Klenk grew up with a strong desire to become a surgeon, at least until he discovered gliding at the nearby Hermuthausen grass strip. Under the terms of the Treaty of Versailles, Germany was not allowed to build powered aircraft and so in the 1920s young pilots and engineers turned to gliding in order to enjoy the skies. This led Klenk, who also knew Willi Messerschmitt through his flying, to begin training as an aviation technician.

When he was 19, war broke out and he was soon in the Luftwaffe, flying his friend Messerschmitt's designs. Most of the time he was based in the north of Germany, close to the Danish border, but later saw action on the Italian front. When the war ended, he completed his studies and decided to open his own engineering business and began souping-up cars for those with money to spend. Among his early products was a Porsche which he rebodied for Heinrich Sauter.

He decided to go racing himself and, like many others at the time, found that the potent pre-war BMW 328 offered the best available starting point for a racing car. So he stripped down a 328 and built his own racing special, similar to many other "eigenbaus" at the time. His own car was not really competitive and so he purchased a Veritas-Meteor (basically another eigenbau) from Karl Kling. The car was unusual in that it had streamlined bodywork, but his results were fairly impressive for a newcomer and he ended the year seventh in the West German Formula 2 Championship.

This drew him to the attention of Mercedes-Benz's celebrated racing manager Alfred Neubauer and he was invited to join the factory team for the Mille Miglia, as co-driver for Karl Kling in the Mercedes 300SL. Their team-mates were Rudi Caracciola, the pre-war Grand Prix ace, and Ernst Kurrle. Klenk decided that the best way to get the best performance was to get to know the route as much as possible in advance and put considerable effort into creating his so-called "gebetbuch" (prayer book) listing all the features on the 1,000-mile course. This proved to be very efficient and they were leading comfortably when they were slowed by a puncture, with a wheel that refused to budge and so they lost the victory to a Ferrari, but recovered to finish second. The two were then entered for the Le Mans 24 Hours alongside another of the pre-war Grand Prix stars Herrmann Lang, who shared his 300SL with Fritz Reiss and the Theo Helfrich/Helmut Niedermayr duo. The Kling/Klenk car retired in the ninth hour with electrical problems, but the other two Mercedes finished 1-2.

The decision, early in 1952, to switch the World Championship to Formula 2 rules, meant that large numbers of BMW eigenbau racers could compete in Grands Prix and Klenk decided that summer to enter the German GP at the Nürburgring. He qualified eighth and finished 11th, which was a commendable effort.

In November he was back with Kling for the Carrera Panamericana, alongside Lang/Edwin Grupp and John Fitch/Eugen Geiger.

On the opening day of the 1,900 mile race through Mexico, their 300SL collided with a low-flying vulture, which came through the windscreen and knocked out Klenk, who was not wearing a helmet. After fixing up the mess and making sure that Klenk was compos mentis, they went on to win the event.

In the months that followed, Klenk re-engineered his Veritas-Meteor and renamed it the Klenk-Meteor. The plan was to enter the car in the German GP that summer. He and Kling started 1953 on the Mille Miglia with an Alfa Romeo, as Mercedes decided not to take part. In July, he was second in the Avusrennen in the Klenk-Meteor but soon afterwards crashed while testing a Mercedes 300SL at the Nürburgring. He broke his thigh and knee. He offered the Klenk-Meteor to the 25-year-old Hans Herrmann for the German GP, allowing the youngster to make his F1 debut. Herrmann qualified 14th, easily the best of the locals, and finished ninth.

Sadly, Klenk's injuries were sufficiently bad to end his career, leaving him with a severe limp for the rest of his life. He would go to become the competition manager of the Continental tyre company and later worked for the firm's public relations department. He continued to run his own car preparation business in Stuttgart before retiring to live at Vellberg, not far from his home village, where he died in 2009, at the age of 89.

A story about pasta

If you go to your local supermarket, in search of something Italian, the chances are that you will go home with pasta and a sauce in a jar. It is more than likely that these will carry the name Barilla, as the Italian firm is the world's largest pasta company – and the market leader in Europe in pasta sauces.

These days Barilla is a conglomerate of dazzling proportions. It has 16 different brands, producing 1.9 million tons of food every year from 29 different factories. It employs 8,400 people and turns over an impressive $3.7 billion a year. In 2015, the company built its own railway into its biggest factory at Pedrignano, in order for its "Grain Train" to reduce the number of trucks required every day – cutting its emissions by 94 percent.

Barilla is a company that dates back to 1877 when Pietro Barilla opened a bakery and pasta shop in the city of Parma. This was passed on to his sons Riccardo and Gualtiero 33 years later. They built the first factory, producing eight tons of pasta and two tons of bread each day.

In 1947, Riccardo's sons Gianni and Pietro took over the business and focussed on the pasta, closing down the bread making business, although they later moved into packaged bakery products. By 1969, they had built the largest pasta factory in the world, producing 1,000 tons of pasta in all shapes and sizes every day. There was a brief period from 1971 when the firm was sold to an American company, although the family still ran the business, but in 1979 Pietro

Barilla bought it back. Pietro died in 1993, leaving the business to his three sons: the chairman Guido and his brothers, the vice chairmen, Luca and Paolo.

Paolo Barilla is a familiar name for racing fans as his name appears on the list of Le Mans 24 Hours winning teams. That was back in 1985 when he was sharing a New Man-sponsored Joest Racing Porsche 956 with Klaus Ludwig and "John Winter", a pseudonymous German timber merchant called Louis Krages. It was a good result, but Barilla wanted to be an F1 driver.

It was a story that goes back to the mid-1970s when the then 14-year-old Paolo decided that he wanted to become a racing driver. He did well in karts and in 1980 switched into Formula Fiat Abarth, racing against the likes of Emanuele Pirro, Roberto Ravaglia and Alessandro Nannini. He moved up to Italian Formula 3 in 1981 with a new Martini-Alfa Romeo MK34 run by Ravarotto Racing and won his third and fourth races (at Vararo and Enna) but ended the year only third in the standings.

He then moved to Formula 2 in 1982, joining the Minardi team, alongside his old Formula Fiat Abarth rival Nannini. He had some top 10 finishes but was overshadowed by Nannini. In 1983, he did just one Formula 2 race while racing Lancia sports cars in selected World Endurance Championship races. He stayed with Lancia in 1984 but then in 1985 joined Joest Racing and had a strong season, including winning Le Mans.

That led to the opportunity to test for the Toleman F1 team at the end of the year at Estoril. He would go on to test for Benetton in 1986 and 1987 while also scoring more wins in sports cars, winning the Miami IMSA race with Bob Wollek in Bruce Leven's Bayside Disposal Porsche 962 and the Fuji 1000 for Joest in 1986.

In 1987, he returned to Formula 3000 with Pavesi, while also being a member of the Alfa Corse World Touring Car Championship team but then had to go to Japan in 1988, competing for Toyota Team TOM'S in the Japanese Sports Car Championship. While there, he played a vital role in rescuing Denmark's Kris Nissen from a burning car at Fuji, diving into the flames in his everyday clothing, having been spectating nearby when the crash occurred. At the end of that year, he agreed a deal to be Minardi's test driver in 1989, while also continuing with TOM'S in Japan (winning the Fuji 1000 again) and competing in Japanese Formula 3000 with Nakajima Racing.

That autumn, Pierluigi Martini damaged his ribs (some say by falling down the steps of the team motor truck) in Estoril and Barilla was asked to race in Japan. He was then signed to race for the Faenza team in 1990, alongside Martini before being replaced for the last couple of races by Gianni Morbidelli.

Although that was the end of his active F1 career, he did do a considerable amount of development work for Bridgestone in Japan with a secret Reynard F1 prototype in the years that followed.

In the end, however, after the death of his father, he turned to the pasta business and, as part of Barilla's expansion into the US in the 1990s, Barilla became a personal sponsor of CART champion Alex Zanardi.

The Barilla family owns one of the most extraordinary modern art collections, having invested heavily in such pictures when prices were at a reasonable level, although the word is that they have in the past invested as much as $100 million to buy a Picasso...

A force behind the scenes

Credit is not always given where credit is deserved, particularly when it comes to engineers in motor racing. Everyone is keen to be associated with a successful car, but a poor car is something that no-one wants to be linked to. It is often hard to say who designed what, particularly today when there are hundreds of engineers involved in the design of each car. But even in the old days the difference between technical director and chief designer caused problems.

One man who did not get very much recognition was France's Paul Carillo, who played a significant role in the sport, although most of the credit for his work went to the ebullient (and very clever) Gérard Ducarouge. The two worked together a lot but people only seem to remember "The Duke". Carillo was 17 years older than Ducarouge and 10 years older than Bernard Boyer, the other Matra engineer who was often mentioned in relation to the success. In truth, they were all working together.

Born on January 1924, Carillo was trained in aviation. He learned the business with Charles Gourdou, who had been an aircraft manufacturer in the 1920s and 1930s with Jean Leseurre. The Gourdou-Leseurre firm went out of business in 1936 but Gourdou went on working in the aviation business, manufacturing parts, particularly propellers. In 1942 the factory began making parts for Messerschmitts, which got him into trouble after the war when he was arrested as a collaborator. Very rapidly some of Charles de Gaulle's intelligence people appeared on the scene and explained to the accusers that Monsieur Goudou was actually one of the good guys and had been using his business as a way to monitor the V1 rocket development programme, which he saw on his visits to Stuttgart, reporting it all back to London.

In 1947, to further his researches, Gourdou built a small windtunnel at his workshops at Saint-Maur, in the south-eastern suburbs of Paris. He tested experimental designs, notably the Makhonine Mak-123, before deciding to sell the factory and retire.

Carillo moved on to a job with the Societe Industrielle pour l'Aéronautique (SIPA), an aircraft manufacturer which had been established by Emile Dewoitine. That did not last very long and he moved on to the Société Nationale de Constructions Aéronautiques du Centre (SNCAC), another aviation business, which had been formed by the nationalisation and merger of the Farman and Hanriot firms in the mid-1930s. This designed military aircraft but it survived only until 1949, at which point the 25-year-old Carillo moved on to Avions Hurel-Dubois in Meudon. That business proved to be a little more stable and he would stay with the firm for the next 13 years, designing civil aircraft.

While he was working there French motorsport was developing with Alpine and Gordini leading the way. There was also Deutsch et Bonnet (DB) building some road-going sports cars and building racing specials for Le Mans. In 1961, Charles Deutsch and René Bonnet agreed to split up. Deutsch wanted to stay with Panhard and Bonnet felt it was better to partner with Renault. So Deutsch formed CD (his initials) and Bonnet established Automobiles René Bonnet. In the years that followed, Panhard CDs and René Bonnet Djets raced one another at Le Mans, although neither troubled the dominant Ferraris.

In February 1963, Carillo joined René Bonnet to work on the development of the Djet. Eighteen months later René Bonnet was taken over by the aerospace company Matra in order to create a car division, Matra Automobiles.

Matra wanted to use racing to promote its new business and Carillo was set to work to design the MS1, a single-seater based on a Formule 2 René-Bonnet, powered by a one-litre Renault engine, which had been raced in F2 that season by Jean-Pierre Beltoise and Gérard Laureau.

The resulting car was a Formula 3 featuring a Ford 105E engine, tuned by Holbay, which first appeared at Monaco in 1965 in the hands of Jean-Pierre Jaussaud and Eric Offenstadt. There was soon a second model called the MS2 and at Reims the MS1 scored its first victory in the Coupe Internationale de Vitesse de Formule 3, with Jean-Pierre Beltoise driving. Beltoise and Jaussaud finished 1-2 in the French F3 championship that year. In addition to the F3 project Matra Sports ran a sportscar programme with the Djet, driven by Beltoise and Henri Pescarolo, while also building a prototype called the MS3. The engineering team at Matra grew with Gérard Ducarouge playing a bigger role and Bernard Boyer but Carillo remained a key player.

In 1966, Matra entered F2 with a BRM-engined MS5 chassis for Beltoise and Jo Schlesser, while Ken Tyrrell did a deal to run cars under the Matra International banner for Jackie Stewart and Jacky Ickx. Suddenly, Matras were appearing everywhere and in January 1967 Matra boss Jean-Luc Lagardère met Elf boss Jean Prada at Monaco and it was agreed that Elf would finance the construction of a Matra 3-litre V12 F1 engines. That year Matra Sport ran Beltoise and Servoz-Gavin in Carillo-designed MS5s, powered with Cosworths, while Tyrrell enjoyed more success with Ickx winning the F2 title. Things were less successful in sports cars with the new MS8 (MS630) crashing at Le Mans and killing the young Roby Weber, but Pescarolo won various races with the car.

In 1968, the company entered F1 with the Matra-powered MS10 for Tyrrell's Stewart and Servoz-Gavin, while the Matra-powered MS11 was raced by Beltoise. Stewart won three races and finished second in the World Championship.

Beltoise won the European F2 Championship that year as well.

The big year was 1969, however, as Stewart won six races and the World Championship with the MS80 while Beltoise was fifth, both using Cosworth engines. In F2, Servoz-Gavin won the title and the sports cars began to show more pace.

It was at this point that Matra sold its car division to Chrysler France. Matra became Matra-Simca. Matra's insistence on using the V12 meant that Tyrrell decided to become a March customer and then went on to build its own cars. Matra ran V12-engined MS12s. The focus began to switch to winning Le Mans. The F1 programme stopped after poor seasons in 1971 and 1972 with Beltoise and Chris Amon. But in the sports car world the company achieved huge success, winning Le Mans in 1972, 1973 and 1974 and the World Championship of Makes in the latter two years. Boyer and Ducarouge got all the glory.

And then the axe fell, Matra announced it was closing down its competition department. The whole thing was sold to Guy Ligier and the staff started work on a JS5 Formula 1 car, which would be powered by the Matra V12s.

The car made its F1 debut in 1976 with Jacques Laffite driving and the following year the JS7 – a development of the original car – won the Swedish Grand Prix.

The same design team produced the JS9 in 1978 but it was the decision to switch to Cosworth engines in 1979 that really produced a breakthrough with the JS11 fighting for the World Championship with Ferrari, Brabham, Williams and Renault.

The car was revised as the JS11/15 in 1980 and enjoyed more success with Laffite and Didier Pironi but a new alliance with Talbot in 1981 meant a switch back to Matra V12s and although Laffite won twice the JS17s were not as competitive as they might have been.

The 1982 season with the JS19 was disappointing and the team began to run short of money as Talbot gave up on the idea of F1. Ligier became frustrated and fired Ducarouge, while Carillo, who was then nearing the age of 60, faded from the F1 scene.

Martini not on the rocks

The village of Pigna nestles at the bottom of a steep wooded valley a few miles inland from the Italian Riviera in Liguria. It is close to the French border if you have lots of energy and good walking boots, but the roads from Pigna lead down to the coast, to Ventimiglia and San Remo.

It was in this quiet place that Renato Martini was born in 1934. He was five when the Second War War began and when was 12 his father decided to move the family to Jersey, in the Channel Islands, in order to get work. For the next seven years Tico, as he was known, grew up as an islander. His father was the had waiter of a hotel in Saint Helier.

At 17, Tico learned to drive and his father gave him a small car. He decided to go home to Italy and worked in an Alfa Romeo garage in San Remo before returning to Jersey in 1955 to help his father. He acquired a Cooper 500cc racing car and began taking part in races on the sands around the island. Among his rivals was a local entrepreneur called Bill Knight and, in 1959, Tico began working as a mechanic for Knight. A year later, Bill opened the Belle Vue Pleasure Park at Les Quennevais, just south of the airport, where he laid out a kart track. Martini worked on keeping the karts in good condition. He decided to try building his own kart and in 1962 made a big impression when he put a 650cc Triumph Tiger motorcycle engine into a tube framed chassis. The machine broke the hill record at the celebrated Bouley Bay hillclimb.

Over in France, the Magny-Cours racing circuit was in the process of setting up a racing school. The enterprising Bill Knight bid for the deal and was granted the concession. He hired Irishman Henry Morrogh, who had a celebrated racing school in Italy and he agreed to be the director of the school. Martini was sent from Jersey to run the technical side of the business. He spent the next two years living in a caravan. Then Morrogh decided to move to the United States and Martini took over running the whole business. The school name was changed to Winfield, Knight's business in the UK and for the next four years things developed well. In 1966, however, Knight decided to hand the business on to his two sons Mike and Richard. Martini argued that in order to cut down costs, the school should build its own racing cars, rather than buying them. The brothers agreed and so Tico built a run of five Martini MW1s. The MW2 followed in 1969 with nine cars being built and several being used that year in the Formula France championship, with one in Formula 3 for Jacques Laffite, who raced under the Winfield Racing banner. The Formula France car won its first race at Albi that year thanks to Jean-Luc Salomon. This meant that there was demand for more cars in 1970 and Martini built 26 MK4s for the new Formula Renault, changing the designation of the cars from Martini Winfield (MW) to Mike Knight (MK). There was also an MK5 Formula 3 car for rising star Jean-Luc Salomon. That year François Lacarrau gave Martini its first title in Formula Renault but there was a shock in Formula 3 when Salomon was killed in an accident at Rouen. By the end of the season, the MK5 was also a winner, thanks to the efforts of Jean-Pierre Jaussaud.

In the course of the 10 years that followed, Martini cars won 200 victories in 280 races in Formula Renault. The first Formula 3 title did not come until 1973 when Laffite dominated the French Championship. Despite the fuel crisis, it was a great year for Martini with a total of 38 cars built but plans to build an F2 car stalled and the French Formula 3 Championship was cancelled. Fortunately money was pouring in from Formula Renault.

A deal was put together for an F2 car in 1975 with funding for Laffite from Elf and the Swiss additive Ambrozium H7. The team used Schnitzer BMW engines and Hugues de Chaunac's ORECA organisation was taken on to run the team. Laffite won six races and swept to the championship. A second would follow for René Arnoux in 1977.

De Chaunac and Martini decided that it was a good time to enter Formula 1 and began preparations, moving to premises that were three times larger than the original factory. It was the era of the Cosworth kit-car and Martini designed the MK23, a simple car for a Cosworth DFV and a Hewland gearbox for the 1978 season. There was not much funding and the team had just 12 staff. Arnoux had backing from Elf and RMO, an employment agency based in his hometown of Grenoble. Not being a member of the Formula One Constructors Association made things more complicated but the car was ready for the third race of the year, in South Africa in March. There were 30 cars battling for a place on the 26-car grid and Arnoux could do no better than 27th and so the team decided to miss the next race in Long Beach, to improve the car. They failed to qualify in Monaco, where there were only 20 starters, but the bad news was that Arnoux was still only 27th, but in Belgium René set the 19th best time and made its debut, finishing the race in ninth. Engine failures in testing meant that the team missed the next two races and so was not seen again until the French GP. The car had been heavily modified and Arnoux qualified 18th and was able to finish 14th but there was then a setback when Martini was refused an entry at the British GP. When he qualified, Arnoux looked a solid runner but getting into the races was tough. He finished ninth in Austria and then crashed in the Dutch GP and as money had run out, it was decided to end the programme there. The sport was going through the ground-effect revolution and Martini did not have the money to work out that could be done.

Arnoux had done enough and was hired by Renault for 1979 but Martini and de Chaunac turned their attention to a bright new French star in Formula 3 – Alain

Prost. The MK27 was a good car and Prost was exceptional and completely dominated the European Formula 3 Championship and leapt straight into a McLaren F1 drive.

In the years that followed, Martin won French Formula 3 titles with Alain Ferté (1980), Philippe Streiff (1981), Michel Ferté (1983), Olivier Grouillard (1984), Pierre-Henri Raphanel (1985) and Yannick Dalmas (1986). In the European Championship there was a title for Ivan Capelli in 1984 and there was a German title for Volker Weidler in 1985. Martini continued to dominate in French Formula Renault but as competition in F3 increased from Ralt, Reynard and Dallara. Then organisers started switching to single chassis supply deals. Martini ran cars in Formula 2 and Formula 3000 but without much success and although there was plenty of business in French national racing, hillclimbs and historics, Martini decided to sell the business when he reached his 70th birthday in 2004. Guy Ligier absorbed the business into his empire.

In retirement, Tico spends his time flying (he has a landing strip in the field next to his house) and singing...

A not-so famous place in Belgium

In the mid-1960s, the venerable old Spa Francorchamps circuit was becoming a place that Formula 1 feared. Driving through the open countryside on roads with no protection at average speeds of 150 mph was challenging and the drivers, who were becoming increasingly worried about safety, began to demand changes. It meant that Spa was living on borrowed time. In 1969, the Belgian Grand Prix was called off after the Spa organisers refused to pay for work that the Grand Prix Drivers' Association insisted was necessary. Across Belgium, the reality began to dawn that Spa might be dropped from the World Championship and if that happened the Belgian Grand Prix would likely end up at Zolder, which was in Flanders, the Flemish part of the country.

Belgium is an odd country, with two predominant cultural and linguistic groups: the Flemings in the north (who represent 57 percent of the population) and the Walloons in the south (who constitute 32 percent). The rest are in Brussels. The Flemings speak Flemish, which is a form of Dutch, while the Walloons speak their own version of French. Not surprisingly, there is intense competition between the two communities and the politics of the country is wildly complicated.

Back in the late 1960s, Jules Bary, the mayor of Nivelles, a town to the south of Brussels, not far from Waterloo, was a leading light in Wallonian politics. He wanted to make sure that the Walloons held on to the Grand Prix and so suggested the idea of a F1 track, near the village of Baulers, north-east of Nivelles, on the road towards Waterloo. The local council liked the concept and the local chamber of commerce thought it would be a great idea. They got together and established a company called Circuit Automobile Permanent Européen de Nivelles-Baulers (CAPENB). The local authorities were keen to help and was granted the firm a 69-year lease on public land on which to build the circuit, on the understanding that the facility would remain a permanent racing circuit for at least 27 years. With the agreements in place, CAPENB approached Robert Benoît, a member of the Royal Automobile Club of Belgium who was in the construction business, and also ran a karting facility in Brussels, and asked if he would build the new circuit.

The design, which was soon nicknamed "The Revolver" as it looked a little (but not a lot) like a hand-gun, was laid out on flat land. The track was relatively quick, with a long curling corner at one end, two fast straights, with fast esses in the middle of the back straight, which led down to a hairpin. There was plenty of run-off area, something that pleased the F1 drivers.

While all this was going on, Spa held another race in 1970, with a temporary chicane installed in the Malmedy corner to slow things down, but a year later the circuit failed to meet new FIA safety requirements and failed to get a licence for F1. The Grand Prix was cancelled again. Spa did not have the money to do the work...

By then Nivelles was under construction and it was decided that in order to keep everyone happy the Belgian Grand Prix would alternate between Nivelles in Wallonia and Zolder in Flanders. The first race at Nivelles took place in the summer of 1972, with a huge crowd of around 100,000 turning up to watch Emerson Fittipaldi winning the race for Lotus. The race had a couple of important side-effects: many of the fans that day felt that the cars were a long way from the public. The drivers were ambivalent. The track was not very interesting. The second impact was that a local association was formed to fight for the circuit to be closed, because of the noise and local disruption.

However, the real problem came in 1973 with the Oil Crisis when the Arab oil producing states refused to sell oil to countries that had supported Israel in the Yom Kippur War. The price of oil quadrupled and the crisis did serious damage to the world economy hard. Early in 1974 CAPENB was declared bankrupt. Bernie Ecclestone, the boss of the Formula One teams organisation, agreed to promote a race at Nivelles that summer. It was won by Fittipaldi again, but this time driving a McLaren. The Grand Prix went back to Zolder in 1975, but there were hopes of hosting another Grand Prix at Nivelles in 1976 although money was still hard to find. The track had started to deteriorate and there was no money to fix the surface and so the Grand Prix switched to Zolder. It did not help that André Cools, a Wallonian socialist, who was a big player in the provincial politics in the 1970s and 1980s, came from Liege and was keen to see Spa revived. That needed money. However in 1978, the old Spa track was abandoned and by the early 1980s the circuit would be reopened in a shortened form.

Nivelles continued to host events for bikes, cars and karts and in 1980 played host to the World Karting Championship in which Peter de Bruijn defeated a youngster called Ayrton Senna da Silva. The following year, however, the track's licence expired and it was closed. By the end of the year the site had been reclassified by the local authorities. It was no longer a racing circuit. The site would remain abandoned for nearly 20 years until the land was acquired by a regional authority and transformed into the Portes de l'Europe-Nivelles Business Park. Some of the roads in the park follow the old circuit... but the rest is abandoned.

A remarkable family

Henry Costin was a bit of a character. He joined the army in his youth, serving with the Rifle Brigade before being promoted to the rank of Corporal and transferring to a role as a gymnastics instructor. In 1910, tired of army life, he answered an advertisement to join an expedition to explore the jungles of South America, with Colonel Percy Fawcett. The two did a number of expeditions together, mapping uncharted territory before returning to England when the First World War broke out in 1914. Both served in the Royal Artillery on the Western Front.

Towards the end of the war, Henry married and although Fawcett wanted to return to the jungles when the war ended, Costin decided not to join him in an expedition to find the fabled Lost City. Fawcett disappeared without trace.

Costin settled in the London suburb of North Harrow and set himself as a marbler and grainer, painting walls to look like marble and wood. Such was his skill that he was soon much in demand and was commissioned to undertake work in residences of the wealthy and the famous, including Buckingham Palace. In the years that followed, four children arrived: Frank (1920), Eric (1922), Michael (1929) and Mary (1932). The three boys all attended Salvatorian College in Harrow Weald.

Frank was fascinated by flying and at 16 joined General Aircraft at the London Air Park in Hanworth as an apprentice fitter. In 1937, he moved into the drawing office and studied for a BSc at Acton Technical College. After completing his apprenticeship, he moved on to join Airspeed Ltd in Portsmouth in 1940, working for the celebrated aeronautical engineer-turned-novelist Nevil Shute Norway. He stayed for three years before being recruited by Supermarine, where he worked with Joe Smith on the later development of the Spitfire, specialising in wing design.

At the end of 1944, his brother Eric, who was learning to be a bomb aimer in the Royal Air Force, was killed when the Lancaster in which he was flying broke up in mid-air while on a training mission over Lincolnshire.

When the war ended Frank moved to the Percival Aircraft Company in Luton for a couple of years before setting up his own consulting business. Then in 1951 he was hired by de Havilland to be its had of aerodynamic flight test engineering, in charge of the experimental department at Christchurch, near Bournemouth, before transferring to a similar role in 1953 to Hawarden, near Chester.

His brother Mike, nine years his junior, was then working at De Havilland but he soon departed to join Colin Chapman at Lotus and this led Chapman to approach Frank, as he was looking for an aerodynamicist to help him produce faster cars. Frank agreed to become a consultant for Lotus and designed the bodywork for the Lotus Eight. He then moved on to the Lotus Eleven. In 1955, Chapman and Costin were asked by Tony Vandervell of Vanwall to design the 1956 Grand Prix cars, which set the company on its path to a string of F1 victories and Constructors' Championship success in 1958. He also worked on the roadgoing Lotus Elite, establishing himself as the leading automotive aerodynamicist in Britain.

This led to him working with Zagato on the Le Mans Maserati 450S and then joining forces with Jem Marsh to create a sporting special, called the Marcos (a combination of their names), with a chassis built from marine plywood. The relationship did not last and Costin returned to building gliders. He created the Protos Formula 2 car, with a wooden chassis, and worked on the unusual March 711 Formula 1 car. This was powered by a Cosworth DFV engine, which was produced by a company set up by his brother Mike and Keith Duckworth (hence Cosworth).

He began to lose interest in motor racing after that but was later involved in the Thompson Motor Company in Ireland, designing the TMC Costin, a lightweight sports car built in Wexford between 1983 and 1987, aimed at the Lotus Seven, Caterham, Westfield market. After that enterprise closed down, Costin retired to the west coast of Ireland, where he designed and built his own house, primarily using wood, while continuing with some consulting and also doing charity work.

An accidental F1 programme

Richard Lea and Graham Francis began manufacturing bicycles in Coventry in 1895 and having enjoyed some success, they took on sub-contract work, building cars for Singer Motors. Having learned how to make cars, Lea-Francis launched its own model but it was not a great success. The automobile division was soon closed down and Lea-Francis went back to bicycles in 1909.

Two years later, they began making motorcycles and this led to a return to car manufacturing in the years before World War I. The car business did not survive the war, but in the 1920s Lea-Francis did a deal with Vulcan Motor and began to manufacture some very successful light and sporting cars, using Meadows engines. In 1928, Kaye Don took a Lea-Francis Hyper sports car to victory in the Ulster TT, while the Ace of Spades model enjoyed much success. However, the company fell victim to the Great Depression after the Wall Street Crash in 1929 and spent most of the 1930s in dire financial trouble.

In 1936, it went into receivership. Former Riley employees George Leek and Hugh Rose bought the assets and launched Lea-Francis Engineering, which went public in 1937 to raise money in order to design its own engines. Leek organised the business and left Rose to do the engineering.

Rose was a seasoned engineer in car design and in racing, having started his career as an apprentice at Humber, working for a young Louis Coatalen. The pair then moved on to Hillman and later to Sunbeam before Rose went his own way with a string of roles with small companies before being commissioned to design a straight-four, 1.5-litre engine for Riley in 1933. This was known as the 12/4, which was used in Falcon, Kestrel and Lynx models with much success in the late 1930s.

After moving with Leek to Lea-Francis, Rose designed an engine similar to the Riley but much lighter and more efficient. The 1.4-litre Twelve engine and the 1.6-litre Fourteen that followed were used in Lea-Francis road cars until the war when production stopped and the firm switched to doing war work. Production restarted in 1946 with the company manufacturing revised versions of the pre-war cars and these soon became very popular, particularly with motor racing folk, who saw potential in the engines and used them in a number of different specials.

Jack Turner felt there was more than could be achieved and persuaded Lea-Francis to produce a limited series of aluminium alloy cylinder blocks for racing and a dozen or so were built. Most of these ended up in the hands of Connaught Engineering, which worked with Lea-Francis to modify the engines for the new two-litre Formula 2.

It was something of an accident that Lea-Francis ended up being involved in Formula 1, as the FIA decided that for 1952 the World Championship should be run to Formula 2 regulations. Connaught began competing with a factory team and soon picked up a number of customers as well, including Rob Walker. The cars enjoyed a fair bit of success in British Formula 1 races but were never really powerful enough to compete with Ferrari and Maserati.

And when the new 2.5-litre Formula 1 regulations began in 1954 Connaught switched to Alta engines.

By then Lea-Francis production had ceased, the company unable to compete with Jaguar, Triumph and Aston Martin.

How Formula 1 became Formula 2 (and vice versa)

At the end of the 1951 season, after Juan-Manuel Fangio had secured his first World Championship title on the streets of Pedralbes in Barcelona, Formula 1 found itself in a state of flux.

Alfa Romeo, unable to fund a new car, and faced with increased opposition from Ferrari, indicated that it would not return in 1952. BRM was still struggling and Talbot-Lago's cars were no longer competitive. That meant that it looked like Ferrari would be the only serious contender. The FIA's Commission Sportive Internationale (CSI) has met during the Paris Salon de l'Automobile in the first few days of October (before the Pedralbes race) and had decided that there would be a new 2.5-litre Formula 1, starting on January 1, 1954 and it was expected the 4.5-litre formula would last until then, but the CSI had made no ruling on the matter, saying that the races counting towards the World Championship could be for Formula 1, Formula 2 or even Formula 3. It may now seem odd, but the CSI nominated the races that would be part of the World Championship for Drivers, the so-called Grandes Épreuves, but they did specify what cars would be used. In part this was because of the inclusion of the Indianapolis 500 in the championship, despite the fact that it was run to completely different rules to all the other races.

The uncertainty over the future continued until January when rumours in France began to suggest that the major races would be switching to Formula 2 rules in 1952.

In the middle of January BRM issued a press release saying that it was going to enter a team of its V16-engined cars in all of the Grands Prix and also in non-championship events between them. The problem was that BRM didn't have a very good reputation after not showing up at events which it had committed to be at.

The French were still particularly important in the sport because France not only hosted the Grand Prix de l'Automobile Club de France – scheduled that year for Rouen in early July – but also a series of races known as the Grands Prix de France, including events at Pau (April 14), Marseille (April 27), Paris (May 25), Reims (June 29) Rouen (July 6), Les Sables d'Olonne (July 13), Saint-Gaudens (August 10) and La Baule (August 24). It was announced in mid-February that all of these events would switch to Formula 2 because the promoters were not convinced that F1 regulations would result in good races. Other race organisers began to consider the same thing.

Alfa Romeo did not officially pull the plug on Formula 1 until the second week of March when the board decided that the company should do only sports car races, while working towards a new Grand Prix car for 1954.

The first non-championship race of the year took place a few days later in Syracuse, resulting in a 1-2-3 for Ferrari 500 Formula 2 cars.

At the same time the Swiss GP – the World Championship-opening race – announced that as a result of Alfa Romeo's withdrawal it could not guarantee spectators a decent race unless the race was run to Formula 2 rules. Ferrari was dominant in F2, but at least running with F2 rules would mean bigger entries. If the World Championship was run to F1 rules, Ferrari would dominate with its 375, but the entry would be smaller. The one hope was that BRM would mount a serious challenge and so all eyes were on the Valentino Grand Prix on April 6 where BRM said it would race. The team did not show up and the race was a Ferrari walk-over, with Gigi Villoresi dominating in a Ferrari 375 – exactly as race promoters had feared. The Belgian GP had been planning to stay with F1 rules but after Turin the Belgians switched, while the British followed.

The weekend of April 14 saw the opening round of the French Grands Prix series at Pau, with Alberto Ascari winning in a Ferrari 500, while in England the Richmond Trophy at Goodwood ran to F1 rules and was won by Froilan Gonzealez in a Ferrari 375 F1 car.

Ascari won again in Marseille two weeks later and on May 10, HWM-Alta Formula 2 cars dominated the International Trophy with victory going to Lance Macklin. That same weekend Ferrari finished 1-2 in Naples with Formula 2 cars for Giuseppe Farina and Piero Taruffi.

A week later – on May 18 – the World Championship kicked off with the Swiss Grand Prix at Bremgarten in Bern. Ferrari arrived with three 500s for Farina, Taruffi and Frenchman André Simon. Alberto Ascari was missing as he had gone to Indianapolis to take part in the 500. There were two customer Ferrari 500s for Rudolf Fischer (Ecurie Espadon) and Louis Rosier (Ecurie Rosier). Maserati had planned to send two cars but did not appear, but Gordini had three entries for Jean Behra, Prince Bira and Robert Manzon while HWM appeared with four cars for Macklin, Stirling Moss, Peter Collins and George Abecassis. There were a number of local entries, notably Hans Stuck Sr's AFM and Toni Ulmen's Veritas-Meteor and a trio of Bristol-engined cars with a Frazer Nash for Ken Wharton and two Coopers entered by Ecurie Richmond for Eric Brandon and Alan Brown.

Ferrari dominated, of course, with Farina leading until his car broke down and Taruffi taking over to win, while Fischer came home second with Behra third.

The CSI never actually decided to switch the World Championship to Formula 2 but that autumn, when the body met in Paris, it was decided that all Grandes Epreuves would be run to the new rules, as long as there were more than three manufacturers committed to race.

A man called Velko

When it comes to American Formula 1 teams, people remember Carl Haas's operation, Roger Penske's efforts, Shadow and the Eagles of Dan Gurney, but few remember the adventures of Vel's Parnelli Jones Racing, which took part in 16 Grands Prix between the end of 1974 and the early part of 1976. They forget that the team finished 10th in the Constructors' Championship in 1975, an impressive first season.

It was a story that began in the unlikely setting of Trebinje in Bosnia in the early years of the 20th Century. At the time, Bosnia was not a happy place with ethnic and religious divisions. The Bosniaks were predominantly muslim, the Serbs were largely followers of the Eastern Orthodox Church and the Croats were catholic. It was under the control of the Ottoman Empire, which was crumbling, but there was a strong nationalist movement. In 1908, keen to stop any revolutions, the Austro-Hungarian Empire annexed the region. Thousands of locals decided to depart, to avoid being conscripted into the Austro-Hungarian army – and to find a better life.

Dusan Miletic was one of them. He went first to France and from there sailed to New York on the SS La Touraine, which sailed the Le Havre to New York route. He ended up in a mining town in South Dakota called Lead, where he settled. He met and married another immigrant called Stane Spich in the early 1920s and they started a family.

In the mid 1930s, they decided to move to California, to a new development called Torrance. Their son Velko, who was 10, enrolled at Torrance High School. Despite his roots in the Balkans, Velko was a very American youngster and was excited about the automobiles which were becoming more and more widespread. After school, he started doing odd jobs at local automobile repair shops. It was what he wanted to do.

He graduated from high school at 17, a few months after Pearl Harbor and the following year, when he reached the age of 18 he enlisted in the Army Air Corps serving as an aerial photographer in the Pacific Theatre in the final part of the war.

He then returned home to Torrance and went to work for the Oscar Maples Ford dealership, rising to become the manager and then in 1954 raised money to buy the business.

In order to promote the dealership, Miletic began sponsoring local racers in all manner of different events and happened upon a promising youngster called Parnelli Jones. He was soon sponsoring the youngster, supplying him with engines and chassis for stock car races. In 1956, they decided to compete in a programme of stock car races, in the Pacific Coast Late Model series and NASCAR Grand National races. On the west coast, Parnelli won at Huntington Beach and Gardena and showed well in the Cup races at Merced and San Mateo and so in September they headed off to Darlington, South Carolina for the Southern 500. By 1960, Parnelli was trying his hand in USAC Indycars, with help from Miletic, who introduced him to JC Agajanian. This led to Parnelli joining Agajanian in 1961, scoring his first victory that year and going on to win the Indy 500 in 1963.

As Parnelli grew more successful, he and Miletic became business partners, selling Firestone racing tyres from the dealership, a business which grew to more than 40 stores in the years that followed, while also diversifying into road car tyres and other automotive products.

In 1969, they decided to set up their own racing team, which was called Vel's Parnelli Jones Racing. They hired Al Unser to drive and George Bignotti to run the team. Unser finished second in the championship. They expanded to TransAm in 1970 and Jones won the title while also building off-road machines with which Jones won the Baja 1000. That year, backed by the Johnny Lightning toy company, Unser won the Indianapolis 500 and the USAC title in a VPJ Colt. In 1971 Unser's team-mate Joe Leonard won the title, though Unser won another Indy 500 victory. In 1972, Parnelli hired Team Lotus designer Maurice Philippe and switched from Ford engines to Offenhausers but the result was not a great success. However, at the end of 1973, the team announced that it would be entering F1 in 1974. Philippe designed the VPJ4 and Mario Andretti raced the car which was developed the following year and he scored a couple of useful placings, while the team also ran a successful Formula 5000 programme with

Viceroy-backed Lolas for Unser and Andretti, the pair finishing second and third in the championship.

Much of this was funded by Firestone. When the company withdrew from competition in 1975, it was a big blow. The team took on John Barnard to design an F1 car but money ran out and the F1 programme came to a close. Barnard designed the VPJ6 Indycar and Unser won three races and he and new team mate Danny Ongais won a couple more in 1977. The cars would remain competitive in 1978 and 1979 but with CART and USAC splitting up that year the team withdrew from the sport.

Miletic and Parnelli stayed in business until Vel's death in 1995.

The story of an emblem

If you go to the Piazza Maggiore in Bologna, you will be able to see the Fontana di Nettuno, a larger-than-life bronze statue of the god Neptune, which has stood there since 1567. It may seem an odd story, but this was the inspiration for one of the best-known motor racing emblems, which featured on Grand Prix cars from the late 1920s until the 1960s.

It is a story which begins in the town of Voghera, to the south of Milan, but still a long way from Bologna, where Rodolfo Maserati worked in the late Nineteenth Century as a train driver for the Italian state railways. Rodolfo was passionate about machinery and new technology and he passed this passion on to his six sons, five of whom grew up passionate about engineering.

The eldest, Carlo, was born in 1881 and when he was 17 had already designed his first internal combustion engine for a motorised bicycle. At 19, he joined Fiat but then moved on to Isotta-Fraschini three years later. He recommended that his brother Alfieri join the firm but he then departed and Alfieri followed him. Carlo's dream was to set up his own engineering business. Alas, in 1910 he was struck down by tuberculosis at the age of only 29.

That year another brother Bindo joined Isotta-Fraschini and convinced Alfieri and another brother Ettore to work for the company. But Alfieri had acquired Carlo's ambitions to start his own empire and after three years he left Isotta-Fraschini and moved to Bologna in order to set up his own firm in league with Ettore. Bindo stayed at Isotta-Fraschini. The timing could not have been worse. World War I broke out and soon both Alfieri and Ettore had been called up into the military, leaving their 16-year-old brother Ernesto in charge of the workshop, until the war was over.

It was four years before they were able to start building their first racing specials, which Alfieri drove. The first was a Diatto chassis fitted with a 6.3-litre Isotta-Fraschini engine. This showed well in early events after the war and as the car was developed, Diatto became more and more interested and commissioned the Maserati brothers to prepare a car for Diatto for the 1922 Italian GP. This was promising and so Diatto agreed to fund more racing machines and Maserati designed a new 2-litre engine. But then Diatto ran into financial trouble and had to stop the whole programme. The Maserati brothers decided to buy 10 Diatto 30 Sport models in order to use them as the basis for their own cars. The problem was funding.

Through his racing, Alfieri had met the Marquis Diego de Sterlich, then in his early twenties. The last survivor of a dynasty that could trace its roots back to Austria in a round 1100, the family had settled in Lombardy in the Sixteenth Century, with the main branch then establishing itself in the Abruzzo region. Diego had emerged as the sole heir to the estates of not only the De Sterlich family but also the barony of Aliprandi, as a result of a series of tragedies when he was growing up. His estates amounted to 23,000 acres, with a string of castles and palaces, farms and mills.

He had soon discovered motor racing and had helped to fund the construction of the Autodomo Nazionale at Monza, was a founder member of the Automobile Club d'Abruzzo, which organized the Coppa Acerbo in Pescara, and had began racing himself in 1923.

He agreed to provide the money for the Maserati brothers to buy the Diattos, which were transformed into the first Maserati Tipo 26s, a highly successful racing machine that created demand for customer cars for the road and for racing. This all meant that the company needed a proper emblem and it was de Sterlich who suggested that the Maserati brothers adopt the trident from the fountain of Neptune. It was decided that Mario Maserati, the only Maserati brother who was not mad about cars, and worked as an artist, should be commissioned to design the logo based on the trident.

Twenty years later, although the Maserati brothers had long gone from the company that bore their name, the trident logo became an integral part of the Formula 1 World Championship, notably with the celebrated Maserati 250F…

A high flyer who never quite took off

France's Michel Costa was a man who looked like he was going to have a major career in the automobile industry. He was a talented student and won a place to study mechanical engineering at the prestigious Centre d'Etudes Superieures des Techniques Industrielles, nowadays known as Supméca. He then picked up a Diplôme d'Études Supérieures Techniques in aerodynamics from the Conservatoire National des Arts et Métiers, another top engineering school. In 1972, he was recruited by the research and development department of Chrysler France, which had been named Simca until two years before. He would spend eight years at the firm's R&D division at Carrières-sous-Poissy, to the west of Paris, becoming head of testing. In 1978, however, Chrysler Europe was sold to PSA Peugeot Citroën for $1, taking on the company's debts in addition to the factories and product lines. Peugeot decided to rebrand the firm as Talbot.

Costa had had enough of politics and decided to give it all up and go racing. He would spend the next five years working as a designer and a team manager in the French Formula Renault championship. He made a sufficiently good impression to be approached by the AGS Formula 1 team and agreed to work alongside Christian Vanderpleyn on the Gonfaron team's 1986 Formula 1 challenger – the AGS-Motori Moderni JH21C. This was built around an old Renault Sport RE40 chassis, dating back to 1983, cobbled together with other old Renault parts. This was mated to a Motori Moderni V6 turbo engine. It was not a good car but Costa revised the design and the team fitted a Cosworth engine for 1987. At the end of the year, the team replaced driver Pascal Fabre by Roberto Moreno and the Brazilian scored a point in the end-of-season Australian GP.

The 1988 car was the JH23 and was a much better car and Philippe Streiff scored a number of promising results, but failed to score a point. In August that year Costa, Vanderpleyn and team manager Frederic Dhainaut all quit the team to go to work for Enzo Coloni in Italy – a major blow to AGS,

Vanederpleyn and Costa designed the Coloni C3 which was driven by Roberto Moreno and Pierre-Henri Raphanel. The Coloni was not bad, but with pre-qualifying necessary it rarely made it through into the races and at the end of the year the three Frenchmen left Coloni.

By then, AGS had been sold to French businessman Cyril de Rouvre. He turned to Costa to be technical director and went to work on the design of the JH25 for the 1990 season. De Rouvre poured a lot of money into the team, setting up a completely new factory at the Circuit du Luc. The problem was that de Rouvre began to run out of money. The team still had to get through pre-qualifying at each race and the talented duo of Gabriele Tarquini and Yannick Dalmas both struggled, although Dalmas managed to finish ninth in the Spanish GP at Jerez. Costa started work on the JH26 for 1991 but the money ran out and the team went into receivership. The new car was never built.

The assets were bought by Italians Patricio Cantu and Gabriele Raffanelli who decided to replace Costa with his old boss Vanderpleyn.

Costa got involved in the awful Andrea Moda Formula F1 team, trying to develop the very poor Simtek-built cars, but it quickly became clear that there was little that could be done and he gave up and moved into sports car racing, working with Gérard Larrousse, ORECA and later with Paul Belmondo Racing.

He then faded out of the sport…

F1 in an old swamp

In 1803, 30-year-old Charles Grimes, an enthusiastic deputy surveyor-general of New South Wales set off to explore parts of the southern coast aboard a schooner called HMS Cumberland. The party stopped in Port Phillip Bay and Grimes drew a map, marking the area to the south of the mouth of the Yarra River as being "low swampy country". Later when Melbourne was established, in 1835, the area became known as "South Melbourne Swamp". The water was brackish and people steered clear of the wetlands but demand for land grew and it was not long before attempts were made to drain the swamps to create grazing land. Housing followed as Melbourne grew but the town planners were wise and in 1864 a large section of the swamp was designated as parkland and named after from Queen Victoria's consort, Prince Albert. The last remnant of the marshland was the lake which was excavated in 1875 to create a place for boating, with fresh water being pumped into from the Yarra River to replace the salty old swamp water. As time went on, a number of roads were laid out in the park and then during World War II a part of the parkland was handed over to the Army to become the headquarters of Army Southern Command. The idea of racing in Albert Park had been suggested as early as the 1930s but it was not until 1953 that the Light Car Club managed to get all the permissions required to host a race, which was jointly organised by Army Southern Command.

It was the first time in the post-war era that a big race had been held in a major population centre as previous Grands Prix had taken place at remote airfields. The race that took place was on a three-mile track and featured 40 starters, running cars for Formula Libre rules. It would be won by Doug Whiteford in an imported Talbot-Lago.

There would be further races on the track in March 1955 and a year later and then late in 1956 it hosted the Australian Tourist Trophy and the Australian GP, won by a visiting Stirling Moss with a Maserati 250F. There would be further races in March 1957 and finally in November 1958, but after that, local opposition led to political pressure and the racing in Albert Park was eventually stopped. After that permanent circuits were built at Calder and Sandown Park. It was not until

Adelaide began hosting Formula 1 in 1985 that Melbourne began to ponder doing the same and the idea of race in Albert Park was revived…

Fast footwork by Ron Walker and state premier Jeff Kennett resulted in Melbourne winning the race and the annual trip to cosmopolitan Melbourne has been a favourite with the F1 circus ever since...

F1's only dead-heat

Syracuse is a city that dates back 2,700 years. It sits on the east coast of Sicily, to the south of Catania, looking out to the Ionian Sea. For many years it was the port that was used to sail to Italy's colonies in Africa, notably Tripoli, where in the 1920s and 1930s there was a major Grand Prix race.

That ended in 1940 and after World War II the local Lambretta dealer in Syracuse Vincenzo D'Amico Urso took out one of his scooters for a test at the edge of the city, close to the vast cemetery and the new war cemetery where 1,000 Commonwealth troops are buried, victims of the amphibious and airborne landings in Sicily in July 1943, which marked the start of the Italian campaign. As he rode through the countryside he pondered the idea of how great it would be to have a racing circuit on the roads, to replace Tripoli. He won the support of the local authorities and the Automobile Club of Italy and paid a visit to Enzo Ferrari and convinced him to send cars to the first race, which took place in March 1951. It was timed to offer the teams a touch of Mediterranean weather at the end of the winter and to attract cars by giving them the chance to test new machinery on a fast and sweeping circuit. They would arrive early, test the cars as much as possible and then race in the Grand Prix. It was run to Formula 1 regulations most of the time, although switched to F2 on occasion. The list of winners was impressive with Gigi Villoresi, Alberto Ascari, Giuseppe Farina, Juan Manuel Fangio, Peter Collins, Stirling Moss, John Surtees and Jim Clark all featuring on the list of winners. There was also Tony Brooks, who took a Connaught to an unexpected victory in 1955 and also witnessed Giancarlo Baghetti winning on his F1 debut in 1961, before going on to victories in Naples and at the French GP. In the 1960s the race moved into May and in 1967 it was scheduled for May 21.

It had started out as a good year for Ferrari with a 1-2 in the Daytona 24 Hours, with Lorenzo Bandini and Chris Amon leading home Mike Parkes and Ludovico Scarfiotti. There was another 1-2 in the Monza 1000 at the end of April.

The European F1 season kicked off on March 12 with the non-championship Race of Champions at Brands Hatch, the race being won by Dan Gurney in an

Eagle-Weslake. A month later, on April 15 Denny Hulme won the Daily Express Spring Cup at Oulton Park and a fortnight after that Mike Parkes gave Ferrari a victory at the BRDC International Trophy at Silverstone. The following weekend (May 7) was the Monaco GP, won by Hulme but this was overshadowed by the fiery crash of Ferrari's Lorenzo Bandini at the harbour chicane on the 82nd lap. The Italian died three days later from burns.

It was against this backdrop that the Syracuse GP took place. It was timed that year to follow the Targa Florio sports cars race, which took place on the Piccolo Madonie road circuit, on the north side of the island, on May 14. It was World Sportscar Championship round but the only Grand Prix drivers involved were Jo Siffert, Scarfiotti and Jo Schlesser.

The later than usual date caused a problem in that it clashed with the Grote Prijs van Limborg Formula 2 race at Zolder, where there was some good start money on offer. This meant that Team Lotus, Brabham, McLaren and Matra all opted to race in Belgium rather than travelling all the way to Sicily. So John Surtees, Jim Clark, Jack Brabham, Bruce McLaren, Jean-Pierre Beltoise and Johnny Servoz-Gavin were all in Belgium.

Other F1 drivers, including Denny Hulme, Jochen Rindt, Pedro Rodriguez, Jackie Stewart, Graham Hill, Dan Gurney, Richie Ginther and Chris Amon were all at Indianapolis, taking part in the qualifying for the Indy 500.

The entry for the Syracuse GP was therefore very poor. Ferrari sent two cars, one for Parkes and the other for Scarfiotti. Siffert was there with his Rob Walker Cooper-Maserati, Chris Irwin and Mike Spence with Reg Parnell Lotus-BRMs, while Jo Bonnier ran his own Cooper-Maserati and Silvio Moser was there with an unusual Cooper-ATS. Schlesser was present too but crashed in practice and did not race. The race was run over 56 laps of the 3.5-mile circuit and quickly (and not surprisingly) developed into a fight between the two Ferrari 312s. It was close all the way but on the last lap the two cars arrived at the finish line side-by-side. They were so close in fact that the timekeepers were unable to separate them and it was declared a dead-heat, both being given the same race time – 1h40m.58.4s. It later emerged that they had done it as gesture to honour their fallen team-mate Lorenzo Bandini.

The Formula 1 World Championship has never had a dead-heat, despite an attempt to do it in 2002 when Michael Schumacher backed off in the final metres of the race to allow Rubens Barrichello to draw alongside. The Brazilian ended up winning by inches as the timing registered a difference between the two cars of 0.011sec.

The last Bugatti

Not many people know that Bugatti competed in the FIA Formula 1 World Championship. The company is associated with Grand Prix racing in the 1920s and 1930s when the Type 35 and its successors dominated the sport. But Bugatti did reappear in 1956 at the Grand Prix de l'Automobile Club de France at Reims, with a car driven by Maurice Trintignant. It qualified 18th out of 20 cars, and broke down after 18 laps. The team was not seen again.

Today the last Bugatti resides in the Musée National de l'Automobile in Mulhouse.

Bugatti had slipped out of contention in Grand Prix racing in the early 1930s when the German car companies – funded by the Nazi government – rose to dominance. Unable to compete, the Bugatti competition department turned to the Le Mans 24 Hours and created the celebrated streamlined T57G sports cars, known as the "Tanks", which won Le Mans in 1937 and again in 1939. They did not compete in 1938 because company founder Ettore Bugatti did not see the point, unless someone could beat the distance record set in 1937 at 2,043.02 miles by Jean-Pierre Wimille and Robert Benoist, the great 1920s champion who was by then Bugatti's head of competition.

Delahaye won the race in 1938 but did not beat Bugatti's record, while Benoist and his team decided to build a car for the new Grand Prix formula, which mandated a maximum engine capacity of 4.5-litre, or a supercharged 3-litre power unit. Wimille did his best but there was not enough budget to build a competitive car. The Bugatti Type 59 continued to appear in various different forms until the war broke out in 1939.

Ettore's son Jean Bugatti managed to convince his father to enter a new supercharged T57G sports car at Le Mans in 1939 and Wimille and Pierre Veyron won the race, completing 2,079.17 miles, a new record.

But that autumn Bugatti suffered a terrible tragedy. Jean was testing a Type 57G which was being prepared for the Le Baule Grand Prix, a race on the sands of the fashionable Atlantic resort in southern Brittany, where Wimille was due to drive the car on September 3. The test was done at 10pm at night on public roads near the Bugatti factory in Molsheim. There were only two junctions to worry about and Jean posted people at each one to stop anyone getting on to the road. But a cyclist was let through. He was warned to stay off the road but forgot the instruction, having had a few drinks. When Jean arrived behind him at 125mph, he could only swerve. He lost control and the 57G went straight into a roadside plane tree, killing Jean instantly. Ironically, the La Baule race was called off as World War II began that day.

Ettore Bugatti was still mourning his son when the Germans invaded France in 1940. As an Italian he was expected to assist the German war effort and, faced with the threat of having his factories seized, he came up with a novel solution to the problem. He sold his factories to the Germans for half their real value, bought the La Licorne car company and began building small vans, which he felt might sell during the war. He set up an experimental department in Paris and began work on cars for the post-war era. His staff, led by Benoist, were very active in resistance work, which led to a number of them being arrested.

When the war ended in 1945, one of the pre-war Type 59s, which had been fitted with 4.7-litre engine and used for hillclimbs in 1939, was taken out of its hiding place and raced to victory by Wimille in the Grand Prix de la Liberation in the Bois de Boulogne. But there was little good news for Bugatti in that era as the new government seized the Bugatti factory in Molsheim, believing that Bugatti had been a collaborator. He battled against the judgement against him. In 1947, the factory was finally returned to the family and Bugatti was cleared. A few days later he died at the age of 62.

The company he had founded continued, but switched to manufacturing aircraft parts to stay afloat. This was lucrative work and in 1955 it was decided to try to restart the automobile business and revive the Bugatti name in Grand Prix racing. The company hired Italian Gioacchino Colombo, who had designed the Maserati 250F. He created a new car called the Bugatti Type 251. The team appeared at the French GP in 1956 but the car was not competitive. Worse still, it didn't seem to have any potential to be competitive.

At the same time, there was a big reduction in French military spending after the country's withdrawal from Indochina, after its defeat at Dien Bien Phu. This meant that there was no money for Bugatti to invest in cars. The firm struggled on until 1963 before being sold to Hispano-Suiza and eventually becoming part of the Messier company, a subsidiary of the French government's Société Nationale d'Etude et de Construction de Moteurs d'Aviation (SNECMA).

Nearly a Grand Prix driver

Colin Chapman is always remembered as the engineering genius who ran Team Lotus, but few people remember that he actually drove a Grand Prix car – and qualified fifth for the French Grand Prix in 1956. He was then 28 years of age and had enjoyed some success in sports car races in Britain while climbing the ladder to Formula 1 as an engineer. At the end of 1955 he was commissioned by Vanwall to design a new F1 car, this would be the basis for the successful models that followed, but Chapman still had the ambition to be an F1 driver. The team was running Maurice Trintignant and Harry Schell in 1956, but when BRM decided not to go to the French GP in July, Tony Vandervell decided to ask Mike Hawthorn to drive for him. He needed to replace Trintignant, as he had been contracted to drive for the revived Bugatti team, which made its first (and last) appearance at Reims. Vandervell also decided to run a third car at Reims and asked Chapman if he would like to give it a try. Chapman accepted and did a terrific job, setting the fifth fastest time in qualifying, ahead of the Maseratis of Jean Behra, Stirling Moss, Gigi Villoresi and Olivier Gendebien. Quite an achievement. On the second day of practice, however, he was following Hawthorn around when they arrived at the Thillois hairpin, at the end of the long back straight. They braked but Chapman's left front locked on, which led to him crashing into the back of his team-mate and punting him off. Hawthorn described "a terrific crash at the back of the car", which sent him up the escape road, while Chapman's bonnet flew off and his car went off on to the grass and hit a small concrete post before bouncing into a rather larger one.

Hawthorn got out of his car and ran back to see if Chapman was OK and was relieved to find that he was unhurt. But the car was a mess. The chassis was bent, the radiator smashed and the bodywork was mangled. Chapman was very upset but when they got back to the pits team boss Tony Vandervell simply shrugged, said "that's motor racing" and began to organise getting the two cars fixed. The problem was that the team could not fix the damage at the circuit. Things were so bad with Chapman's car that it would need to go back to the factory to be straightened out. So he was out for the weekend. The team pulled the fuel tank out of the car and put it into Hawthorn's and thus there were only two cars ready to race on Sunday. Chapman had to watch.

After the crash, Chapman's insurance company said that it would be best if he did not race cars any longer, and so he decided to focus all his efforts on running his car company and designing great racing cars…

An unlikely tale

British motor racing leads the world, particularly in Formula 1, where most of the teams are British-based, even if they fly foreign flags. McLaren, Mercedes, Racing Point, Red Bull Racing, Renault and Williams are all headquartered in the UK. AlphaTauri and Haas have significant departments based in the Britain.

Today, only Alfa Romeo and Scuderia Ferrari have no British department, although both have a significant number of British staff members. Given that Britain's automobile industry is today nothing to compare to what one finds in France, Germany and Italy, that is perhaps a little strange, but it is clear evidence of the importance of industrial clustering, where local competence and know-how lead to a specific area becoming the centre of an industry.

A similar example, perhaps, would be the marmalade industry which for many years was centred on the Scottish port of Dundee because it was there that marmalade was first invented, after a Spanish ship loaded with oranges took refuge after being damaged in a storm. The cannot Scots figured out to preserve the fruit – and started an industry as a result.

What very few people know is that British motor racing did not begin at Brooklands, the world's first permanent racing facility, which was built in 1907. Five years prior to that, the first British motor racing event took place in the unlikely setting of Bexhill-on-Sea.

Bexhill-on-Sea is a seaside resort on the south coast. The original village of Bexhill was a mile inland from the sea but the Earl De La Warr, who owned the entire place, decided to transform the coast into an exclusive holiday destination. A sea wall was built, followed by De la Warr Parade, and then luxurious hotels and houses. After the Earl died in 1896, his son, Viscount Cantelupe, became the new Earl, at the age of 27. He was an investor in the Dunlop tyre company and decided to create a bicycle boulevard along the seafront from the Sackville Hotel to Galley Hill, a slight rise to the east of the new development, to help promote the resort and to spread the word about Dunlop tyres. In 1902, as a further piece of promotion, he turned the road into a race track, which being on private land was not affected by Britain's speed limit of 12 mph. That effectively meant that there could be no road racing. The Great Whitsuntide Motor Races took place on Monday May 19, 1902, a bank holiday and there were more than 200 entries. Thousands of curious spectators arrived to watch the races and to see visiting French driver Léon Serpollet winning on one of his steam cars, which recorded the highest speed of 54mph. The event was a huge success and the Earl continued to organise an annual event until 1907.

It all seems rather unlikely these days, with Bexhill being a very sedate resort with shingle beaches, with wooden breakwaters with some good hard sand when the tide is low. There are beach huts and in places a greensward. It's not overcrowded like nearby Hastings and is calm and peaceful.

Not motor racing country at all…

Britain's first NASCAR driver

Name a British driver who competed in Formula 1 and in the Daytona 500. Tough one, huh? Well, here's a clue. He built his own Formula 1 cars as well. OK, he was decorated during World War II. He came from Manchester. Not an easy one, is it?

The answer is Brian Naylor, or at least JB Naylor was he was known. He was born in the village of Leigh in Lancashire, to the west of Manchester, but moved to Stockport on the eastern side of the city. When war broke out in 1939, he was 16. Two years later he joined the merchant navy and served as a radio operator, returning home decorated for his exploits.

 After the war he went into the automotive business and established a string of companies including a successful car dealership on the A6 road, which ran from London to Carlyle, passing through Stockport, where it is known as Wellington Road. This provided the money he needed to start competing and in 1953 – when he was 31 – he bought a MG TD and went racing.

He waltzed through a number of other cars and was soon scoring some good results in British races. This led to the purchase in 1955 of a Maserati 150S sports car. He would later take the Maserati engine and used it in a Lotus Eleven, which was a great success and he won 27 victories in Britain with the unusual car. He also went abroad and competed in various European events.

The following year, he upgraded to a Maserati 200S engine, which was a 2-litre unit. This was also quite successful but he ended the season at Goodwood when he suffered a suspension failure and crashed heavily, breaking a leg. The car was a write-off and so Naylor and his mechanic Fred Wilkinson built their own version of the Lotus for 1958, beefing up the tubular chassis. The car was called the JBW-Maserati, the JB coming from Naylor's initials and the W from Wilkinson. It was quite successful in minor races, winning 14 times. Naylor even shared the car with Stirling Moss in one race at the Roskilde Ring in Denmark when Moss's own Maserati failed.

They then decided to build a JBW Formula 1 car, while also putting together a Ferrrai-engined sports car. The F1 car was based on the Cooper F2 design and was fitted with a Maserati 250F engine. It ran in three British F1 races, retiring in the International Trophy and the British GP and being a non-starter in the Gold Cup at Oulton Park after a crash in practice. It had some success in Formula Libre events. That year, Naylor was invited to co-drive Graham Whitehead's

Aston Martin DBR1 at Le Mans. This resulted in a big accident when Naylor rolled the car at Maison Blanche, but he escaped unhurt.

The F1 programme expanded in 1960 with more races, some of them on the Continent and was even shipped out to California for the United States GP at Riverside, but it was unreliable and never scored any decent results.

At the Italian GP, which was boycotted by most of the British teams because of the danger of the Monza high banking, Naylor met NASCAR boss Bill France and the two hit it off. This led to an invitation from France for Naylor to try to lap Daytona at more than 180mph in a Cooper Monaco-Ferrari sports car. As a result of this, France organised for him to drive a Pontiac prepared by Smokey Yunick in the Daytona 500 in February 1961. He qualified seventh in the qualifying race but retired early. He seems to have then bought a ride in a Ford and started 58th and last for the 500. He raced for 85 of the 200 laps before going out with an engine failure.

There was a second JBW in 1961 for the new 1.5-litre Formula 1 regulations, with the old Maserati 150S engine being used. It was off the pace. For the Italian GP Naylor fitted the car with a Coventry Climax engine but this blew up after a few laps. That summer he returned to Daytona and tested Art Arfons's Green Monster land speed record car at Daytona…

Towards the end of the year, however, Naylor was diagnosed to have a heart problem. He was only 38 but decided it would be best to retire from racing.

In the years that followed, he spent much time messing up in boats, having retired from business due to his poor health. He ran a café in Marbella in southern Spain until 1989 when he was killed in an explosion while working on a boat, believed to have been caused by a build-up of gas.

The yellow Rolls-Royce

In 1966, an imposing and rather elegant 1931 Rolls-Royce Phantom II rolled into the paddock at Silverstone. It featured a Sedanca de Ville coachwork, painted bright yellow, created by the Barker company in South Audley Street in Mayfair. This was no ordinary car.

She had a movie career behind her, having co-starred with Rex Harrison, Omar Sharif, Ingrid Bergman, Shirley MacLaine, George C Scott, Alain Delon and Jeanne Moreau in the 1965 movie "The Yellow Rolls-Royce", released by MGM, directed by Anthony Asquith and written by Terence Rattigan.

The car featured a curtained compartment behind where the chauffeur sat and a large box on the back for luggage. The car drew to a stop and the chauffeur jumped out and proceeded to busy himself with the luggage box, extracting a card table, four folding chairs, a table cloth, silverware (proper stuff), bone china and crystal glass. He then opened a bottle of champagne, returned to the car and opened the door. Four racing drivers emerged, wearing their overalls, although each sported a yellow bow tie and a black top hat. They sat down and enjoyed a impromptu lunch of caviar and crackers, with champagne whenever their glasses were empty. No-one paid them much attention. People didn't go to national motor races in those days to have picnics. They went to watch racing…

It was a Formula 3 event and Charlie Crichton-Stuart, Piers Courage, Charles Lucas and Jonathan Williams were all taking part. The chauffeur was another racer called Anthony Horsley, known as "Bubbles". They were a wealthy group: Crichton-Stuart was one of the Bute family, who owned most of Scotland. Charlie was slightly older than the others and had been an RAF pilot. He was often to be found in the company of the stunning model-turned-movie star Shirley Anne Field. Lucas, who was known as "Luke" came from a wealthy land-owning family, which had a fortune based on construction, his great-grandfather having built the Albert Hall, Covent Garden Opera House, Cliveden House, Alexandra Palace and many other celebrated landmarks. He had been at school (Eton, of course) with Courage, who was the heir to the Courage Brewery, although he was known as "Porridge" to his pals.

Piers was soon to be married to Sally Curzon, daughter of BRDC President Earl Howe, the former Grand Prix driver. Jonathan Williams was less well-heeled but lived in Crichton-Stuart's apartment in Pinner Road, Harrow, where Lucas, Courage, Horsley and Williams were often to be found, when not racing. This was also the home of a youngster called Frank Williams, who slept on the sofa, when he wasn't off racing. Other visitors to the establishment include Innes Ireland and Jochen Rindt.

Crichton-Stuart would go on to be one of the early members of Williams Grand Prix Engineering, when Frank finally managed to land some money for his F1 team. Courage, alas, died in a crash in 1970 at Zandvoort, driving a Williams de Tomaso.

Lucas ran the Lotus Formula 3 team for a while before deciding to give up racing and sold the business, which later became Titan Cars. He would go on to become the van driver for Hesketh Racing, the Formula 1 team run by Lord Hesketh, which helped James Hunt on his way to success, and was managed by Lucas's "chauffeur" "Bubbles" Horsley…

Something of a Bohemian

For centuries Germans settled in the Czech-speaking Bohemian crown lands in Bohemia, Moravia and Silesia, to the south of the Sudeten mountains, which formed a natural border between Poland and the Czechs. They made up around 30 percent of the population in these regions and were known as German Bohemians, and later as Sudeten Germans. The region became part of the Austro-Hungarian empire in 1867. The town of Novy Jicin, known to the Germans as Neutitschein, was not far from Ostrava, between Brno and the Polish border, was home to a furniture-maker called Karl Neubauer. Novy Jicin was close to the village of Kopřivnice (known as Nesseldorf to the Germans), where in 1897 the Nesseldorfer Wagenbau-Fabriksgesellschaft was founded, to build wooden carriages for the road and for the railways.

In 1897, the firm decided to build an automobile named the Präsident, to be powered by a Benz engine. This was at the instigation of Baron Theodor Liebig, from a wealthy textile family, who was one of the early owners and racers of Benz machinery.

The company was always looking for help from skilled carpenters and so Karl Neubauer was often to be found there, helping to create the wooden bodies required for the Präsident. Karls' son Afred, who was nicknamed Friedl, saw his first Präsident when he was seven and was fascinated by automobiles from then onwards. After attending the local schools he attended the nearby imperial cavalry cadet school in the famous garrison town of Hranice na Moravě (Weißkirchen in German) and then, aged 19, was transferred to the Imperial Artillery School at Traiskirchen, to the south of Vienna before being promoted to the rank of Sergeant and joining the Kaiser Franz Josef Regiment.

At the time, the Imperial Austrian Army was just beginning to look at replacing horses with motorised transportation and the 21-year-old Sergeant Neubauer was sent to the Austro-Daimler headquarters in Wiener Neustadt to discuss the possibilities with Austro-Daimler's chief designer Ferdinand Porsche, another Sudeten German. Although there was a gap of 15 years in age, the two men hit it off.

War broke out not long afterwards and young Neubauer was put in command of two motorised mortar units and despatched to the Balkans, where he took part in campaigns in Serbia, Montenegro and Albania. He was commissioned and appointed a Lieutenant and was ordered to join a commission that was looking into developing new vehicles for the Austrian artillery. This revived his friendship with Porsche and after Austria was defeated Porsche offered him a job as the director of road testing for the Austro-Daimler company.

After the end of the war, Neubauer was no longer an Austro-Hungarian and officially became Czech, the state of Czechoslovakia having been established in October 1918.

In 1922, Neubauer was despatched to Sicily to take part in the Targa Florioin an Austro-Daimler Sascha. He finished 19th, three places behind an Italian youngster called Enzo Ferrari, who had been racing an Alfa Romeo.

But change was ahead. In April 1923 Porsche was offered the role of technical director of Daimler-Motoren-Gesellschaft (DMG) in Stuttgart, Austro-Daimler's parent company. Two months later, Neubauer followed Porsche to DMG. Neubauer was sent off to Sicily again in 1924 to take part in the Targa Florio, teamed with veteran Mercedes Grand Prix drivers Christian Werner and Christian Lautenschlager. They finished first, 10th and 15th, with Neubauer bringing up the rear. Later that year, Werner and Neubauer were joined for the Italian GP by aristocrats Count Giulio Masetti and Count Louis Zborowski. Sadly, Zborowski crashed into a tree in the middle of the race, and the Mercedes team withdrew.

It was a difficult time for the car industry and that year DMG formed "a community of interests" with rival Benz & Cie, which led to a full merger in June 1926 to form Daimler-Benz AG. Before the final merger Neubauer was named racing manager for DMG, his organisational skills having been considered better than his abilities behind the wheel.

The Benz merger brought new management with Benz employees Wilhelm Kissel becoming CEO and chief engineer Hans Nibel sharing control of the technical development with Porsche. Neubauer managed the sporting activities, running Porsche's Mercedes-Benz SSK in sports car events, with occasional outings in Grands Prix with stripped down cars for Rudi Caracciola. While this was going on, Neubauer became a German citizen in 1928.

At the end of the year, there was another big change when Porsche decided to move to Steyr, leaving Nibel as technical director of Daimler-Benz AG. This time Neubauer did not follow, staying on to run competition activities, although these stopped completely at the end of the year when the Wall Street Crash caused an economic crisis that would become the Great Depression.

Daimler-Benz withdrew from competition but Neubauer found a way to run low-key programmes with the SSKs at Le Mans in 1930 and 1931, with occasional Grand Prix appearances for Caracciola and others. He also kept an eye open for new talents and, by the middle of 1931, Caracciola was able to give Daimler-Benz a major victory at Avus in a stripped down SSK sportscar. Nibel began to make plans for a new Grand Prix team and designed the Mercedes-Benz W25, which was funded by money from the new Nazi government in Germany.

And so it was that Alfred Neubauer found himself at the head of the mighty Mercedes Grand Prix programme of the 1930s, battling with rival German firm AutoUnion, in what has become known as the age of the titans.

World War II ended that era, with Neubauer managing Mercedes factories during the war years. He would begin campaigning for a return to competition in the early 1950s, when Mercedes ran three of the old pre-war cars in odd races. He then got the go-ahead to create a sports car programme with the Mercedes 300SL, with much success and in 1954 Mercedes returned to Grand Prix racing when the new 2.5-litre formula began. The W196 was a dominant car and in 1955, Juan-Manuel Fangio won the Formula 1 World Championship for the company.

But that summer disaster struck at Le Mans. Pierre Levegh, driving a works Mercedes-Benz 300 SLR ran into the back of a slower car that veered into his path, avoiding the Jaguar of Mike Hawthorn, which made a late decision to pit. Levegh's car flew into the wall and disintegrated into the crowd. There were at least 80 people killed, including Levegh, with another 120 injured. It was, and remains, motor racing's worst disaster and led to the banning of all racing in Switzerland and major changes in the way the sport could operate.

At the end of the year, Mercedes quietly withdrew from the sport. It would not return until the late 1980s. Neubauer was then 64 and was close to retirement age.

He lived to a ripe old age, long enough to see Mercedes begin to return the sport…

The Duke turns the tide

Paolo Pavanello was involved in racing in Italy in the early 1970s leading up to becoming the manager (and a shareholder) in the AFMP Euroracing team, partnered by March Engineering's agent in Italy Sandro Angeleri, racing driver Martino Finotto and March Engineering itself. That all went bad wrong when Angeleri was arrested in 1977 and jailed for drug smuggling. The team collapsed and Pavanello salvaged the operational end of the business and transformed it into Euroracing, running Piercarlo Ghinzani to victory in the Italian Formula 3 championship in a March-Alfa Romeo in 1979.

The team won the European Formula 3 title in 1980 with Michele Alboreto and then again in 1981 with Mauro Baldi. March then decided to withdraw from Formula 3 and so Pavanello took the two March 813 chassis he owned and rebuilt them as Euroracing 101s, which were then raced with much success in 1982 by Oscar Larrauri, who won the European title, and a young Emanuele Pirro.

At the time, Alfa Romeo – which was then owned by the Italian government's holding company Finmeccanica –, was suffering serious financial losses and was looking to reduce its involvement in Formula 1. The decision was taken to hand over the chassis design to Euroracing, leaving Carlo Chiti's Autodelta to develop the engines.

Pavanello took control of things late in the day and so had little choice but to have Autodelta designer Gérard Ducarouge update the carbon composite 182 that he had designed the previous year, which had shown promise but was never properly developed. The result was the Alfa Romeo 183T which was raced by Andrea de Cesaris and Baldi.

It was clear that Pavanello wanted to get his own people involved. At the French Grand Prix, the opening European round of the World Championship, held in April at Paul Ricard, de Cesaris's car was found to have an empty fire extinguisher bottle in practice and was disqualified. Ducarouge was blamed and was dismissed by Pavanello. There were then races in quick succession in San Marino, Monaco and Belgium.

At the time, John Player Team Lotus has slipped into the doldrums. The Lotus 93T, the first Lotus to be fitted with Renault F1 turbo engines, had been designed in the autumn of 1982 by a team led by Lotus founder Colin Chapman, who had done a deal for Renault turbo engines that summer. In mid-December Chapman had suddenly died, at the age of just 54. The team finished off the design but what was not widely known at the time was that the Renault deal allowed for just one car to run with its engines for the first half of the season. Perhaps it was because the team was focussed on developing an active suspension system, but the car was designed with a standard-sized fuel tank, while rival teams worked out that with refuelling they could build smaller and lighter cars. Team Lotus's new boss Peter Warr had the difficult task of informing Nigel Mansell that he would be racing the older car, with the less-powerful Cosworth engines. It did not go down well.

The 93T was not very competitive and highly unreliable in the early part of the year. Warr decided that new technical leadership was required. He made contact with Ducarouge, offering him the job of being technical director. The Duke, who also had an offer from Renault, decided to join the British team. The Gauloises-puffing Frenchman arrived like a whirlwind at Ketteringham Hall in May and concluded straight away that the 93T must be scrapped and a new car built.

Working with Martin Ogilvie, Lotus's chef designer, he set out to create a lighter more nimble car, based on a modified version of the Lotus 92 monocoque. His target was to have two of the new cars for the British GP at Silverstone on Saturday, July 16.

There was a gap of four and a half weeks after the Canadian GP on June 12, which helped the team get the work done and not only were there two new cars ready to go at Silverstone but they were quick as well. After the first qualifying session on Thursday, de Angelis was third on the provisional grid, behind Alain Prost's Renault and René Arnoux's Ferrari. Mansell, on the other hand, was suffering from a misfire which would not go away. On the Friday de Angelis dropped one place to fourth as Arnoux and his team-mate Patrick Tambay grabbed the front row. Mansell continued to struggle and ended up a disappointed 18th on the grid. In the race, however, de Angelis disappeared after just one lap with a turbo failure, but Mansell drove steadily through the field, making a late pit stop to emerge in fifth place and then hunted down Arnoux to grab fourth. He could not catch Tambay and had to settle for fourth place, amid great excitement for British fans…

Team Lotus was back on an upward path again.

A big day, and big oops

The Australian GPs of 1995 and 1996 followed on from one another. The event had switched from the end-of-season party in Adelaide, to the season-opener in Melbourne. The 1995 race, had the biggest crowd in modern F1 history, with a four-day attendance of 520,000 people and a race day crowd of 210,000. It is often remembered as the race at which Mika Häkkinen crashed at Brewery Bend on Friday afternoon, after suffering a rear left puncture and crashed so heavily that his helmet hit the steering wheel and then the side of the cockpit. He was fortunate that two of the doctors working at the corner intensive care specialist Jerome Cockings and neurologist Stephen Lewis were on the scene immediately, as Professor Sid Watkins was still on his way to the scene in the medical car. They realised that Häkkinen had suffered a fracture at the base of his skull and was not getting sufficient oxygen. They performed a trackside tracheotomy on the Finn, before he was transported to the Royal Adelaide Hospital.

The event went on as planned and by the end of qualifying on the Saturday, the two Rothmans Williams-Renaults of Damon Hill and David Coulthard qualifying 1-2 on the grid, the two split by 0.123s, with Hill ahead and Coulthard 0.211s ahead of the Benetton-Renault of Michael Schumacher.

At the start on Sunday, Coulthard jumped into the lead and held off Hill until the first pit stops on lap 19. He has recently scored his first F1 victory, at the Portuguese GP, but the 24-year-old was still learning. He arrived at the pit lane entrance and slowed, changing down from third to second gear rather late. The engine gave him an unexpected push and DC braked to counter-act this, but the pit lane was dusty. The Williams was travelling too quickly. The brakes locked up and Coulthard slid into the inside of the pit wall, which turned to the right quite dramatically at that point. The nose was knocked off and broke the left front suspension of the car.

Coulthard was out…

Hill won the race, lapping the entire field twice after 81 laps.

And that was the end of the Grand Prix in Adelaide.

Less is more?

The 1966 World Championship began on May 22 in Monaco. It was a late start because of the new 3-litre formula, which meant not just new car-engine combinations but also a number of new teams. Not everyone was ready.

The biggest change was that Jaguar, which had owned Coventry Climax since 1963, had agreed a deal to be merged into the British Motor Corporation (BMC). It was a time when the British manufacturing was in decline. Mergers and takeovers were being promoted by the government in order to ensure that Britain retained a strong presence in the automobile industry. Jaguar owner Sir Williams Lyons was nearing retiring and his only son John had been killed in 1955 in a head-on collision with a US Army truck near Cherbourg, in France, when he was driving to Le Mans, leaving Sir William without a successor.

As part of the restructuring, it was decided to withdraw Coventry Climax from F1. The rights to the engines were sold to Bob King's Racing Preparations in Wembley and although the engines continued to be used by some teams, they quickly became uncompetitive. Ferrari had a reliable V12 engine, concocted from a 3.3-litre sports car unit that was reduced to three-litres to meet the regulations. Jack Brabham had commissioned Repco to revamp an obsolete GM engine block to create a Repco V8, while BRM had decided to build a complicated H16 engine.

There were big changes as well at Cooper. Charles Cooper had died at the age of 70 in October 1964. His son John was still recovering from a huge crash on the Kingston Bypass, which had left him with a fractured skull. Wheeler-dealer Roy Salvadori had just sold his car business to the Chipstead Motor Group, the UK's Maserati importer, and he convinced Chipstead boss Mario Tozzi-Condivi to buy Cooper. Tozzi-Condivi then asked Maserati to revive its old V12 engine from 1957 to provide engines for the team.

Bruce McLaren had left Cooper and had started his own team, his plan being to use a Ford Indianapolis V8 engine, derived from the 406, while had commissioned Weslake Engineering to design a V12. Honda too was working on a new V12 but it was not ready.

It was a similar story with Team Lotus, as Ford had agreed to fund a new engine build by Cosworth Engineering, but the DFV was not ready. So Lotus did a deal to use the BRM H16s.

The usual pre-season non-championship races started only in April with Syracuse, which John Surtees won in a Ferrari, a good effort as John was still recovering from the serious injuries he had suffered in September 1965 when he crashed a Lola T70 sports car at Mosport Park. In mid-May the International Trophy at Silverstone saw Jack Brabham's Brabham-Repco victorious.

A week later in Monaco, there was much excitement as John Frankenheimer and his movie crew were busy filming. Jim Clark was on pole in a Lotus, using an old Climax engine, with Surtees alongside in an interim Ferrari 246, which was basically an old 158 fitted with a 2.4-litre engine. Stewart was third in his BRM.

Surtees led the first 14 laps of the race, chased by Stewart, until the Ferrari suffered a differential failure. Stewart then took over. It was, not surprisingly, a race with a very high retirement rate, due to the all the new cars, and in the end Stewart won by 40 secs, with Graham Hill third a lap behind. The only other classified runner was Bob Bondurant, who was five laps down in a BRM. Two other cars were still circulating: Guy Ligier in a Cooper-Maserati, who was 25 laps behind, and Jo Bonnier, in a similar car, who was two laps behind him. The race held the record for the fewest number of classified finishers in the history of the World Championship until the Monaco GP in 1996 when only three cars got to the finish line.

From dumper trucks to F1

George Fowell Ltd was a company based in the unglamorous Birmingham suburb of Smethwick. It manufactured small plant machinery: dumper trucks, mini steam rollers and cement mixers. These were branded GF. The founder's oldest son Gordon began working for the family business in the late 1950s, designing dumper trucks. In his spare time, he competed with a Lotus Eleven sports car. The arrival of the Mini in 1959 gave Gordon Fowell an idea: why not diversify the business and have GF build a lightweight GT coupé, based on the Mini sub frame and running gear.

It was in the same era in which Lamborghini was transforming itself from being a tractor manufacturer to becoming a supercar company so perhaps there was sound logic in the idea. The only difference was that Lamborghini had more money to play with. The GF coupé was given the rather exotic name of Gitane, the French word for gipsy. Creating the prototype proved to be sufficiently difficult to convince GF to give up on the idea, although the Gitane that was built was use quite successfully in hillclimb events in the late 1960s. By then Gordon had come up with another idea: to start a company with a racing journalist called Alan Philips to create and sell audio tapes of racing engines. The business was called Goral. It is not really clear why David Yorke, the celebrated team manager, who had made his name with Vanwall and the JW Automotive Gulf GT40 team, who had gone on to be an advisor for motorsport to the Martini & Rossi drinks company, commissioned Goral to build an F1 car for Martini for the 1973 season. The most likely explanation is that Fowell had decided to draw his own F1 design, probably just for fun, and that Yorke found himself in need of an F1 car in a hurry, heard about what Fowell was doing – and decided to give him a try. Whatever the case, choosing a designer without any previous F1 experience, with a background in dumper trucks, was a little eccentric.

At the time Martini was sponsoring a new F1 team called Tecno. It had a good record in the junior formulae but had embarked on a Formula 1 the hard way, building its own flat-12 engines, rather than buying Cosworths, as everyone else was doing. The first season – 1972 – was not a success and so Tecno's owners Luciano and Gianfranco Pederzani commissioned New Zealander Alan McCall to design a new car for them. Yorke and Count Gregorio Rossi seem to have decided it would be wiser to build a car in the UK…

While this was all going on, McCall talked Chris Amon into joining Tecno. He was a top F1 driver who had been left without a drive when Matra quit F1. He did a deal to race with March Engineering, but fell out with the management before the 1973 season had even begun. McCall's Italian-built car was ready in May, in time for the fifth race of the F1 season, at Zolder in Belgium. The car was heavy but reliable. Amon finished three laps behind. It was enough to finish sixth and score a point, which looked like a pretty decent result, if only on paper.

The Goral car – known as the E731 – did not appear until the British GP in mid-July where Amon tried it for the first time in practice. It seems that the British end of the team indulged in some skulduggery, trying to show that the British car was better than its Italian cousin – and the result was that Luciano Pederzani stormed off, never to return.

Yorke then recommended that Martini & Rossi do a deal with Bernie Ecclestone's Brabham for 1974. Before the money ran out, the Tecno E731 appeared again in Holland and Austria, but then the team closed its doors. That left Amon in need of a drive once again. He had seen Jack Brabham, Bruce McLaren and John Surtees all start their own F1 teams and decided that he would give it a go, reasoning that a half-decent chassis with a Cosworth engine and a Hewland gearbox ought to be able to qualify for races. He found funding from British racer John Dalton and asked Fowell to design him a new car which was then built by John Thompson's TC Prototypes.

The E731 had been a very low car and the AF101 followed that concept. In an effort to create a narrower chassis (and thus reduce the frontal area) Fowell placed the fuel tank between the driver and the engine, rather than having the fuel in both of the sidepods, as was then the fashion.

Aerodynamics was still a rudimentary art in F1 but Fowell asked Professor Tom Boyce, a Canadian academic who worked at Imperial College in London, for help. Boyce was a clever man, with a Masters in plasma physics and a doctorate in combustion kinetics, although these were unusual qualifications for a racing car designer.

He had rallied an MG in Canada before moving to the UK in 1961 and after that had competed in (and completed) the London-Sydney Marathon, in an MGB, as co-driver of journalist Jean Denton. His first work in racing car design had been in 1970 and 1971 when he shaped the body of the Jerboa SP sports car, built around an old Ginetta G12. This enjoyed limited success in prototype events in Europe.

The Amon appeared (briefly) at the International Trophy race in April 1974 and a couple of weeks later was present for the Spanish GP. Amon qualified the car 23rd despite serious brake vibrations, which led to a failure in the race. The team missed the Belgian GP but then reappeared at Monaco, where Amon qualified 20th but did not start because the car was not ready in time for the race. Chris Amon Racing then missed the next four races and the team had concluded that the AF101 was not sufficiently rigid, which meant it flexed and consequently was not reliable nor easy to drive. Trying to strengthen the car made it too heavy and the car could not qualify when it reappeared in August in Germany.

The team ran out of money and closed down after the Italian GP.

Fowell disappeared from F1 but later designed the Sana Formula Atlantic car, with some success.

In the end he gave up racing – but later made a fortune by designing and developing the PowerJog running machine, with a new company called Sport Engineering Ltd, based in Stirchley.

How not to be a Ferrari driver

Not all racing drivers are sane and balanced individuals. Some of them are rather difficult personalities and often that is a part of the reason that they are successful – or not.

France's Jean Behra was just such a man. He was a quick driver but never won a Grand Prix, although the driver from Nice won a series of victories in non-championship races. He rose to prominence with Equipe Gordini in the early 1950s, scoring his first podium in Switzerland in 1952. In 1955, he switched to the Maserati factory team and that year finished second in Argentina and collected four second places, ending the year fourth in the World Championship. He was second again in Argentina the following year but then moved on to a season with BRM in 1958, which resulted in just one third place, before he was recruited by Ferrari for 1959, to replace the retiring Mike Hawthorn. He found himself racing teamed up with British drivers Tony Brooks and Cliff Allison.

The problem for Behra was that Brooks was very fast and he fell into the age old trap of believing that the team was favouring Brooks. That made little sense, but sometimes drivers have to resort to such thinking when they come up against someone young and quicker. It's the only way they can handle it. Behra was then 38 and Brooks 27 but although Ferrari never designated a number one driver, both Brooks and Behra seemed to believe they were team leader.

In reality, Brooks was…

Things came to a head at the European Grand Prix at Reims in early July. Ferrari sent five cars to the race for Brooks, Behra, Phil Hill and Olivier Gendebien being joined by Dan Gurney. It was a blistering ly hot day and Behra dropped out of the race with an engine problem after showing well in the early laps, setting a number of fastest laps. Brooks streaked away to victory, averaging an impressive 127 mph.

Behra was frustrated. When he climbed out of the car he spoke to the French journalist Pierre About, the F1 correspondent of L'Equipe, France's big daily sports newspaper. He claimed that not only had Ferrari given him a bad engine but the chassis was also not right and the car handled badly as a result. Legend has it that there was an altercation in the pits and Behra is supposed to have laid out Ferrari team manager Romolo Tavoni with a single punch.

But that is not what actually happened.

On the Monday after the race, Enzo Ferrari heard what had been published in L'Equipe and was not happy with the criticism. He had not travelled to the race from Italy and so telephoned Tavoni, who had stayed on in Reims in order to collect the prize at a prize-giving lunch, which was a quite normal thing in those days. Ferrari told Tavoni to see Behra and tell him to retract what he had said.

Tavoni duly did as he was told instructed and met Behra at the restaurant where the prize-giving was taking place. Behra lost his temper, called Tavoni stupid and punched him in the face twice. Tavoni did not return the blows – but was not happy with his difficult driver.

There are two stories about how Ferrari found out: firstly that one of the engineers told him about the altercation; or secondly that it was Enzo's wife Laura who was there with the team. Whatever the case, Behra was summoned to Maranello for a meeting at 10 o'clock on the Tuesday morning.

Enzo Ferrari decided that he would invite some Italian journalists and L'Equipe's Italian correspondent for a press conference at midday. He explained to Behra that he wanted an apology for Tavoni and asked the pugnacious Frenchman to tell the media that he was happy with his car, telling Behra that he would never have sent a kinked chassis to a race, because it made no sense to do such a thing. Behra refused to do was Ferrari had asked. Enzo repeated the request. Behra refused again. Ferrari then called in the head of the finance department Ermano della Casa and told him to settle up Behra's accounts, pay anything outstanding, and terminate the contract. Their relationship was over.

A couple of weeks later Behra went to Berlin to race a Porsche sports car and was killed in a gruesome accident on the high banking at Avus…

An extraordinary individual

Charles and Frank Purley sold fish before taking over a small electrical repair business which they turned into the Longford Engineering Company Ltd manufacturing munitions at a facility on Longford Road in the seaside resort of Bognor Regis on the south coast of England, not far from Chichester.

It was a profitable but rather short-term business because when the war ended in 1945, the company needed to find something else to do, so they began experimenting with refrigerators and manufactured their first fridge in 1946.

They were soon doing so well that they bought a new site on the Shrimpney Road, where they built a mass production facility in 1947. Today the factory site has been turned into a large supermarket and car park, but there is a nod to history with the access road, known as Fridge Way. They changed the name of the company to LEC Refrigeration at the end of 1954 and this expanded quickly, becoming a public company in 1964, generating millions every year. They were making so much money that they bought 50 acres of land and built their own landing strip, known as Lec Airfield.

Charles' son David was born at the end of the war. He attended a couple of boarding schools, being expelled from one prior to becoming the Lec company pilot for a few months before falling out with his father and going to be part of a demolition gang, working on tall buildings. He then decided that he enlist the army and signed up at a recruiting office. He spent two years at the Royal Military Academy at Sandhurst before being commissioned in December 1966, and joining the 1st Battalion of the Parachute Regiment early in 1967 as a 2nd Lieutenant. He survived a close call during training when his parachute became entangled with that of his instructor and he rode his way to the ground on the top of the other instructor's parachute. Later that year, he was sent to Aden where he spent several months in action against rebel forces. While still in he army, he was introduced to racing by a neighbour Derek Bell and bought a powerful AC Cobra sports car, which he would soon write-off at Brands Hatch. He then bought a Chevron sportscar and decided that racing was more exciting than soldiering and resigned his commission at the end of 1969 and set up his own Formula 3 team with a Brabham BT28. The team was funded by the family and called Lec Refrigeration Racing. He won his first F3 victory after just a few weeks, beating James Hunt by a tenth of a second in the Grand Prix des Frontières at Chimay in Belgium. He would not win again until he returned to Chimay a year later.

In mid 1971, he switched to an Ensign. His results improved and he won two races in Britain at the end of the year. For 1972 he concentrated on Formula 2 with a March 722 and finished third at Pau, but he returned to Chimay to win his third consecutive Grand Prix des Frontières.

He switched to Formula Atlantic in 1973 but made his F1 debut that year at Monaco in a March 731. Later, his efforts to save Roger Williamson from a burning car at the Dutch GP led to the award of a George Medal for bravery. He left Formula 1 and spent 1974 racing in Formula 5000 and became increasingly successful and won the British title in 1976.

That winter he commissioned designer Mike Pilbeam to build a Lec F1 car and in 1977 qualified for several Formula 1 races. In practice at Silverstone, he suffered a stuck throttle and crashed with incredible violence. His life was saved by rescue crews at the scene of the crash but it took many months for him to recover from multiple fractures to his legs, pelvis and ribs. He did eventually have a second Lec F1 car built and did one or two events and then raced a Shadow in the 1979 British F1 series but then he quit racing. He underwent a series of painful operations to try to repair his damaged legs and then settled down to run the family business – and to do aerobatics in his spare time. In the years that followed, he survived two crash landings, but in the summer of 1985 his Pitts Special stunt plane went down in the sea, off the coast. It was an accident that even David Purley could not survive.

A similar tale

William Ronald Flockhart was tall, good-looking, fair-haired and something of a lady-killer. He came from a comfortable background in Edinburgh where he attended Daniel Stewart's College before going on to study engineering at Edinburgh University. After graduating he joined the Corps of the Royal Electrical and Mechanical Engineers (REME), being commissioned in January 1944 and seeing active service in the Italian campaigns later that year. He would remain in the REME until 1951, but when the war ended, he began competing in motorcycle scrambling before switching to cars in 1948, starting out with an MG before trying out single-seaters with a 500cc Cooper. He also learned to fly in a Tiger Moth.

He left the army in 1951 and went to work in a textile business in Edinburgh, but racing had by then become a passion and he began competing in Formula Libre and in hillclimbs with pre-war ERAs. Some success led to him being offered a BRM drive in 1953. He left his job and turned professional. He made his F1 debut at the British GP in 1954, sharing a Maserati 250F with Prince Bira. Alhough he did a lot of testing for BRM, his F1 career was rather intermittent but it was in sports cars that he really made an impact, winning the Le Mans 24 Hours in an Ecurie Ecosse Jaguar D-Type in 1956. He appeared a few weeks later at the British GP in a BRM but the engine failed quickly. The Le Mans victory led to an invitation to drive for Connaught at the Italian GP and he made a big impression by finishing third behind Stirling Moss and a Ferrari shared by Peter Collins and Juan Manuel Fangio. He won Le Mans a second time in 1957 but then crashed a BRM at the French GP and suffered burns. A year later he crashed while taking part in practice for a sports car race at Rouen, hitting an ambulance in his Lotus 15 and suffering from crushed vertebrae and broken ribs. He was back in action in 1959 and beat Jack Brabham and Bruce McLaren to win the Lady Wigram Trophy in January and finished sixth at the French GP. In the autumn he won the Silver City Trophy F1 race at Snetterton (beating Brabham again).

In 1960, he was recruited by Team Lotus after the death of Alan Stacey at Spa and finished sixth at the French GP. At the end of the year he raced a factory Cooper in the United States GP at Riverside.

It was then that United Dominions Trust, which was sponsoring the UDT Laystall F1 team, asked him to try to break the record of flying between Sydney and London using a World War II Mustang fighter. He had to abandon his attempt after suffering engine problems in Athens.

He was back out in New Zealand in 1962 to race for Lotus and to prepare for a second Sydney-London record attempt with another Mustang. As part of his preparations he set off from Melbourne's Morabbin Airport to fly to Bankstown in Sydney on April 12. He ran into cloud in the Dandenong Ranges, to the east of Melbourne and crashed near the village of Kallista. He was 38.

Three weeks of disaster

History has a way of isolating events from one another, leaving future generations to miss the continuity of events and thus it is hard to understand the atmosphere in a certain place at a certain time.

This was certainly true of a three week period in 1955 when the motorsport world went through a traumatic period.

It began in Monaco on Sunday May 22 when Grand Prix racing returned to the streets of the principality for the first time in five years. Mercedes was dominant with team-mates Juan Manuel Fangio and Stirling Moss running 1-2 until halfway through the race when Fangio dropped out with transmission trouble. Moss looked to have victory in his hands but 20 laps from the finish his engine blew. A few minutes later the new leader Alberto Ascari, World Champion of 1952 and 1953, made a mistake at the chicane, his Lancia smashed into and over the barriers and flew into the harbour with a not inconsiderable splash. For a few seconds there was a sense of horror and then Ascari's pale blue helmet appeared and the driver was quickly taken aboard a small boat, his only injury being a broken nose. The race went on and Ferrari's Maurice Trintignant scored his first F1 victory – at the age of 37.

In Britain the focus was on politics with a general election due to take place on Thursday, May 26. As the British were going to the polls, Ascari paid a visit to Monza, decided to test a Ferrari sports car and was killed in an inexplicable accident. The same day Sir Anthony Eden became the British Prime Minister, at the head of a strong Conservative government.

The World Championship that year included the Indy 500, although none of the Europeans went to America. In fact, it was a triple header of races with Monaco followed on May 30 by the Indy 500 with the Belgian GP on June 5.

At Indy, Bill Vukovich was in dominant form. He had won the 500 in 1953 and 1954 and was looking for a hat-trick and had built up a lead of 17 secs when on the 57th lap he came up to lap three slower cars, driven by Rodger Ward, Al Keller and Johnny Boyd. Ward lost control and hit the wall. His car flipped and came back on to the race track, hitting Boyd and punting his car into the path of Vukovich. He hit the wall and the car cart-wheeled over the wall, landing on top of a group of parked cars, where it burst into flames. Vukovich was dead.

The Grand Prix teams were in Belgium a few days later. Lancia had withdrawn from Formula 1 in the days after Ascari's death and Fangio and Moss finished 1-2 for Mercedes. The big names then headed down to Le Mans to prepare for the 24 Hours on June 12. History relates that in the late afternoon Mike Hawthorn made a late decision to pit in his Jaguar and pulled across the track rather took rapidly. Lance Macklin in an Austin Healey tried to avoid him and went into the path of the Mercedes-Benz of Pierre Levegh, which hit the English car and few into the wall and disintegrated when it hit a tunnel support, sending wreckage into the packed area in front of the grandstands. At least 83 people were killed (including Levegh himself) and a further 120 were injured, many of them seriously. No-one knows the full total of those killed as some did not survive their injuries but such was the scale of the accident that the injured were sent to 11 different hospitals.

The accident led to the banning of motor racing in several countries, although only Switzerland maintained the ban in the long term…

The Lion Heart

Formula 1 has existed as a World Championship since 1950, but there were one or two famous names from the pre-war era who are listed as "Formula 1 drivers", although there is no official definition of what a "Formula 1 driver" must have done to qualify for such status. One such racer was France's Raymond Sommer, who competed in Grand Prix racing in the 1930s, he never won a Grande Epreuve, he did win the French GP in 1936, when it was held as a sports car race. He was also a factory driver in various events for Gordini, Talbot-Darracq, Ferrari and even BRM. They called him "Cœur de Lion" – Lion Heart – a title that he shared with the English King Richard I.

Sommer's life spanned the history of Grand Prix racing until the Formula 1 World Championship came along. He was born in the summer of 1906, a few weeks after the first Grand Prix de l'Automobile Club de France was held at Le Mans.

His father was a well-to-do carpet manufacturer from Pont-à-Mousson, a town in the Moselle valley in Lorraine. His father Roger had been an aviation pioneer and even manufactured his own flying machines. Raymond's competitive urges were nurtured with boxing but he was then sent off to study in Manchester to learn English before starting working for the family firm. It was then he decided that he wanted to be a racing driver and he did his first race in 1931, at the age of 24. He enjoyed almost instant success with an Alfa Romeo 8C roadster, winning Le Mans in 1932 and 1933. He did his first Grand Prix races, although not Grandes Epreuves, and won the Grand Prix de Marseille at Miramas in his first year. He was signed by Maserati for 1933 but afterwards tended to run his own Alfa Romeos, winning at Comminges and Montlhéry in 1935 with an ex-factory Alfa Romeo P3. In 1936 he won the Spa 24 Hours and was French racing champion in 1937 and 1939. After a war which involved being an active resistant, he tried to get the French government to fund a Grand Prix challenger in the late 1940s with the CTA-Arsenal, designed by the government-owned Centre d'Etude Technique de l'Automobile et du Cycle (abbreviated to CTA) and built by the Arsenal de l'Aéronautique, another state-owned firm. The car was not a disastrous failure as the government-employed engineers refused to listen to engineers who knew about racing.

He gave up in 1947 and signed to drive for Ferrari in 1948 but then went his own way again with a privately-owned Lago-Talbot. He was signed to race for BRM in the first race of the new Formula 1 World Championship at Silverstone in 1950 but the team failed to appear and so he raced Ferraris at Monaco and Bremgarten. In Belgium, he went back to his own Lago-Talbot and found himself leading the race at one point as the thirstier Alfa Romeos pitted, but his engine failed. The French GP ended early with an overheating engine but at Monza on September 3, he qualified eighth for the Italian GP and ran well until he suffered a gearbox failure.

A week later, he went to the little-known Haute Garonne GP at Cadours, in the south-west of France, having borrowed a Cooper from Harry Schell. It was a very minor race with only around 14,000 spectators but he accepted the invitation to help promote the event. He broke down in the first heat but won the second and so qualified for the final and soon took the lead but then on the eighth lap he failed to appear. The word filtered back that he had gone off and the car had somersaulted several times before hitting a tree. Sommer was dead.

Investigations would later reveal that he had suffered a steering failure.

A year later, the organisers at Cadours unveiled a monument in his honour, funded by a public appeal. Later an identical monument was erected in Pont-à-Mousson.

www.ingramcontent.com/pod-product-compliance
Lightning Source LLC
Chambersburg PA
CBHW031957080426
42735CB00007B/424